POWERSCORE
TEST PREPARATION

LSAT
LOGIC
GAMES
BIBLE
WORKBOOK

The best resource for practicing PowerScore's famous Logic Games methods!

Published by
PowerScore Publishing, a division of PowerScore Incorporated
57 Hasell Street
Charleston, SC 29401

Author: David M. Killoran

Manufactured in Canada
January 2010

ISBN: 978-0-9801782-8-9

Also Available...

PowerScore LSAT Logical Reasoning Bible

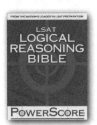

One of the most highly anticipated publications in LSAT history, the *PowerScore LSAT Logical Reasoning Bible™* is a comprehensive how-to manual for solving every type of Logical Reasoning question. Featuring over 100 real Logical Reasoning questions with detailed explanations, the Bible is the ultimate resource for improving your LSAT Logical Reasoning score.

Available on the PowerScore website for $49.99.
Website: www.powerscore.com/pubs.htm

PowerScore LSAT Reading Comprehension Bible

The Reading Comprehension Bible provides the complete guide to reading difficult passages, increasing comprehension, understanding argumentation, and effectively attacking different question types. It includes complete explanations of passages and questions drawn from actual LSATs, guides to passage diagramming, and multiple practice drills.

Available on the PowerScore website for $46.99.
Website: www.powerscore.com/pubs.htm

PowerScore LSATs Deconstructed Series

The PowerScore LSATs Deconstructed Series™ offers comprehensive, question-by-question analysis of real LSATs. Each book provides a practice test as well as detailed explanations of every question and answer choice for the Logical Reasoning, Reading Comprehension, and Analytical Reasoning sections of an actual LSAT, administered by the LSAC. The concepts presented in *The PowerScore LSATs Deconstructed Series™* reflect techniques covered in PowerScore's live courses and have consistently been proven effective for thousands of our students.

Available on the PowerScore website.
Website: www.powerscore.com/pubs.htm

Also Available...

PowerScore Logic Games Bible Flashcards

The Games Bible Flashcards relay and test foundational concepts such as games terminology, game-type recognition, and rule language, as well as advanced conceptual approaches including conditional reasoning, formal logic, and numerical distribution. Mini-challenges allow test takers to develop the skills necessary to create effective diagrams and draw sound logical inferences. Each set includes 140 cards that test the concepts and approaches to logic games taught in the LGB and in PowerScore LSAT courses.

Available on the PowerScore website only for $24.99.
Website: www.powerscore.com/pubs.htm

PowerScore Logical Reasoning Bible Flashcards

The Logical Reasoning Bible Flashcards introduce and test concepts taught in our courses and in PowerScore's LSAT Logical Reasoning Bible. The flashcards cover everything from foundational definitions and question type recognition to more advanced Logical Reasoning skills, including causal reasoning, conditional reasoning, and understanding formal logic. The LRB Flashcards can be used as a stand-alone study aid, or as an ideal complement to the renowned Logical Reasoning Bible.

Available on the PowerScore website only for $29.99.
Website: www.powerscore.com/pubs.htm

PowerScore LSAT Private and Telephone Tutoring

PowerScore Private Tutoring gives students the opportunity to work one-on-one with a PowerScore tutor for the most specialized learning experience. Whether you need personalized lesson plans or you want a review on a few concepts, PowerScore can create a tutoring experience that will address all of your LSAT difficulties.

Our tutors have all scored in the 99th percentile on an actual LSAT. Aside from mastering the test themselves, every PowerScore tutor can clearly explain the underlying principles of the LSAT to any student.

PowerScore offers individual tutoring hours or tutoring packages. Please visit www.powerscore.com, or call 1-800-545-1750 for more information.

PowerScore Law School Admissions Counseling

While your LSAT score and GPA will undeniably be major factors during your admissions cycle, to truly separate yourself from the rest of the applicant pool you must assemble the most powerful application folder possible. To do this you must have an outstanding personal statement, top-notch letters of recommendation, and flawless overall presentation.

PowerScore has gathered a team of admissions experts—including former law school admissions board members, top lawyers, and students from top-twenty law schools—to address your admissions counseling and personal statement needs and help you get to where you want to be.

Please visit www.powerscore.com, or call 1-800-545-1750 for more information.

CONTENTS

CHAPTER ONE: INTRODUCTION

CHAPTER TWO: PRACTICE DRILLS

CHAPTER THREE: INDIVIDUAL LOGIC GAMES

Chapter Four: Logic Games Sections

Appendix

Endnotes

About PowerScore

PowerScore is one of the nation's fastest growing test preparation companies. Founded in 1997, PowerScore offers LSAT, GMAT, GRE, and SAT preparation classes in over 150 locations in the U.S. and abroad. Preparation options include Full-length courses, Weekend courses, Virtual courses, and private tutoring. For more information, please visit our website at www.powerscore.com or call us at (800) 545-1750.

For supplemental information about this book, please visit the *Logic Games Bible Workbook* website at www.powerscore.com/lsatbibles.

CHAPTER ONE: INTRODUCTION

Introduction

Welcome to the *PowerScore LSAT Logic Games Bible Workbook*. This book is designed for use after you read the *PowerScore LSAT Logic Games Bible*; the purpose of this workbook is to help you better understand the ideas presented in the *Games Bible*, and to allow you to practice the application of our methods and techniques. This is not a how-to manual, but rather a traditional workbook designed to reinforce the skills and approaches that will enable you to master the games section of the LSAT.

If you are looking for a how-to manual, please refer to the *PowerScore LSAT Logic Games Bible*, which provides the conceptual basis for the setups, rule diagramming, and general strategies you will be practicing here. In the discussions of game approaches and techniques in this workbook, we will assume that you have read the *Logic Games Bible* and are familiar with its basic terminology.

To help you practice the application of your Logic Game skills, this book is divided into three sections:

Section One: Practice Drills

The first section of this workbook contains drills which test isolated analytical abilities, designed to reinforce and improve the specific skills necessary to successfully attack the Logic Games section. The set of drills is followed by an answer key explaining each item.

Section Two: Individual Games

The second section of this workbook contains ten individual LSAT Logic Games, each of which comes from an actual LSAT and is used with the permission of Law Services, the producers of the LSAT. At the end of the section is a comprehensive explanation of each game, including a discussion of the setup, each rule diagram, inferences, and a complete explanation of every question. This is an excellent section for testing and reinforcing your game skills on days when your time is limited.

Section Three: Complete Game Sections

The final portion of this workbook features five complete LSAT Logic Games sections, followed by full explanations of each game and every corresponding question. This section gives you the opportunity to emulate actual testing conditions, allowing you to apply the full range of your Logic Game strategies while also focusing on your pacing under time pressure.

Each of the three sections is easily located using the black sidebars that mark each section. The sidebars in the second and third sections also contain additional information that help you to identify each game and section number.

As you finish each item, we suggest that you carefully read the corresponding explanation. Examine the correct answer choice, but also study the incorrect answer choices. Look again at the problem and determine which elements led to the correct answer. Study the explanations and setups provided in the book and check them against your own work to assess and improve vital game skills. By doing so you will greatly increase your chances of performing well on the Logic Games section of the LSAT.

Finally, in our LSAT courses, in our admissions counseling programs, and in our publications, we always strive to present the most accurate and up-to-date information available. Consequently, we have devoted a section of our website to *Logic Games Bible Workbook* students. This free online resource area offers supplements to the book material and provides updates as needed. There is also an official book evaluation form that we strongly encourage you to use. The exclusive *LSAT Logic Games Bible Workbook* online area can be accessed at:

www.powerscore.com/lsatbibles

If we can assist you in your LSAT preparation in any way, or if you have any questions or comments, please do not hesitate to email us at lsatbibles@powerscore.com. Additional contact information is provided at the end of this book. We look forward to hearing from you!

CHAPTER TWO: PRACTICE DRILLS

Chapter Notes

This section contains a set of drills designed to achieve the following goals:

1. Reacquaint you with the language used in LSAT rules, and with the PowerScore rule representations.

2. Isolate and test certain skills that are used in Logic Games, and refresh and refine your abilities to apply those skills.

3. Expose you to a variety of game situations and game concepts.

We believe the best approach is to complete each drill, and then check the answer key in the back, examining both the questions you answered correctly and the ones you answered incorrectly.

These drills have no timing restrictions. Instead of worrying about speed, focus on a complete understanding of the idea under examination. Later in this book there will be timed exercises to give you practice with the timing element.

Rule Origin Drill

Each of the following items presents a Logic Game rule in diagram form, followed by five lettered answer choices. Select the answer choice that contains language that produces the *exact* rule diagram in the problem. *Answers begin on page 32*

1. J ———▶ W

   (A) Jin is selected unless Walter is selected.
   (B) Jin is selected if and only if Walter is selected.
   (C) Jin is selected if Walter is selected.
   (D) If Walter is not selected then Jin is not selected.
   (E) Either Jin or Walter must be selected.

2. R̄/S̄

   (A) Rena is not seated at the same table as Suki.
   (B) Rena and Suki sit in consecutive seats.
   (C) Neither Rena nor Suki are selected for the dinner.
   (D) If Rena is not selected for the dinner, then Suki is not selected for the dinner.
   (E) Rena and Suki appear at the same meals.

3. J ◀——▶ L
         at lst 1

   (A) A family eats at restaurant J during the day if, but only if, they eat at restaurant L that same day.
   (B) Restaurants J and L have at least one dish in common.
   (C) Restaurants J and L have exactly one dish in common.
   (D) Restaurants J and L serve exactly the same dishes.
   (E) At least one family eats at either J or L, or both.

4. G ◀—|—▶ H

   (A) Neither Greta nor Harrison speak at the fundraiser.
   (B) Greta and Harrison cannot speak in consecutive time slots at the fundraiser.
   (C) If Greta speaks at the fundraiser, Harrison cannot speak at the fundraiser.
   (D) If Greta does not speak at the fundraiser, Harrison speaks at the fundraiser.
   (E) Greta and Harrison cannot speak at any fundraiser with another speaker.

5.   C
     - - - - > F
     D

(A) Calliope and Dennison both are slower than Flipper.
(B) Calliope is faster than Flipper, and Dennison is slower than Flipper.
(C) Dennison is faster than Flipper, and faster than Calliope.
(D) Flipper is slower than Dennison, and Calliope is faster than Dennison.
(E) Calliope and Dennison both are faster than Flipper.

6. | P   Q/R |

(A) Putnam must sit immediately next to Quince and Roe.
(B) Putnam sits immediately next to either Quince or Roe.
(C) Putnam and Quince sit immediately next to Roe.
(D) Either Quince or Row sits immediately behind Putnam.
(E) Either Quince or Row sits immediately ahead of Putnam.

7. M > N > O
          or
    O > N > M

Assume no ties are possible.

(A) Either M is taller than N, or else N is taller than M, but not both.
(B) Either N is taller than O, or else N is taller than M, but not both.
(C) Either N is taller than O, or else O is taller than N, but not both.
(D) Either O is taller than M, or else O is taller than N, but not both.
(E) Either M is taller than O, or else M is taller than N, but not both.

8. | T/V / Y |

(A) T or V, but not both, cannot be the stop ahead of Y.
(B) Either T or V is the stop chosen ahead of Y.
(C) Whenever T or V is chosen as a stop, then Y is not chosen as the next stop.
(D) Whenever T or V is chosen as the first stop, then Y is not chosen as the second stop.
(E) Y cannot be a stop chosen after T or V.

Pure Sequencing Diagramming Drill

Use the Pure Sequencing Diagramming Guidelines from page 280 of the *Logic Games Bible* to set up sequencing chains for the given sets of variables and rules. The rules for each item may yield more than one chain. *Answers begin on page 34*

1. Rules: L is taller than M.
             N is shorter than M.
             L is shorter than J and K.
             O is taller than N.

Question 1.1

Which one of the following could accurately list the three tallest variables, in order from first to third tallest?

(A)   J, L, M
(B)   J, L, O
(C)   J, K, M
(D)   K, O, J
(E)   K, L, O

Pure Sequencing Diagramming Drill

2. Rules: T is larger than W.
                     W is smaller than V.
                     T is not larger than S.
                     X is larger than W.
                     X is larger than Y.

A. Which variables in the chain could be largest?

B. Which variables in the chain could be smallest?

3. Rules: B and D are heavier than E.
                     J is lighter than B.
                     C is heavier than D.
                     B is lighter than A.
                     E is heavier than F and H.
                     K is heavier than H.
                     G is lighter than F.

A. Which variables in the chain could be heaviest?

B. Which variables in the chain could be lightest?

PRACTICE DRILLS

4. Rules: C is shorter than A and B.
                  B and D are taller than E.
                  F is taller than A.

Question 4.1

Which one of the following could be an accurate list of the two smallest variables?

(A)   A, E
(B)   B, C
(C)   B, E
(D)   C, D
(E)   D, E

5. Rules: R is faster than S.
              U is slower than T.
              Q is faster than R and T.
              W is faster than R.
              T is slower than X.
              P is faster than Q.

Question 5.1

Which one of the following must be false?

(A)   S is sixth fastest.
(B)   W is sixth fastest.
(C)   X is sixth fastest.
(D)   Q is fifth fastest.
(E)   P is third fastest.

Basic Linear Rule Diagramming Drill

In the space provided, supply the best symbolic representation (if any) of each of the following rules. If applicable, show any corresponding implications (Not Laws, dual-options, etc.) on the linear diagram provided. Assume a one-to-one relationship for each problem, with no ties possible.
Answers begin on page 36

1. G is recorded earlier than H and J.

recording positions =   1   2   3   4   5   6

2. Exactly one day separates the interviews of Y and Z.

days =   1   2   3   4   5   6

3. C must sit 3 chairs behind D, and E must sit 1 chair before C.

chairs =   1   2   3   4   5   6

4. If S speaks, S speaks the day before T.

days =   1   2   3   4   5   6

5. The factory that is inspected second is also inspected first.

inspections =   1   2   3   4   5   6

Basic Linear Rule Diagramming Drill

6. If J performs, then K performs earlier than L.

performances = $\frac{}{1}$ $\frac{}{2}$ $\frac{}{3}$ $\frac{}{4}$ $\frac{}{5}$ $\frac{}{6}$

7. R's sole trip will occur between S's two trips.

trips = $\frac{}{1}$ $\frac{}{2}$ $\frac{}{3}$ $\frac{}{4}$ $\frac{}{5}$ $\frac{}{6}$

8. A sits in either the first or last seat.

seats = $\frac{}{1}$ $\frac{}{2}$ $\frac{}{3}$ $\frac{}{4}$ $\frac{}{5}$ $\frac{}{6}$

9. Y is inspected after X is inspected but before Z is inspected.

inspections = $\frac{}{1}$ $\frac{}{2}$ $\frac{}{3}$ $\frac{}{4}$ $\frac{}{5}$ $\frac{}{6}$

10. M and T are not performed on consecutive days.

days = $\frac{}{1}$ $\frac{}{2}$ $\frac{}{3}$ $\frac{}{4}$ $\frac{}{5}$ $\frac{}{6}$

In the space provided, supply the best symbolic representation (if any) of each of the following rules. If applicable, show any corresponding implications (Not Laws, dual-options, etc.) on the linear diagram provided. Assume a one-to-one relationship for each problem, with no ties possible. *Answers begin on page 39*

1. Both green vehicles are inspected before the Ford car.

colors = __ __ __ __ __ __

cars = __ __ __ __ __ __
            1   2   3   4   5   6

2. Martina reviews the Thai restaurant, which is reviewed immediately after the French restaurant.

cuisine = __ __ __ __ __ __

reviewer = __ __ __ __ __ __
             1   2   3   4   5   6

3. An activity is assigned to each time period, and the activity selected for the afternoon of day 3 must be the same as the activity selected for the morning of day 4.

afternoon = __ __ __ __ __ __

morning = __ __ __ __ __ __
            1   2   3   4   5   6

Advanced Linear Rule Diagramming Drill

4. Kim cannot compete in the morning sessions, and Rosen cannot compete in the afternoon sessions.

afternoon =   ___   ___   ___   ___   ___   ___

morning =   ___   ___   ___   ___   ___   ___
            1   2   3   4   5   6

5. The Great Dane dog is shown before the Siamese cat, which is shown before the Calico cat.

dogs =   ___   ___   ___   ___   ___   ___

cats =   ___   ___   ___   ___   ___   ___
        1   2   3   4   5   6

Grouping Rule Diagramming Drill

In the space provided, supply the best symbolic representation (if any) of each of the following rules. If applicable, show any corresponding implications on the diagram provided. *Answers begin on page 42*

1. Of the three applicants W, X, and Y, exactly two are interviewed.

— —— —— —— —
Group of 5 Interviews

2. R and S cannot be selected together.

— —— —— —— —
Group of 5 Selections

3. Every member is assigned to exactly one of the two groups, and L and N cannot be assigned to the same group.

```
 __   __
 __   __
 __   __
 __   __
  1    2
```

4. If D is assigned to group 2, then E is assigned to group 2.

```
 __   __
 __   __
 __   __
 __   __
  1    2
```

Grouping Rule Diagramming Drill

5. If Q is not selected then T is selected.

___ ___ ___ ___ ___

Group of 5 Selections

6. Either G or H, but not both, must perform.

___ ___ ___ ___ ___

Group of 5 Performances

7. Group 2 and group 3 do not have any members in common.

___	___	___
___	___	___
___	___	___
1	2	3

8. R and S cannot be assigned to the same group as each other.

___ ___ ___ ___
___ ___ ___ ___
1   2   3   4

Two Rule Inference Drill

In the space provided, supply the best symbolic representation of each of the following rules. Link the rules if possible, and, if applicable, show any corresponding inferences. Assume that all provided spaces must be filled with exactly one variable. *Answers begin on page 44*

Answers begin on page 44

1. If Q is on the stage, then R is on the stage.
   R is not on the stage unless P is not on the stage.

2. The third car sold is either S or T.
   W is sold immediately before X.

   cars =   ___ ___ ___ ___ ___ ___
             1   2   3   4   5   6

3. D's performance and E's performance are separated by exactly one performance.
   G performs immediately after F.

   performances =   ___ ___ ___ ___ ___
                     1   2   3   4   5

4. M cannot be in a group unless N is in the same group.
   Q and R cannot be in different groups, and all variables must be in one of the two groups.

   ___ ___

   ___ ___
    1   2

Two Rule Inference Drill

5. R's call is made at some point before S's call.
   T's call is made exactly two calls ahead of R's call.

calls = $\underline{\quad}$ $\underline{\quad}$ $\underline{\quad}$ $\underline{\quad}$ $\underline{\quad}$ $\underline{\quad}$
         1   2   3   4   5   6

6. Every variable is in a group, and H cannot be in group 1 unless K is in group 1.
   J is in group 2 only if L is in group 2.

$$\frac{\overline{\qquad}}{\underline{\qquad}} \quad \frac{\overline{\qquad}}{\underline{\qquad}}$$
   1   2

7. If A is not interviewed then B must be interviewed, and if B is interviewed then A cannot be interviewed.
   Of the six interviewees, if B is not interviewed then exactly two other interviewees cannot be interviewed.

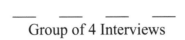

Group of 4 Interviews

8. J and K cannot audition together.
   When K auditions, L must audition.

Numerical Distribution Identification Drill

Each of the following game scenarios contain rules that lead to one or more numerical distributions. For each problem identify each of the possible fixed or unfixed numerical distributions created by the rules. *Answers begin on page 49*

1.   Eight books are assigned to three students. Each student is assigned at least two books.

2.   Ten drinks are served to two bar patrons. Each patron is served at least one drink but no more than seven drinks.

3.   Six bones are given to three dogs—a Greyhound, a Mastiff, and a Terrier. Each dog must be given at least one bone, and the Terrier is given exactly one less bone than the Mastiff.

4.   Eleven cookies are placed in four jars. Each jar contains at least one cookie but no more than five cookies.

5.   Eight tables are assigned to four different servers—servers A, B, C, and D. Each server is assigned at least one table. Server A is assigned exactly twice the number of tables as Server B.

6.   Twelve students are assigned to five different floors in a dormitory. At least two students are assigned to each floor.

7.   Seven animals are placed into three cages. Each cage contains at most five animals.

8.   Thirteen toys are given to four children—W, X, Y, and Z. Each child is given at least two toys, and Y is given exactly three times as many toys as W.

9.   Twenty-one pills are placed into six bottles. At least three pills are placed in each bottle.

10.   Seven appointments with a doctor are scheduled over four days—Monday, Tuesday, Wednesday, and Thursday. At least one appointment must be scheduled for each day, and there is exactly one more appointment on Wednesday than there is on Thursday.

Each of the following items presents a scenario and corresponding rules similar to those found in actual Logic Games. Using the space provided, diagram the setup and include a representation of all sequences, blocks, not-blocks, and Not Laws™. Occasionally, a problem will contain a corresponding question. Use your knowledge of the rules and the setup to answer the question. After you complete *each* item, check your work against the diagram in the answer key, and carefully read the comments concerning each diagram. *Answers begin on page 51*

1. A manager must schedule six employees—Kwame, Lars, Marina, Noriko, Oliver, and Paulo—during a single workweek, Monday through Saturday. Each employee will be scheduled for exactly one day, and exactly one employee works each day. The schedule must observe the following constraints:

    If Noriko works on Tuesday, then Marina works on Saturday.
    Either Oliver or Paulo works on Wednesday.
    Kwame works on Monday or on Saturday.

2. Five birds—a parrot, a quail, a raven, a sparrow, and a thrush—are placed in five separate cages numbered one through five. Each bird will be placed in exactly one cage, and each cage contains exactly one bird in accordance with the following conditions:

    The raven is placed in the second cage.
    There is exactly one cage between the cage holding the parrot and the cage holding the quail.

    Question 2.1. Which one of the following must be true?

    (A) Either P or Q is placed in the first cage.
    (B) Either S or T is placed in the first cage.
    (C) Either S or T is placed in the fourth cage.
    (D) Either P or Q is placed in the fifth cage.
    (E) Either S or T is placed in the fifth cage.

Basic Linear Setup Practice Drill

3. Six speakers—B, C, D, F, G, and H—are scheduled to speak at a political rally. Each speaker will speak exactly once, and no two speakers will speak at the same time. The schedule must satisfy the following requirements:

> C speaks immediately after B.
> F must be the second speaker.
> B speaks at some time before D.

4. An opening act is selecting the songs for an evening's concert. Seven songs—G, H, J, K, N, O, and P—will be played one after another, not necessarily in that order. Each song will be played exactly once, according to the following conditions:

> G must be played exactly three songs before K.
> The fourth song played is either N or O.
> H must be played immediately before J.

5. A building manager must assign seven companies—Q, R, S, T, W, X, and Y—to seven different floors of the building—floors 1, 2, 3, 4, 5, 6, and 7. The assignments must comply with the following restrictions:

    Q must be assigned to the floor directly above R.
    S must be assigned to floor 2.
    X must be assigned to the floor directly below W.
    T must be assigned to floor 5.

Question 5.1. Each of the following cannot be true EXCEPT:

(A)   R is assigned to the floor directly below T.
(B)   S is assigned to the floor directly below Q.
(C)   R is assigned to the floor directly above W.
(D)   T is assigned to the floor directly below R.
(E)   Y is assigned to the floor directly above S.

6. Each of six tennis players—Gemma, Hiroko, Jun, Kurt, Lenisha, and Mahita—is assigned to exactly one of seven tennis courts in preparation for a tournament. The courts are consecutively numbered 1 through 7, and each court is assigned no more than one player. Court assignments must meet the following requirements:

    Kurt is assigned a lower-numbered court than Hiroko.
    Courts 1, 2, and 3 cannot be empty.
    Lenisha and Mahita must be assigned higher-numbered courts than Hiroko.
    Jun cannot be assigned to court 1, 3, or 5.

7. There are exactly seven houses numbered 1 through 7 on a street. Each building is occupied by exactly one of seven families: the Pearsons, the Quarles, the Rodriguezes, the Sesays, the Tangs, the Valerios, and the Zolkins. All of the houses are on the same side of the street, which runs from west to east. House 1 is the westernmost house. The following restrictions apply:

   House 4 is occupied by either the Quarles or Rodriguezes.

   The Rodriguezes and the Tangs do not live in consecutively numbered houses.

   The Quarles live to the west of the Tangs.

8. A researcher must test exactly eight products—B, C, D, F, G, H, J, and K—one at a time, not necessarily in that order. The tests must be made in accordance with the following conditions:

   K is tested exactly two products earlier than F is tested.

   Either J or K must be tested fourth.

   Either F or G must be tested sixth.

   Only if D is tested first is J tested fourth.

Advanced Linear Setup Practice Drill

Each of the following items presents an Advanced Linear game scenario. Using the space provided, diagram the game and corresponding rules. Use your knowledge of rule representation to properly display each rule and inference. *Answers begin on page 59*

1. A bicycle manufacturer produces six bike models—T, U, W, X, Y, and Z—in three different colors—black, red, and silver. Each bike is produced at a different time, and each bike is exactly one color. The production adheres to the following conditions:

   The only silver bike is produced immediately before the only red bike.
   The fourth bike produced is X or Y.
   Model W is silver.
   The second and fourth bikes are black.

2. Seven runners—K, L, N, O, P, R, and S—finish a race in order from 1 though 7. There are no ties, and four of the runners are male and three are female. The runners finish in accordance with the following requirements:

   P finishes immediately ahead of S.
   The fourth place runner is L or N.
   S is a female.
   No two male runners finish in consecutive positions.

3. A lawyer schedules ten depositions over the course of five days: Monday, Tuesday, Wednesday, Thursday, and Friday. Exactly one deposition is scheduled for the morning of each day and exactly one deposition is scheduled for the afternoon of each day. The ten individuals being deposed are A, B, C, D, F, G, H, J, K, and L. The depositions must be scheduled according to the following conditions:

   A and B cannot be deposed in the afternoon.

   H's deposition is scheduled for an earlier time than K's deposition.

   C and D cannot be deposed in the morning, and D is not deposed on Monday afternoon.

   K and L must be deposed on consecutive mornings.

   H is deposed on the afternoon of the day following G's morning deposition.

4. A design company is placing pieces of art on the floors of two office buildings, Building A and Building B. Each building has exactly six floors, numbered 1 through 6. Each floor contains exactly one piece of art, and each artwork is made of glass, plaster, or steel only. The art placements must comply with the following restrictions:

   Artworks of the same type cannot be displayed on the same numbered floor of the two buildings.

   The artwork on floor 3 of Building A is identical to the artwork on floor 4 of Building B.

   The artwork on floor 6 of Building A is not made of plaster.

   Steel artworks and glass artworks cannot be displayed on consecutively-numbered floors.

Unified Grouping Theory Classification Drill

Each of the following items provides a Grouping game scenario. In the space provided, supply the most accurate classification of the game using the categories defined by the Unified Grouping Theory (Defined/Partially Defined/Undefined, Fixed/Moving, Balanced/Unbalanced, Overloaded/Underfunded). *Answers begin on page 64*

1. Seven doctors are being considered for positions at a hospital. Only doctors who are interviewed will be hired.

   Classification: _____

2. Nine agents are divided among exactly three firms—firm 1, firm 2, and firm 3. Each firm will be assigned exactly three agents, and each agent will be assigned to only one firm.

   Classification: _____

3. Exactly eight students are assigned to two classes, class A and class B. Each student is assigned to exactly one class.

   Classification: _____

4. The members of four committees will be selected from among seven candidates. Each committee must have exactly two members. Each applicant must be assigned to at least one committee, and applicants can be assigned to more than one committee.

   Classification: _____

5. Exactly six of nine reviewers are selected to review exactly four restaurants, with each selected reviewer reviewing exactly one restaurant and each restaurant being reviewed by at least one reviewer.

   Classification: _____

Unified Grouping Theory Classification Drill

6. A dinner reservation for at least four people will be made at a local restaurant. The diners will be selected from a group of ten people.

   Classification: _____

7. Exactly six of eight weight lifters are assigned to two weight lifting teams of three weight lifters each.

   Classification: _____

8. A summer school offers at least one of seven courses.

   Classification: _____

Grouping Setup Practice Drill

Each of the following items presents a scenario and corresponding rules similar to those found in actual Logic Games. Using the space provided, diagram the setup and include a representation of all rules and inferences. Each problem contains a corresponding question or questions. Use your knowledge of the rules and the setup to answer the question. After you complete *each* item, check your work against the diagram in the answer key, and carefully read the comments concerning each diagram. *Answers begin on page 66*

1. Six waiters—S, T W, X, Y, and Z—are assigned in pairs to wait on four tables—tables, A, B, C, and D. The assignment of the waiters will meet the following conditions:

    Each waiter must be assigned to at least one table.

    S cannot be assigned to table A.

    W is assigned to table B only if Y is assigned to table D.

    S and T must be assigned to the same table.

2. Seven horses—A, B, C, D, F, G, and H—are in a horse paddock at various times. The horses are in the paddock in a manner consistent with the following conditions:

    If C is in the paddock, then D is not in the paddock.

    Every time F is in the paddock, C is in the paddock.

    D is in the paddock only when G is in the paddock.

    If A is not in the paddock then B is in the paddock.

Grouping Setup Practice Drill

3. At a music festival, eight bands—Cage, Deadbolt, Fluster, Gravel, Hammer, Irony, Kernel, and Lunar—are assigned to two stages—the Main Stage and the Side Stage. Each band must be assigned to a single stage. The assignments are made in accordance with the following conditions:

   At least four bands are assigned to the Main stage, and at least three bands are assigned to the Side Stage.

   Kernel cannot be assigned to the Side Stage unless Deadbolt is assigned to the Main Stage.

   Fluster and Gravel are not assigned to the same stage.

4. Eight senators—J, K, L, M, O, P, Q, and R—serve on three subcommittees—Defense, Finance, and Policy. Each subcommittee has three members, except for the Finance subcommittee, which has two members. The following is known about the three subcommittees:

   P serves on the Defense subcommittee.

   Q serves on the Finance subcommittee.

   K and L serve on the same subcommittee.

   J serves on a subcommittee if and only if M serves on the same subcommittee.

For each of the following items, classify the question stem as Global or Local, and then identify the truth characteristic of the correct answer and then the truth characteristic of the four incorrect answers. Also note any additional characteristics of the question stem, and remember to always convert false into true. *Answers begin on page 71*

Example: "Which one of the following must be true?"

　　　　　　 Classification: Global, Must Be True
　　　　　　 Four Incorrect Answers: Not Necessarily True

1. Question: "If L is the third car sold, then which one of the following could be true?"

　　　　　　 Classification: _____

　　　　　　 Four Incorrect Answers: _____

2. Question: "Which one of the following could be false?"

　　　　　　 Classification: _____

　　　　　　 Four Incorrect Answers: _____

3. Question: "Which one of the following is a list of all the musicians who could be in the band at a particular time?"

　　　　　　 Classification: _____

　　　　　　 Four Incorrect Answers: _____

4. Question: "If more green shoes than yellow shoes are selected, then which one of the following cannot be true?"

　　　　　　 Classification: _____

　　　　　　 Four Incorrect Answers: _____

5. Question: "If K is displayed fifth, then each of the following could be true EXCEPT:"

　　　　　　 Classification: _____

　　　　　　 Four Incorrect Answers: _____

PRACTICE DRILLS

Question Stem Classification Drill

6. Question: "If T and R each received a rating of "excellent," then which one of the following cannot be false?"

   Classification: _____

   Four Incorrect Answers: _____

7. Question: "Each of the following must be false EXCEPT:"

   Classification: _____

   Four Incorrect Answers: _____

8. Question: "What is the minimum number of animals that could be in the barn at any given time?"

   Classification: _____

   Four Incorrect Answers: _____

9. Question: "Suppose that the condition requiring W to perform earlier than Y is replaced by a new condition requiring that Y performs earlier than W. If all of the other original conditions remain in effect, which one of the following cannot occur?"

   Classification: _____

   Four Incorrect Answers: _____

10. Question: "There is only one acceptable group of five speakers that can be selected if which one of the following pairs of speakers is selected?"

    Classification: _____

    Four Incorrect Answers: _____

PRACTICE DRILL EXPLANATIONS

1. The correct answer choice is (D). Answer choice (D) provides the contrapositive of the rule diagram, but as with any rule where both terms are negative, you should take the contrapositive and show the rule with both terms positive. Answer choice (B) would be properly diagrammed as J ◄──────► W, so although it would include the diagram in question, the diagram in question would be only partially correct, and thus (B) is not the correct answer. Answer choices (A) and (E) produce identical diagrams of J̸ ──────► W, and answer choice (C) produces the Mistaken Reversal of the rule in this problem.

2. The correct answer choice is (A). Answer choice (A) leads to a rule representation that must reflect the fact that R and S cannot be together. In a Grouping game, one method of displaying that situation is through a Not-block. Answer choice (B) would likely produce a rotating horizontal RS block. Answer choice (C) would produce two Not Laws on the dinner group. Answer choice (D) would produce a S ──────► R diagram. Answer choice (E) would likely produce a positive block.

3. The correct answer choice is (B). The rule diagram requires language that shows commonality between J and L, but also the fact that there is a minimum of 1 item in common. Answer choices (A), (C), and (D) each show commonality between J and L and lead to the diagram of J ◄──────► L, but all three answers fail to capture the "at least one" idea and are thus incorrect. Answer choice (E) fails to show that just one of J or L could be visited.

4. The correct answer choice is (C). The rule representation indicates that G and H cannot be together. Answer choice (C) indicates that if G speaks at the fundraiser, then H does not. Via the contrapositive, if H speaks, then G does not, and so G and H cannot speak at the same fundraiser, which is best represented by the rule diagram in this problem. Answer choice (A) would best be shown by two Not Laws. Answer choice (B) would produce a rotating horizontal Not-block. Answer choice (D) produces a double not-arrow where both terms are negated (the polar opposite of the rule represented here). Answer choice (E) means that G or H must speak alone, which, although it is then true that G and H cannot speak together, would be better represented by a rule indicating that G and H are separately alone.

5. The correct answer choice is (E). Remember, the ">" symbol simply means "to the left of," and in Linear diagrams "faster" would be towards the left.

   Answer choice (A) produces the following diagram:

   $$\begin{array}{c} C \\ F > - - - - \\ D \end{array}$$

   Answer choice (B) produces the following diagram:

   $$C > F > D$$

   Answer choice (C) produces the following diagram:

$$F$$
$$D > - - - -$$
$$C$$

Answer choice (D) produces the following diagram:

$$C > D > F$$

6. The correct answer choice is (D). The block representation indicates that Q *or* R is next to, *and behind* P (if Q or R were simply next to P, there would be a rotating block display, either with a circle or with both possible blocks shown). Answer choice (A) places P next to *both* Q and R, creating a QPR or RPQ block. Answer choice (B) places Q or R next to P, but not behind P. Answer choice (C) places P and Q next to R, creating a PRQ or QRP block. Answer choice (E) improperly reverses the order of the variables in the rule diagram.

7. The correct answer choice is (B). The wording in the answer choice creates two separate and mutually exclusive chains. Because N is taller than O or M, but not both, when N is taller than one of the two, the other must then be taller than N. This creates two different chains, effectively breaking the game into two directions depending on which scenario applies. Since the two are mutually exclusive, one and only one of the chains is in operation at any given time, hence the "or" between the two sequences.

Answer choice (A) is incorrect because it never addresses O. Answer choice (C) is incorrect because it never addresses M. Answer choice (D) would produce the following diagram:

$$N > O > M$$
$$\text{or}$$
$$M > O > N$$

Answer choice (E) would produce the following diagram:

$$N > M > O$$
$$\text{or}$$
$$O > M > N$$

8. The correct answer choice is (C). The rule diagram captures the scenario where neither T nor V can be immediately followed by Y. This rule would be best produced by the language in answer choice (C). Answer choices (A) and (B) suggest that one of T or V is ahead of Y, but that is not possible. Answer choice (D) is incorrect because if the variables were tied to exact position, this rule would be shown as a conditional relationship with subscripts, as in: $T/V_1 \longleftarrow\!\!\!+\!\!\!\longrightarrow Y_2$

Answer choice (E) is incorrect because the language it uses ("a stop") does not create a block rule, but rather a sequential rule.

1.   Diagram:

```
                    O ◄─┐
   J              - - - - │
   - - - - > L > M > N
   K
```

Question 1.1. The correct answer is (D). Although O appears to be a variable that will be short, the only restriction on O is that O is taller than N. Thus, O can be among the three tallest variables. J and K must also be among the three tallest variables, and thus the order K, O, J is viable. Several of the other answers (answers A, B, and E) fail to include J or K, both of which must be among the three tallest. Answer choice (C) is incorrect because M cannot be among the three tallest variables.

2.   Diagram:

```
      S ≥ T
   - - - - - -
      V      > W
   - - - - - -
      X
        └─ - - - -
           ► Y
```

Largest: S, T, V, X   (T could only tie for the largest)

Smallest: W, Y

3.   Diagram:

```
           ┌─► J
           │ - - - -
   A > B              F > G
   - - - - - >  E  > - - - - - - -
   C > D                H
                     - - - - ┐
                       K ◄──┘
```

Heaviest: A, C, K

Lightest: G, H, J

4.   Diagram:

$$F > A$$
$$\text{------} > C$$
$$\textcircled{B} \quad \text{----}$$
$$\text{------} > E$$
$$D$$

B is circled because it is linked to both C and E.

Question 4.1. The correct answer is (E). Answer choice (A) can be eliminated because A is taller than C, so A can only be among the two shortest when the other variable is C.

Variable B cannot be a part of the correct answer because B is always taller than both C and E. Thus, answer choices (B) and (C) can be eliminated.

Similar to (A), answer choice (D) can be eliminated because D is taller than E, so D can only be among the two shortest when the other variable is E.

5.   Diagram:

$$W$$
$$\text{----}$$
$$R > S$$
$$P > Q > \text{------}$$
$$T > U$$
$$\text{----}$$
$$X$$

Question 5.1. The correct answer is (D). The question stem asks for an answer that Cannot Be True (remember, convert "false" to "true"), and so any answer choice that Could Be True can be eliminated.

One key to this question is understanding the range of possibilities for W and X. Either W or X could be fastest, but they can also be relatively slow: W must only be faster than R and S, and X must only be faster than T and U. Thus, W or X could be sixth fastest, and both answer choices (B) and (C) can be eliminated. P could also be slower than both W and X, so P could be third fastest, and answer choice (E) can be eliminated.

Answer choice (A) can also be eliminated because S could be faster than both T and U, leaving S sixth fastest.

Answer choice (D) is correct; Q must always be faster than R, S, T, and U, and so Q could only be fourth fastest at worst.

Each item shows the appropriate rule representation, and then any relevant inferences or representations on the diagram.

1.
$$G >\begin{matrix} H \\ - - - - \\ J \end{matrix}$$

recording positions =

1	2	3	4	5	6
H̶ J̶				Ø̶	Ø̶

2. | Y/Z ___ Z/Y |

No Not Laws can be drawn from this rule.

days =

1	2	3	4	5	6

3. | D ___ E C |

The diagram above is correct. If C sits *three* chairs *behind* D, then the diagram is | D ___ ___ C |. If E sits one chair before C, then the diagram is | E C |. Those two rules combined create the diagram above.

Due to the size of the block, it can only be placed in three different positions: 1-4, 2-5, or 3-6. Depending on the other rules in the game, you could show those three possibilities, or, alternately, show the Not Laws:

chairs =

1	2	3	4	5	6
C̶ E̶	C̶ E̶	C̶	D̶	D̶	D̶ E̶

4. S ⟶ | S T |

days =

1	2	3	4	5	6
					S̶

The rule indicates that "if" S speaks, then S speaks the day before T. Thus, S does not necessarily have to speak. As such, T could speak on day 1 as long as S does not speak. If S does speak, S could never speak on day 6, hence the Not Law on that day.

5.　　2 ⟶ 1

$$\text{seats} = \overline{\;1\;}\!\leftarrow\!\overline{\;2\;}\quad\overline{\;3\;}\quad\overline{\;4\;}\quad\overline{\;5\;}\quad\overline{\;6\;}$$

The most useful representation is the one in the diagram itself. If we had more information about the game, we might be able to determine that seats 1 and 2 are in a block, but in the absence of that information the best representation is with an arrow.

6.　　J ⟶ K > L　　　　No Not Laws can be drawn from this rule.

$$\text{performances} = \overline{\;1\;}\quad\overline{\;2\;}\quad\overline{\;3\;}\quad\overline{\;4\;}\quad\overline{\;5\;}\quad\overline{\;6\;}$$

Not Laws can be drawn only once J is known to perform. Otherwise, we cannot be certain that K > L, and thus no inferences follow.

7.　　S > R > S

$$\text{trips} = \overline{\;1\;}\quad\overline{\;2\;}\quad\overline{\;3\;}\quad\overline{\;4\;}\quad\overline{\;5\;}\quad\overline{\;6\;}$$
$$\quad\;\;\cancel{R}\qquad\qquad\qquad\qquad\qquad\quad\cancel{R}$$

Because R is "bracketed" by S, R cannot go on the first or last trip. S could go on any trip, and thus no Not Laws can be shown for S. The only way to create Not Laws for S would be to use subscript designations for the first and second trip, as in S_1 and S_2. Then, an S_1 Not Law would be placed on trips 5 and 6, and an S_2 Not Law would be placed on Trips 1 and 2. However, due to the possibility of confusion we have elected not to show those Not Laws (you could—the choice is yours) and instead to use the S > R > S sequence.

8.　　A ⟶ 1/6

$$\text{seats} = \overset{A/}{\overline{\;1\;}}\quad\overline{\;2\;}\quad\overline{\;3\;}\quad\overline{\;4\;}\quad\overline{\;5\;}\quad\overset{/A}{\overline{\;6\;}}$$

Not Laws could be placed on seats 2, 3, 4, and 5, but since A is already shown in the diagram in seat 1 or seat 6, that would redundant.

9.   X > Y > Z

        inspections = $\underline{\quad}$ $\underline{\quad}$ $\underline{\quad}$ $\underline{\quad}$ $\underline{\quad}$ $\underline{\quad}$
                          1   2   3   4   5   6
                          ~~Z~~   ~~Z~~   ~~X~~   ~~X~~
                          ~~X~~   ~~Y~~

The language of this rule can be confusing, but it is often used by Law Services. Let's take a closer look at the potential problem.

In the rule, some students do not realize that the phrase "after...but before" applies entirely to Y, the initial variable. Thus, the rule as stated actually contains two separate relationships:

                           X > Y
            and
                           Y > Z

Combining the two produces the rule diagram: X > Y > Z.

The meaning would be clearer if Law Services restated the rule as, "Y is inspected after X, and Y is inspected before Z is inspected." Regardless, be on the lookout for confusing language, and read every rule carefully.

10.   No Not Laws can be drawn from this rule.

        days = $\underline{\quad}$ $\underline{\quad}$ $\underline{\quad}$ $\underline{\quad}$ $\underline{\quad}$ $\underline{\quad}$
                   1   2   3   4   5   6

In most cases not-blocks (as in this item) and rotating blocks (as in item #2) do not allow you to make initial inferences. However, once other rules are added to the blocks, inferences often follow.

Each item shows the appropriate rule representation, and then any relevant inferences or representations on the diagram.

1. G
    - - - - > F
    G

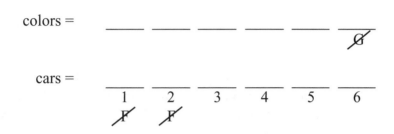

Because both green vehicles are inspected prior to the Ford car, the Ford cannot be inspected first or second, and the green cars cannot be inspected last. The Not Laws are shown on the appropriate stack for each variable set. Note that if the rule said "*Two* green cars are inspected before the Ford car," then there would be no "G" Not Law on the color row because perhaps there are more than two green cars, and as long as two are inspected before F, one or more would be inspected after F (that would then create extra F Not Laws on the car row, however).

2.   ┌─────┐
     │ F T │
     │ _ M │
     └─────┘

cuisine =   ___ ___ ___ ___ ___ ___
            T̸   F̸

reviewer = ___ ___ ___ ___ ___ ___
             1   2   3   4   5   6
            M̸

As is often the case in Advanced Linear games, the rule connects two variable sets. Martina and the Thai restaurant create a vertical block, and the French and Thai restaurants create a horizontal block. Combining the two creates the representation above. As the French restaurant always is reviewed before the Thai restaurant, the French restaurant cannot be reviewed last. As Martina reviews the Thai restaurant after the French restaurant, they cannot go first, and Not Laws are placed on the appropriate row.

3.

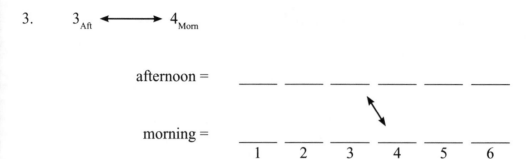

Most students will represent the rule as $4_{Morn} \longrightarrow 3_{Aft}$. There is nothing incorrect about this representation, but it does not capture the full meaning of the rule. Because an activity must always be assigned to the morning of day 4, whatever that activity is will also be the activity assigned to the afternoon of day 3. Thus, if we establish what activity is assigned to the afternoon of day 3, then that *must* also be the activity assigned to the morning of day 4. For example, let us say that one of the activities is Skiing. If Skiing is assigned to the morning of day 4, then Skiing must also be assigned to the afternoon of day 3, and this matches the wording of the rule. However, consider what occurs if Skiing is first assigned to the afternoon of day 3. What options are available for the morning day 4? Could another activity be assigned, such as Painting or Climbing? No, because if one of those activities were assigned, then that activity would also have to be assigned to the afternoon of day 3. Thus, because the activity assigned to the afternoon of day 3 is Skiing, the activity assigned to the morning of day 4 must also be Skiing. Therefore, the proper representation of the rule is with a double-arrow.

The double-arrow should also be represented on the diagram itself. By doing so, you make it less likely that you would forget the operational effects of the rule during the game.

4. K ⟶ M~~orn~~   *or*   K ⟶ Aft

    R ⟶ ~~Aft~~   *or*   R ⟶ Morn

afternoon = ____ ____ ____ ____ ____ ____ ~~K~~

morning = ____ ____ ____ ____ ____ ____ ~~K~~
             1   2   3   4   5   6

The K portion of the rule can be diagrammed in two ways, as K cannot compete in the morning, or alternately that K must compete in the afternoon. The same holds true for the R portion of the rule, with the times reversed. The choice is yours, although we have a slight preference for the "K ⟶ Aft" and "R ⟶ Morn" representations, especially when combined with Side Not Laws on the main diagram (which should be shown regardless of which representation you choose).

5. $G_D > S_C > C_C$

dogs = ____ ____ ____ ____ ~~G~~ ~~G~~

cats = ____ ____ ____ ____ ____ ____
             1   2   3   4   5   6
            ~~C~~ ~~C~~   ~~S~~
            ~~S~~

The rules link the two variable sets, creating a sequence that spans both rows. Use subscripts for cat and dog to easily identify the animal type, and then place the appropriate Not Laws under each row.

1.   2 of W, X, and Y

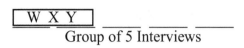
Group of 5 Interviews

The most efficient representation of this rule is directly in the diagram, with a block taking up two spaces (any two spaces will do, although spaces at the far left or far right of the group seem most intuitive and the least confusing). This representation allows you to visually "reserve" the two spaces for W, X, and Y.

2.   R ←——+——→ S

Group of 5 Selections

The rule is shown with the double-not arrow since there is no vertical element in the setup. No representation can be made on the diagram itself

3.

L/N   N/L
 1   2

Remember to show the L/N dual-option in the diagram. L and N are represented in a block to the side since there is a vertical element in the setup.

4. $D_2 \longrightarrow E_2$

        $E_1 \longrightarrow D_1$

        1   2

Many students diagram this rule as a block, but that is incorrect. While both variables are assigned to group 2 when D is assigned to group 2, and via the contrapositive both variables are assigned to group 1 when E is assigned to group 1, the variables do not always have to be in the same group. For example, D could be assigned to group 1 and E could be assigned to group 2 without violating the rule. Note also the power of a contrapositive in a two-value system game.

5.   Ø ——→ T

   X̸ ——→ Q

<u>Q/T</u> __   __   __   __
   Group of 5 Selections

This can be a tricky rule. If Q is not selected then T is selected, and via the contrapositive it T is not selected then Q is selected. Thus, Q and T cannot both not be selected (which can be represented as Ø ←→ X̸) and at least one of Q and T *must* be selected. This is represented on the diagram as a Q/T dual-option, but remember that it is possible for *both* Q and T to be selected (remember, the rule only addresses what occurs when one of them is not selected; if both are selected there is no rule violation).

6.   G ←—|—→ H

<u>G/H</u> __   __   __   __
   Group of 5 Performances

Reserve one space for the choice of G or H since exactly one must perform.

7.   2 ←—|—→ 3

   __   __   __
   __   __   __
   ‾‾   ‾‾   ‾‾
   1   2 ←|→ 3

This rule is best shown internally with a double-not arrow between group 2 and group 3 (or you can place a not-block around 2 and 3 if you prefer).

8.   ┌─┐
   │R̸│
   │S│
   └─┘

   __   __   __   __
   ‾‾   ‾‾   ‾‾   ‾‾
   1   2   3   4

Compare this representation to the representation in item #2. Because there is a vertical component to this diagram, we have chosen a vertical not-block.

1. Rule 1:   Q ———→ R

    Rule 2:   R ←—|—→ P

    Combined: Q ———→ R ←—|—→ P

    Inference: Q ←—|—→ P

The first rule is a standard conditional rule. The second rule is a bit trickier to diagram because it features the indicator "unless" and two "nots." Using a single arrow, the diagram for the second rule is:

R ———→ P̸

This representation can be turned into the double-not arrow representation above.

When the two rules are combined, we can draw the very common grouping inference that Q and P cannot be on the stage at the same time:

Q ←—|—→ P

2. Rule 1:   3 ———→ S/T

    Rule 2: | W X |

On the diagram:

cars =   ___ ___ S/T ___ ___ ___
          1   2   3   4   5   6
          X̸   W̸   X̸   W̸

The first rule is best displayed directly on the diagram, as an S/T dual-option on space 3. The block rule yields two Not Laws automatically: X cannot be the first car sold, and W cannot be the last car sold. The combination of the two rules also yields two more Not Laws: W cannot be sold second (no space for X to be sold third), and X cannot be sold fourth (no space for W to be sold third).

In fact, the WX block is very limited in this game, and can only be placed in spaces 1-2, 4-5, and 5-6. The presence of other rules might suggest attacking the game by Identifying the Templates or Possibilities.

3.   Rule 1: | D/E ___ E/D |

        Rule 2: | F G |

On the diagram:

performances =

___	___	___	___	___
1	2	3	4	5
~~G~~				~~F~~

The first rule is a rotating split-block, and the second rule is a standard block. The second rule yields two Not Laws: G cannot be the first performance, and F cannot be the last performance. At this point it may seem as if there are no further inferences that can be drawn, but the two blocks create a significant restriction in the game that should be explored further. For example, the DE split block can only be placed in three positions, and those positions then restrict the movement of the FG block:

DE in 3-5:	F	G	D/E		E/D
~~DE in 2-4:~~		~~D/E~~		~~E/D~~	
DE in 1-3:	D/E		E/D	F	G
	1	2	3	4	5

As shown above, placing the DE block in spaces 2-4 does not allow for the placement of the FG block, and thus the DE block cannot be placed in 2-4. Therefore, the DE block must be in spaces 1-3 or 3-5 (meaning D or E is always in space 3), and the FG block must be in spaces 4-5 or 1-2. The final, unnamed variable would then fill in space 2 or 4.

---

4.   Rule 1:   ☐ M
                   N

      Rule 2:   ☐ Q
                   R

      Inference: ☐ M ⟷⊣ ☐ Q
                      N   R

Although stated in conditional terms, the first rule has the functional effect of creating a block. If M cannot be in a group unless N is in the same group, then M and N must be in the same group together. Similarly, if Q and R cannot be in different groups, they must be in the same group.

The size of these two blocks makes it impossible for the two to be in the same group, and thus we can draw the inference that the two blocks cannot be together. This can be shown on the diagram:

Of course, because the blocks take up two spaces in each group, there is only one space remaining in each group, and the other two, unnamed variables would have to be in separate groups as well.

5.   Rule 1:   R > S

        Rule 2: | T ___ R |

        Combined: | T ___ R | > S

        On the diagram:

        calls =   ___ ___ ___ ___ ___ ___
                    1   2   3   4   5   6
                    S̶   S̶   S̶   T̶   T̶   T̶
                    R̶   R̶   R̶

        The block-sequence configuration is fairly common in Logic games. Because the
        relationship involves three variables and four spaces, it produces a number of Not Laws. The
        configuration is also limited in placement, as the TR block has only three options: 1-3, 2-4,
        and 3-5.

6.   Rule 1: $H_1 \longrightarrow K_1$

        Rule 2: $J_2 \longrightarrow L_2$

        As this is a two-value system game, the contrapositive of any conditional rule typically yields
        useful information. The contrapositives of the two rules above are as follows:

        Contrapositive of Rule 1: $K_2 \longrightarrow H_2$

        Contrapositive of Rule 2: $L_1 \longrightarrow J_1$

        Because there are only three spaces in each group, any combination of the two rules that
        produces four variables in a group would be a violation. Thus, H and L cannot be in group 1
        together because H requires K, and L in group 1 requires J. Similarly, J and K cannot be in
        group 2 together because J requires L, and K in group 2 requires H. These two inferences can
        be shown as follows:

Two Rule Inference Drill Answer Key—page 17

7. Rule 1: ~~A~~ ⟷ B

   Rule 2: ~~B~~ ⟶ 2 out

The first rule creates a double arrow statement wherein when A is not interviewed then B must be interviewed, and when B is interviewed then A cannot be interviewed. Only two possible scenarios exist under this rule: A is not interviewed and B is interviewed, or, via the contrapositive of the rule, A is interviewed and B is not interviewed. Thus, exactly one of A and B must be selected, and normally we would represent that fact with an A/B dual-option on the diagram.

However, the second rule creates a situation that impacts the first rule. If B is not selected, then two other variables are also not selected, for a total of three variables not selected. As the rules indicate that there are only six interviewees, and the diagram shows there are only four interviews, the second rule would create a situation where not interviewing B would leave only three interviewees for the four interviews. As this is unacceptable, we can conclude that B must be interviewed and A is not interviewed:

B ___ ___ ___

Group of 4 Interviews

~~A~~

8. Rule 1: J ⟷|⟷ K

   Rule 2: K ⟶ L

   Combined: J ⟷|⟷ K ⟶ L

   Inference: No useful inference

Compare this item to item #1. The rules involved are the same, but because the relationships are different, this pair of rules does *not* produce an inference that is useful during Games.

The only inference that can be drawn is that "Some Ls are not Js," but during a game inferences involving "some" are typically worthless. If this were a Logical Reasoning question, the inference might very well play a role in the correct answer, but this is not the case in Games because we typically need inferences involving absolutes such as "must" or "cannot."

Commit to memory the difference between the first item and this item. During an actual game you want to be sure that you are drawing valid inferences, and not unknowingly relying on false inferences.

1.   Eight books are assigned to three students.

    Unfixed: 4-2-2
                    3-3-2

2.   Ten drinks are served to two bar patrons.

    Unfixed: 7-3
                    6-4
                    5-5

3.   Six bones are given to three dogs—a Greyhound, a Mastiff, and a Terrier.

Fixed:

G	M	T
3	2	1
1	3	2

4.   Eleven cookies are placed in four jars.

    Unfixed: 5-4-1-1
                    5-3-2-1
                    5-2-2-2
                    4-4-2-1
                    4-3-3-1
                    4-3-2-2
                    3-3-3-2

5.   Eight tables are assigned to four different servers—servers A, B, C, and D.

Fixed:

A	B	C	D
4	2	1	1
2	1	4	1
2	1	1	4
2	1	3	2
2	1	2	3

6.   Twelve students are assigned to five different floors in a dormitory.

        Unfixed: 4-2-2-2-2
                        3-3-2-2-2

7.   Seven animals are placed into three cages.

        Unfixed: 5-2-0
                        5-1-1
                        4-3-0
                        4-2-1
                        3-3-1
                        3-2-2

        Careful, the rules do not stipulate that a cage must contain a minimum number of animals, just a maximum.

8.   Thirteen toys are given to four children—W, X, Y, and Z.

        Fixed:

W	X	Y	Z
2	3	6	2
2	2	6	3

9.   Twenty-one pills are placed into six bottles.

        Unfixed: 6-3-3-3-3-3
                        5-4-3-3-3-3
                        4-4-4-3-3-3

10.   Seven appointments with a doctor are scheduled over four days—Monday, Tuesday, Wednesday, and Thursday.

        Fixed:

M	Tu	W	Th
1	1	3	2
3	1	2	1
2	2	2	1
1	3	2	1

Note: Most of the problems in this drill are diagrammed with horizontal setups. In many cases these problems could be diagrammed with vertical setups, although some games should be shown horizontally, such as one about houses on a street. Also, if you encounter a Not Law in the answer key that appears incorrectly placed, put that variable into that position and observe the consequences. This will allow you to better understand the interaction taking place between the variables and the rules.

<u>Drill #1</u>. Whenever a game introduces the days of the week as a variable set, always use the days of the week as the base. As the two variable sets both contain six members, and each member is either used or filled, the two variable sets are in a one-to-one relationship (1-1-1-1-1-1).

The base diagram appears as follows:

K L M N O P^6
   *

$\frac{\text{K/}}{\text{M}}$	$\frac{}{\text{Tu}}$	$\frac{\text{O/P}}{\text{W}}$	$\frac{}{\text{Th}}$	$\frac{}{\text{F}}$	$\frac{\text{/K}}{\text{S}}$

$N_{Tu} \longrightarrow M_S$

$W \longrightarrow O/P$

$K \longrightarrow M/S$

The relationships can be linked by connecting the two rules that reference Saturday:

If Noriko works on Tuesday, then Marina works on Saturday, and Kwame must work Monday. This can be diagrammed as:

$$N_{Tu} \longrightarrow M_S \longrightarrow K_M$$

If Kwame works on Saturday, then Marina cannot work on Saturday, and Noriko cannot work on Tuesday. This can be diagrammed as:

$$K_S \longrightarrow \cancel{M_S} \longrightarrow \cancel{N_{Tu}}$$

Either relationship reduces to:

$$N_{Tu} \longleftarrow\!\!\!|\!\!\!\longrightarrow K_S$$

<u>Drill #2</u>. There are two variable sets in this problem: the five birds and the five cages in which they are placed. Since the cage numbers in which the birds are placed have an inherent sense of order, they are chosen as the base. Again, the two variable sets are in a one-to-one relationship (1-1-1-1-1).

P Q R S T[5]
   * *

R ———→ 2

$$\underline{} \quad \overset{R}{\underline{2}} \quad \underline{3} \quad \underline{4} \quad \underline{5}$$

| P/Q __ Q/P |

The split-block has only two spacing options: 1-3 and 3-5. The following diagram shows each option drawn out:

Option #2—Block in 3-5:   ___ R P/Q ___ Q/P

Option #1—Block in 1-3:
$$\underset{1}{P/Q} \quad \underset{2}{R} \quad \underset{3}{Q/P} \quad \underset{4}{} \quad \underset{5}{}$$

Of course, in each instance only two spaces are open, and only two variables are unaccounted for: S and T. Thus, S and T form a dual-option in the open spaces in each scenario:

Option #2—Block in 3-5:   S/T R P/Q T/S Q/P

Option #1—Block in 1-3:
$$\underset{1}{P/Q} \quad \underset{2}{R} \quad \underset{3}{Q/P} \quad \underset{4}{S/T} \quad \underset{5}{T/S}$$

The two templates contain four solutions each, and thus there are only eight solutions in this game.

Although this problem is too simple to appear as an entire Logic Game, it is indicative of the type of "endgame" situations that occur after several variables have already been placed in a question.

Question 2.1. The correct answer is (C). As shown by the two templates above, S or T is always fourth.

Answer choice (A) is incorrect because S or T could be placed in the first cage.
Answer choice (B) is incorrect because P or Q could be placed in the first cage.
Answer choice (D) is incorrect because S or T could be placed in the fifth cage.
Answer choice (E) is incorrect because P or Q could be placed in the fifth cage.

Drill #3. In this problem the speaking order should be chosen as the base, and the variables are in a one-to-one relationship (1-1-1-1-1-1).

B C D F G H [6]

$\boxed{BC} > D$

G/H	F		B/C	D/	/D
1	2	3	4	5	6
~~D~~		~~D~~	~~D~~	~~B~~	~~B~~
~~B~~		~~C~~			~~C~~
~~C~~					

The first point of interest in this problem is in the representation of F. Since F must speak second, it automatically follows that F cannot speak first, third, fourth, fifth, or sixth. An argument could thus be made that F Not Laws should be shown on those slots. This representation would be correct, but since F is already placed, this would be redundant. However, if you find yourself continually missing these types of inferences, you can certainly show the F Not Laws.

The second point of interest is in the placement of the BC block. Because of the space requirements for the block, and the fact that D speaks later than the block, the block must be placed in positions 3-4 or 4-5. Accordingly, either B or C must always speak fourth and therefore no other student can speak fourth. This dual-option is represented by B/C in the fourth slot.

The next piece of relevant information in this problem concerns D. Because D must speak later than the block, D must speak fifth or sixth, and this is represented on the diagram with a split-option.

The final piece of relevant information in this problem concerns G and H. Although we cannot be sure of the exact placement of these two variables, we can deduce that one of the two must always occupy the first space (because all other speakers have been eliminated from the first space).

Drill #4. In this problem the order of song performance is chosen as the base, and the variable sets are in a one-to-one relationship (1-1-1-1-1-1-1).

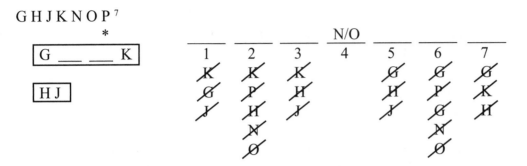

The first rule presents a tricky block that is often mis-diagrammed. If G is played *three songs before* K, then there are actually two songs between G and K. To best understand the rule, start with K and then count three spaces going to the left. G is placed in that third space, producing the block above.

Because the GK block requires so much space, the options for placing that block are limited. In fact, the GK block can only be placed in spaces 2-5 or 3-6:

Option #2—Block in 3-6: ____ ____ G N/O ____ K ____

Option #1—Block in 2-5: ____ G ____ N/O K ____ ____
            1   2   3   4   5   6   7

Of course, in each option the HJ block is limited in placement as well:

Option #2—Block in 3-6: H J G N/O ____ K ____

Option #1—Block in 2-5: ____ G ____ N/O K H J
            1   2   3   4   5   6   7

The remaining two open spaces in each diagram are then filled by P and the remainder of the N/O dual-option. Thus, we can deduce that spaces 2 and 6 are highly restricted and a number of Not Laws follow for each. For example, P must be in space 1, 3, 5, or 7, and thus can never be placed in space 2 or 6.

<u>Drill #5</u>. Of the two variable sets, the floors of the building should be chosen as the base because they have the greatest sense of inherent order. The variable sets are in a one-to-one relationship (1-1-1-1-1-1-1), and in this case the best representation is vertical since that is the way the floors of buildings exist in the real world.

Q R S T W X Y [7]

```
          *                    7 ____
 ┌───┐   ┌───┐                 6 ____
 │ Q │   │ W │                 5 _T__
 │ R │   │ X │                 4 ____
 └───┘   └───┘                 3 ____
                               2 _S__
                               1 ____
```

The diagram above shows the basic rule representations. A quick glance at the diagram reveals that the two blocks must be assigned to floors 3-4 and 6-7:

```
        7 ┌──┐
        6 │  │
        5  T
        4 ┌──┐
        3 │  │
        2  S
        1 ___
```

Accordingly, Y, the only remaining variable, must be assigned to floor 1.

Question 5.1. The correct answer is (D). If the QR block is assigned to the top two floors, T would be assigned to the floor directly below R. Each of the remaining answer choices puts a fixed variable on the "wrong" side of the block, or attempts to place the two blocks consecutively.

<u>Drill #6</u>. Of the two variable sets, the courts should be chosen as the base since they are numbered and stand consecutively. The game is Underfunded with only six players for the seven courts (6 into 7). However, this shortage can be alleviated by representing the "missing" player with an "E" variable for empty. Whenever there is a shortage of variables (in this case, the players) available to fill a set number of spaces (in this case, the courts), you can always combat this problem by representing the missing variable with an E (or if the given variables already include E, use another letter, such as X). With the shortage of variables eliminated, the variable set relationship can be seen as a one-to-one (1-1-1-1-1-1-1).

G H J K L M E ^{7}
*

$$
\begin{array}{c}
\qquad\qquad\quad L \\
K > H > \text{----} \\
\qquad\qquad\quad M
\end{array}
$$

G/K						
1	2	3	4	5	6	7
~~E~~	~~E~~	~~E~~	~~K~~	~~K~~	~~K~~	~~K~~
~~L~~	~~L~~	~~J~~		~~J~~	~~H~~	~~H~~
~~M~~	~~M~~					
~~H~~						
~~J~~						

In all game types, one of the basic methods for identifying inferences is to examine the points of restriction in the game. In games with Not Laws, that involves looking closely at the slots with the greatest number of Not Laws. In this case, it becomes apparent that court 1 is the most restricted court in the problem. In fact, since five of the seven variables cannot be assigned to court 1 (E is counted as a variable for this purpose), only two players—G and K—are available to play at court 1. This inference would most likely be tested in a game by a question such as, "If K is assigned to court 4, which one of the following must be true?" The correct answer would be "G must be assigned to court 1." In one-to-one Linear games, always examine any space that has a large number of Not Laws, and do not forget that any variable that is already placed is automatically eliminated from all other slots!

In addition, the "K" Not Law on court 4 is correct because placing K on 4 causes a violation of the second rule:

> When K is assigned to court 4, then courts 5, 6, and 7 must be occupied by players H, L, and M (not necessarily in that order). This forces the Empty court (variable "E") to be assigned to court 1, 2, or 3. Unfortunately, that assignment is a violation of the second rule that states that courts 1, 2, and 3 cannot be empty.

<u>Drill #7</u>. The houses should be chosen as the base since they are numbered and stand on the same side of the street. The two variable sets are in a one-to-one relationship (1-1-1-1-1-1-1), and the game should be set up horizontally since that is the way streets exist in the real world.

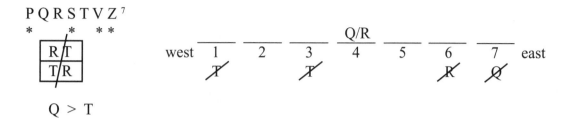

Initially this seems like a fairly simple setup. The rules are easy to represent, and two quick Not Laws follow from the Q > T relationship. In a real game, at this point most students would stop and move to the questions. However, always make sure to examine the linkages in a game before moving to the questions. In this drill, the rules link together on several counts: the first two rules are linked through R, and the third rule is linked to both of the first two rules. When this type of multiple link situation arises, you can expect there will either be some immediate inferences, or that the connections will play a significant role in the game.

The inferences involving T not occupying house 3 and R not occupying house 6 are quite challenging. Let us review each:

<u>T cannot occupy house 3</u>

If T occupies house 3, then Q must live to the west of T in house 1 or 2. From the first rule, R must then occupy house 4, creating a violation as R and T occupy consecutively numbered houses.

<u>R cannot occupy house 6</u>

If R occupies house 6, then from the first rule Q must occupy house 4. From the third rule, T must then live east of house 4 in houses 5 or 7. As either house is consecutively numbered with R in house 6, a violation of the second rule occurs.

<u>Drill #8</u>. The order of testing should be chosen as the base in this problem, and the variable sets are in a one-to-one relationship (1-1-1-1-1-1-1-1).

B C D F G H J K ^{8}

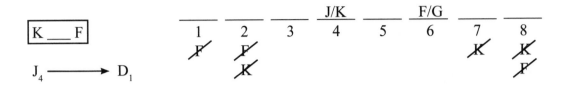

All of the Not Laws above follow from the KF block. Note that because the fourth and sixth tests are already assigned, these affect the block as well.

The interaction of the first, second, and third rules establishes that there are only two possibilities for the fourth and sixth tests: K in four and F in six, or J in four and G in six. Using this information the best attack is to Identify the Templates:

K in 4:

			K		F		
1	2	3	4	5	6	7	8

J in 4, K in 5:

D			J	K	G	F	

J in 4, K in 3:

D		K	J	F	G		
1	2	3	4	5	6	7	8

In the first template, there are no restrictions on the placement of any variable (D can be tested first, even if J is not tested fourth; do not make a Mistaken Reversal!).

In the second set of templates, when J is tested fourth, then D must be tested first. This limits the placement of the KF block to 3-5 or 5-7. The remaining spaces are then taken by B, C, and H.

Note also that the fourth rule is conditional, and uses the necessary condition indicator "only if." We did not show the contrapositive because over time you should begin to understand that the contrapositive inherently follows from any conditional relationship. The rule of thumb is to write out the contrapositive when you feel that doing so will make the game easier for you.

<u>Drill #1</u>. There are three variable sets in this problem: the six production positions, the six bike models, and the colors. Because the production positions have the greatest sense of inherent order, they should be chosen as the base. Consequently, the base diagram should appear as follows:

Colors: B R S ^{3}
Bikes: T U W X Y Z ^{6}

Colors: ____ ____ ____ ____ ____ ____

Bikes: ____ ____ ____ ____ ____ ____
$\quad\quad$ 1 $\quad$ 2 $\quad$ 3 $\quad$ 4 $\quad$ 5 $\quad$ 6

The first rule forms an SR block and indicates that only one silver bike and only one red bike are produced, meaning the other four bikes must be black. The third rule adds in that W is the silver bike, producing an advanced stacked block:

S	R
W	___

The last rule stipulates that the second and fourth bikes are black, meaning that the block can only be produced fifth and sixth (and thus the first and third bikes are black), leading to the following complete setup:

Colors: B B B B $\boxed{\text{S R}}$ ^{6}
Bikes: T U W X Y Z ^{6}
$\quad\quad$ * * $\quad\quad$ *

Colors: $\quad$ B $\quad$ B $\quad$ B $\quad$ B $\quad$ S $\quad$ R

Bikes: $\quad$ ____ ____ ____ X/Y $\quad$ W $\quad$ ____
$\quad\quad\quad$ 1 $\quad$ 2 $\quad$ 3 $\quad$ 4 $\quad$ 5 $\quad$ 6

Drill #2. There are three variable sets in this problem: the seven finishing positions, the seven runners, and the male/female designation. The finishing positions have an inherent order, and they should be chosen as the base, leading to the following base setup:

Sex: M M M M F F F [7]
Runner: K L N O P R S [7]

M/F: ___ ___ ___ ___ ___ ___ ___

Runner: ___ ___ ___ ___ ___ ___ ___
        1   2   3   4   5   6   7

As is often the case in Linear Games, the rules add a considerable amount of information to the diagram. The last rule is the most powerful. Because there are four males and no two males can finish consecutively (and thus each male must be next to a female), the Separation Principle applies and the males must finish 1-3-5-7. The three females then finish 2-4-6:

M/F: M F M F M F M

Runner: ___ ___ ___ ___ ___ ___ ___
        1   2   3   4   5   6   7

With this information in place, the movement of the runners is considerably restricted, and the remaining rules can be diagrammed as follows:

```
 ___   F
  P    S
```

M/F: M F M F M F M

Runner: P/ S/ ___ L/N /P /S ___
        1   2   3   4   5   6   7

4 ⟶ L/N

Because S is a female, and L and N are also females (those are the two options for the fourth spot, which is female), the three females are L, N, and S, and thus the four males are K, O, P, and R.

With the fourth space occupied by L or N, S must finish second or sixth (the only two spots available for a female). Given the limited options for the PS block, one approach would be to show the two templates, one with PS in 1-2 and the other with PS in 5-6.

<u>Drill #3</u>. There are four variable sets in this problem: the days of the week, the morning times, the afternoon times, and the ten individuals being deposed. Because the days of the week have the greatest sense of inherent order, they should be chosen as the base. Consequently, the base diagram should appear as follows:

Depositions: A B C D F G H J K L [10]

Afternoon: ___ ___ ___ ___ ___

Morning: ___ ___ ___ ___ ___
                 M   Tu   W   Th   F

The first and third rules establish four Side Not Laws, and one Not Law under Monday afternoon:

Afternoon: ___ ___ ___ ___ ___   A̶ B̶
                  D̶
Morning: ___ ___ ___ ___ ___   C̶ D̶
                 M   Tu   W   Th   F

The second, fourth, and fifth rules create a powerful block sequence:

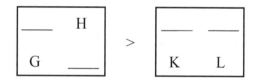

Although you could show the Not Laws that follow from this configuration, doing so is time-consuming, and the visual power of the block is enough so that showing the Not Laws is probably unnecessary. There are, of course, powerful inferences that follow from the limited options available for the blocks. For example, the Thursday morning deposition must be K or L.

At this point, many students stop working, but there is one final set of inferences that can be drawn. Because the blocks establish that G, K, and L are all deposed in the morning, and A and B cannot be deposed in the afternoon and thus must be deposed in the morning, we can conclude that A, B, G, K, and L are the morning depositions, and the remaining five individuals—C, D, F, H, and J—are the afternoon depositions.

<u>Drill #4</u>. There are three variable sets in this problem: the two apartment buildings, the six floors, and the three art types. The best setup for buildings with floors is vertical, and thus the buildings should be the base, and the floors should number 1-6 from the bottom to the top, as in the real world:

G P S [3]

```
6    _____           _____

5    _____           _____

4    _____           _____

3    _____           _____

2    _____           _____

1    _____           _____
       A               B
```

The art types are a repeating variable set. Although no stipulation is made that all three styles will appear in each building, if any given floor cannot be decorated in one of the types, that will leave a dual-option of the other two types.

The first rule establishes a horizontal not-block, with "T" designating "type:"

$$\boxed{T\!\!\!/T}$$

The second rule creates a block on floor 3 of Building A and floor 4 of Building B. Because showing this can be difficult, use a double arrow to represent the rule (and also place the double arrow on the diagram):

$$3A \longleftrightarrow 4B$$

The third rule can be diagrammed as a Not Law on floor 6 of Building A, creating a G/S dual-option on that space.

The last rule establishes a rotating vertical not-block:

Advanced Linear Setup Practice Drill Answer Key—page

When combined, the rules create the following diagram:

G P S [3]

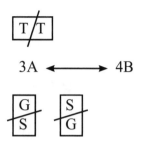

3A ⟷ 4B

1. Classification: Undefined

Since the number of doctors to be hired at the hospital is unknown, the game is Undefined. Since the game is Undefined there is no Moving/Fixed element, nor is there a Balance element.

2. Classification: Defined-Fixed, Balanced

Since each firm contains exactly three agents, the game is Defined-Fixed. Since there are nine agents for exactly nine positions, the game is Balanced.

3. Classification: Defined-Moving, Balanced

Since each of the eight students is assigned to a class, but it is unknown exactly how many students are assigned to each class, the game is Defined-Moving. Since all eight students are assigned to the two classes, the game is Balanced.

4. Classification: Defined-Fixed, Unbalanced: Underfunded

Since each committee contains exactly two members, the game is Defined-Fixed. Since there are only seven candidates for the eight positions, the game is Unbalanced: Underfunded. The seven-into-eight scenario creates a numerical distribution of 2-1-1-1-1-1-1. Remember, each of the seven candidates must be assigned to at least one committee. That means that seven of the eight committee spaces are automatically filled. The remaining space goes to a candidate who is assigned to two committees, and hence the 2-1-1-1-1-1-1 distribution.

5. Classification: Defined-Moving, Unbalanced: Overloaded

Since exactly six reviewers will be assigned to the four restaurants, but it is unknown how many reviewers will review each restaurant (it is either a 3-1-1-1 numerical distribution or a 2-2-1-1 numerical distribution), the game is Defined-Moving. Since there are nine reviewers for the six positions, the game is Unbalanced: Overloaded.

6. Classification: Partially Defined

Since the number of diners is at least four, but it is uncertain exactly how many diners there will be, the game is Partially Defined. Since the game is Partially Defined, there is no Moving/Fixed element, nor is there a Balance element.

7. Classification: Defined-Fixed, Unbalanced: Overloaded

Since each weight lifting team contains exactly three weight lifters, the game is Defined-Fixed. Since there are eight weight lifters for exactly six positions, the game is Unbalanced: Overloaded.

8. Classification: Undefined

Since the number of courses offered at the school is unknown, the game is Undefined. Since the game is Undefined there is no Moving/Fixed element, nor is there a Balance element.

Drill #1. The scenario states that there are six waiters for four tables, so at first this game appears to be Overloaded. However, the scenario states that the waiters are assigned in pairs, and thus there are eight total positions to fill. With only six waiters, some waiters will have to be assigned to more than one table, and thus the grouping classification of this drill is Defined-Fixed, Unbalanced: Underfunded.

Because each waiter is assigned to a table, and there are eight positions, there are two numerical distributions of assignments-to-waiters in this game:

Three tables assigned to one waiter, one to each of the rest:	3-1-1-1-1-1
Two tables assigned to two waiters, one to each of the rest:	2-2-1-1-1-1

The remainder of the setup is relatively straightforward:

S T W X Y Z ^{6}

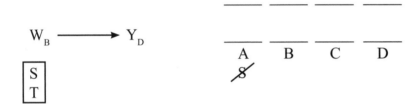

The one inference of note is that if W is assigned to table B, then Y must be assigned to table D, forcing S and T to be assigned to table C (S cannot be assigned to table A):

$$W_B \longrightarrow \boxed{\begin{matrix} S \\ T \end{matrix}}_C$$

<u>Drill #2</u>. This game is classified as Undefined because no specification is made as to how many horses are in the paddock at any given time.

The four rules, as given, can be diagrammed as follows:

1. C ◄——┼——► D

2. D ———► G

3. F ———► C

4. A̸ ———► B

As you diagrammed the rules, you should have been looking for connections. The first and third rules can be combined:

F ———► C ◄——┼——► D

This relationship yields the following inference:

F ◄——┼——► D

Some students attempt to draw an inference from the combination of the first and second rules:

C ◄——┼——► D ———► G

However, this relationship does not yield a usable inference for Logic Games (the inference that it does yield, "Some Gs are not Cs" typically is useful only in Logical Reasoning).

The last rule also bears consideration. If A is not in the paddock, then B must be in the paddock. Via the contrapositive, if B is not in the paddock, then A must be in the paddock. Thus, at all times, either A or B must be in the paddock. Of course, the rule also allows for *both* A and B to be in the paddock but at least one of A and B must be there.

<u>Drill #3</u>. The scenario states that there are eight bands playing two stages at a music festival. The exact number of bands on each stage is not fixed; the Main Stage must be assigned at least four bands and the Side Stage must be assigned at least three bands. These requirements create two fixed distributions:

	Main Stage	Side Stage
Distribution #1:	5	3
Distribution #2:	4	4

Thus, the selection group is Defined-Moving, and as there are eight bands for the eight spaces, the variable pool is Balanced.

The initial scenario appears as follows:

$$C \; D \; F \; G \; H \; I \; K \; L^{\,8}$$

$K_S \longrightarrow D_M$

The second rule bears further examination. At first, this appears to be a standard conditional grouping rule. Thus, the contrapositive of this rule would be:

$$\cancel{D_M} \longrightarrow \cancel{K_S}$$

But, because there are only two stages, and each band must be assigned to one of the two stages, this is actually a two-value system game. Thus, if a band is not assigned to the Main Stage it must be assigned to the Side Stage, and if a band is not assigned to the side stage it must be assigned to the Main Stage. This allows us to restate the contrapositive as follows:

$$D_S \longrightarrow K_M$$

Although D and K do not have to perform on different stages (they could both perform on the Main Stage), should one of them perform on the Side Stage the first rule will come into play and the other band will occupy a space on the Main Stage.

Drill #4. The scenario states that there are eight senators serving on three subcommittees. This makes the game Defined-Fixed. As there is a space for each senator, the final classification is Defined-Fixed, Balanced.

The initial scenario with the first two rules diagrammed appears as follows:

J K L M O P Q R[8]

      *   *

$$\begin{array}{ccc} \underline{\quad} & \underline{\quad} & \underline{\quad} \\ \underline{\quad} & \underline{\quad} & \underline{\quad} \\ \underline{P} & \underline{Q} & \underline{\quad} \\ D & F & P \end{array}$$

The last two rules are fairly easy to diagram as they are both positive grouping rules.

Third rule:

$$\boxed{\begin{array}{c} K \\ L \end{array}}$$

Fourth rule:

$$\boxed{\begin{array}{c} J \\ M \end{array}}$$

The fourth rule can be a bit more challenging, but remember that "if and only if" introduces a double-arrow. The proper conditional diagram is thus:

$$J \longleftrightarrow M$$

In a grouping game featuring verticality, we turn this double-arrow into a vertical block.

Applying the last two rules to the diagram, although we cannot ascertain where each block is placed, we do know that neither block can be on the Finance subcommittee due to insufficient space, and thus one of the blocks must serve on the Defense subcommittee and the other block must serve on the Policy subcommittee. These inferences can be shown as:

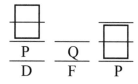

Of course, this leaves only one "open" space on the Finance subcommittee and one open space on the Policy subcommittee. The only two variables available are the two randoms—O and R—leading

---

to the final setup for the game:

J K L M O P Q R [8]
     *   *

  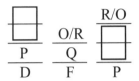

1.   Classification: Local, Could Be True
        Four Incorrect Answers: Cannot Be True

2.   Classification: Global, Not Necessarily True
        Four Incorrect Answers: Must Be True

        Remember, "could be false" is the equivalent of "not necessarily true."

3.   Classification: Global, Could Be True, List
        Four Incorrect Answers: Cannot Be True

        The question asks for a list of musicians; remember to apply proper List question technique.

4.   Classification: Local, Cannot Be True
        Four Incorrect Answers: Could Be True

5.   Classification: Local, Cannot Be True
        Four Incorrect Answers: Could Be True

        Remember, "Except" turns the question around.

6.   Classification: Local, Must Be True
        Four Incorrect Answers: Not Necessarily True

        Remember, "cannot be false" is the equivalent of "must be true."

7.   Classification: Global, Could Be True
        Four Incorrect Answers: Cannot Be True

        Remember, "must be false" is the equivalent to "cannot be true," and then "Except" turns the question around.

8.　　　Classification: Global, Must Be True, Minimum
　　　　Four Incorrect Answers: Not Necessarily True

The classification here is not a mistake. This is a Must Be True question, not a Could Be True question even though the question stem uses the word "could." In asking for the "minimum number of animals," the question seeks a number that Must Be True, that is, the minimum is a global certainty that is always constant and therefore must be true.

9.　　　Classification: Local, Cannot Be True, Suspension
　　　　Four Incorrect Answers: Could Be True

This is a Suspension question because it asks you to suspend one of the original rules of the game. When questions such as this one appear, they always appear at the end of the game. Be wary of Suspension questions if time is low because they force you to re-setup the game and can be time-consuming.

10.　　　Classification: Global, Must Be True, Justify
　　　　Four Incorrect Answers: Not Necessarily True

This is actually a Justify question. The question stem asks you to select the answer choice that will, when added to the existing rules, force only one outcome. The question has been classified as "Must Be True, Justify" because the correct answer must justify (or produce) the desired solution and the four incorrect answers do not necessarily justify the desired outcome.

CHAPTER THREE: INDIVIDUAL GAMES

Chapter Notes

This section contains ten individual Logic Games drawn from actual LSATs. You can use these games in a variety of ways, but perhaps the best approach is to complete each game as a time trial, and then check your work against the complete setup and explanation provided at the end of this section. We do *not* recommend that you do all ten games in a row as this will defeat the purpose of learning from your mistakes and improving your performance. We also do not recommend that you section these ten games out and try to make them in two and a half Logic Games sections. The next section of the book contains complete LSAT Logic Games sections, and those should be done as full timed exercises.

To properly time yourself on these individual games, keep in mind the timing guidelines dictated by the 35-minute format of each LSAT section. The following table displays the amount of time that should be allotted to each game, depending on how many you plan to attempt in a section:

# Games Attempted in a Section	Time per Game Attempted
2	17 minutes and 30 seconds
3	11 minutes and 40 seconds
4	8 minutes and 45 seconds

Thus, if your overall goal in the Logic Games section is to complete all four games, then you should look to complete each individual game in this section in 8 minutes and 45 seconds. If you only expect to complete three games per test, then you should look to finish each individual game in this section in 11 minutes and 40 seconds (although, of course, you should always look to go faster—part of the goal with this book is to give you practice with our methods and techniques in an effort to help you work more quickly and efficiently).

Stay focused, be positive, and good luck!

Six hotel suites—F, G, H, J, K, L—are ranked from most expensive (first) to least expensive (sixth). There are no ties. The ranking must be consistent with the following conditions:

H is more expensive than L.

If G is more expensive than H, then neither K nor L is more expensive than J.

If H is more expensive than G, then neither J nor L is more expensive than K.

F is more expensive than G, or else F is more expensive than H, but not both.

6. Which one of the following could be the ranking of the suites, from most expensive to least expensive?

(A)   G, F, H, L, J, K
(B)   H, K, F, J, G, L
(C)   J, H, F, K, G, L
(D)   J, K, G, H, L, F
(E)   K, J, L, H, F, G

7. If G is the second most expensive suite, then which one of the following could be true?

(A)   H is more expensive than F.
(B)   H is more expensive than G.
(C)   K is more expensive than F.
(D)   K is more expensive than J.
(E)   L is more expensive than F.

8. Which one of the following CANNOT be the most expensive suite?

(A)   F
(B)   G
(C)   H
(D)   J
(E)   K

9. If L is more expensive than F, then which one of the following could be true?

(A)   F is more expensive than H.
(B)   F is more expensive than K.
(C)   G is more expensive than H.
(D)   G is more expensive than J.
(E)   G is more expensive than L.

10. If H is more expensive than J and less expensive than K, then which one of the following could be true?

(A)   F is more expensive than H.
(B)   G is more expensive than F.
(C)   G is more expensive than H.
(D)   J is more expensive than L.
(E)   L is more expensive than K.

A courier delivers exactly eight parcels-G, H, J, K, L, M, N, and O. No two parcels are delivered at the same time, nor is any parcel delivered more than once. The following conditions must apply:

L is delivered later than H.
K is delivered earlier than O.
H is delivered earlier than M.
O is delivered later than G.
M is delivered earlier than G.
Both N and J are delivered earlier than M.

16. Which one of the following could be the order of deliveries from first to last?

(A)   N, H, K, M, J, G, O, L
(B)   H, N, J, K, G, O, L, M
(C)   J, H, N, M, K, O, G, L
(D)   N, J, H, L, M, K, G, O
(E)   K, N, J, M, G, H, O, L

17. Which one of the following must be true?

(A)   At least one parcel is delivered earlier than K is delivered.
(B)   At least two parcels are delivered later than G is delivered.
(C)   At least four parcels are delivered later than H is delivered.
(D)   At least four parcels are delivered later than J is delivered.
(E)   At least four parcels are delivered earlier than M is delivered.

18. If M is the fourth parcel delivered, then which one of the following must be true?

(A)   G is the fifth parcel delivered.
(B)   O is the seventh parcel delivered.
(C)   J is delivered later than H.
(D)   K is delivered later than N.
(E)   G is delivered later than L.

19. If H is the fourth parcel delivered, then each of the following could be true EXCEPT:

(A)   K is the fifth parcel delivered.
(B)   L is the sixth parcel delivered.
(C)   M is the sixth parcel delivered.
(D)   G is the seventh parcel delivered.
(E)   O is the seventh parcel delivered.

20. Each of the following could be true EXCEPT:

(A)   H is delivered later than K.
(B)   J is delivered later than G.
(C)   L is delivered later than O.
(D)   M is delivered later than L.
(E)   N is delivered later than H.

21. If K is the seventh parcel delivered, then each of the following could be true EXCEPT:

(A)   G is the fifth parcel delivered.
(B)   M is the fifth parcel delivered.
(C)   H is the fourth parcel delivered.
(D)   L is the fourth parcel delivered.
(E)   J is the third parcel delivered.

22. If L is delivered earlier than K, then which one of the following must be false?

(A)   N is the second parcel delivered.
(B)   L is the third parcel delivered.
(C)   H is the fourth parcel delivered.
(D)   K is the fifth parcel delivered.
(E)   M is the sixth parcel delivered.

There are exactly six groups in this year's Civic Parade: firefighters, gymnasts, jugglers, musicians, puppeteers, and veterans. Each group marches as a unit; the groups are ordered from first, at the front of the parade, to sixth, at the back. The following conditions apply:

At least two groups march behind the puppeteers but ahead of the musicians.

Exactly one group marches behind the firefighters but ahead of the veterans.

The gymnasts are the first, third, or fifth group.

1. Which one of the following could be an accurate list of the groups in the Civic Parade in order from first to last?

(A) firefighters, puppeteers, veterans, musicians, gymnasts, jugglers
(B) gymnasts, puppeteers, jugglers, musicians, firefighters, veterans
(C) veterans, puppeteers, firefighters, gymnasts, jugglers, musicians
(D) jugglers, puppeteers, gymnasts, firefighters, musicians, veterans
(E) musicians, veterans, jugglers, firefighters, gymnasts, puppeteers

2. If the gymnasts march immediately ahead of the veterans, then which one of the following could be the fourth group?

(A) gymnasts
(B) jugglers
(C) musicians
(D) puppeteers
(E) veterans

3. If the veterans march immediately behind the puppeteers, then which one of the following could be the second group?

(A) firefighters
(B) gymnasts
(C) jugglers
(D) musicians
(E) veterans

4. If the jugglers are the fifth group, then which one of the following must be true?

(A) The puppeteers are the first group.
(B) The firefighters are the first group.
(C) The veterans are the second group.
(D) The gymnasts are the third group.
(E) The musicians are the sixth group.

5. Which one of the following groups CANNOT march immediately behind the gymnasts?

(A) firefighters
(B) jugglers
(C) musicians
(D) puppeteers
(E) veterans

On one afternoon, Patterson meets individually with each of exactly five clients—Reilly, Sanchez, Tang, Upton, and Yansky—and also goes to the gym by herself for a workout. Patterson's workout and her five meetings each start at either 1:00, 2:00, 3:00, 4:00, 5:00, or 6:00. The following conditions must apply:

Patterson meets with Sanchez at some time before her workout.

Patterson meets with Tang at some time after her workout. Patterson meets with Yansky either immediately before or immediately after her workout.

Patterson meets with Upton at some time before she meets with Reilly.

1. Which one of the following could be an acceptable schedule of Patterson's workout and meetings, in order from 1:00 to 6:00?

    (A) Yansky, workout, Upton, Reilly, Sanchez, Tang
    (B) Upton, Tang, Sanchez, Yansky, workout, Reilly
    (C) Upton, Reilly, Sanchez, workout, Tang, Yansky
    (D) Sanchez, Yansky, workout, Reilly, Tang, Upton
    (E) Sanchez, Upton, workout, Yansky, Tang, Reilly

2. How many of the clients are there, anyone of whom could meet with Patterson at 1:00?

    (A) one
    (B) two
    (C) three
    (D) four
    (E) five

3. Patterson CANNOT meet with Upton at which one of the following times?

    (A) 1:00
    (B) 2:00
    (C) 3:00
    (D) 4:00
    (E) 5:00

4. If Patterson meets with Sanchez the hour before she meets with Yansky, then each of the following could be true EXCEPT:

    (A) Patterson meets with Reilly at 2:00.
    (B) Patterson meets with Yansky at 3:00.
    (C) Patterson meets with Tang at 4:00.
    (D) Patterson meets with Yansky at 5:00.
    (E) Patterson meets with Tang at 6:00.

5. If Patterson meets with Tang at 4:00, then which one of the following must be true?

    (A) Patterson meets with Reilly at 5:00.
    (B) Patterson meets with Upton at 5:00.
    (C) Patterson meets with Yansky at 2:00.
    (D) Patterson meets with Yansky at 3:00.
    (E) Patterson's workout is at 2:00.

6. Which one of the following could be the order of Patterson's meetings, from earliest to latest?

    (A) Upton, Yansky, Sanchez, Reilly, Tang
    (B) Upton, Reilly, Sanchez, Tang, Yansky
    (C) Sanchez, Yansky, Reilly, Tang, Upton
    (D) Sanchez, Upton, Tang, Yansky, Reilly
    (E) Sanchez, Upton, Reilly, Yansky, Tang

Exactly six of an artist's paintings, entitled *Quarterion, Redemption, Sipapu, Tesseract, Vale,* and *Zelkova,* are sold at auction. Three of the paintings are sold to a museum, and three are sold to a private collector. Two of the paintings are from the artist's first (earliest) period, two are from her second period, and two are from her third (most recent) period. The private collector and the museum each buy one painting from each period. The following conditions hold:

Sipapu, which is sold to the private collector, is from an earlier period than *Zelkova,* which is sold to the museum.

Quarterion is not from an earlier period than *Tesseract.*

Vale is from the artist's second period.

13. Which one of the following could be an accurate list of the paintings bought by the museum and the private collector, listed in order of the paintings' periods, from first to third?

    (A)   museum: *Quarterion, Vale, Zelkova*
          private collector: *Redemption, Sipapu, Tesseract*
    (B)   museum: *Redemption, Zelkova, Quarterion*
          private collector: *Sipapu, Vale, Tesseract*
    (C)   museum: *Sipapu, Zelkova, Quarterion*
          private collector: *Tesseract, Vale, Redemption*
    (D)   museum: *Tesseract, Quarterion, Zelkova*
          private collector: *Sipapu, Redemption, Vale*
    (E)   museum: *Zelkova, Tesseract, Redemption*
          private collector: *Sipapu, Vale, Quarterion*

14. If *Sipapu* is from the artist's second period, which one of the following could be two of the three paintings bought by the private collector?

    (A)   *Quarterion* and *Zelkova*
    (B)   *Redemption* and *Tesseract*
    (C)   *Redemption* and *Vale*
    (D)   *Redemption* and *Zelkova*
    (E)   *Tesseract* and *Zelkova*

15. Which one of the following is a complete and accurate list of the paintings, any one of which could be the painting from the artist's first period that is sold to the private collector?

    (A)   *Quarterion, Redemption*
    (B)   *Redemption, Sipapu*
    (C)   *Quarterion, Sipapu, Tesseract*
    (D)   *Quarterion, Redemption, Sipapu, Tesseract*
    (E)   *Redemption, Sipapu, Tesseract, Zelkova*

16. If *Sipapu* is from the artist's second period, then which one of the following paintings could be from the period immediately preceding *Quarterion*'s period and be sold to the same buyer as *Quarterion*?

    (A)   *Redemption*
    (B)   *Sipapu*
    (C)   *Tesseract*
    (D)   *Vale*
    (E)   *Zelkova*

17. If *Zelkova* is sold to the same buyer as *Tesseract* and is from the period immediately preceding *Tesseract*'s period, then which one of the following must be true?

    (A)   *Quarterion* is sold to the museum.
    (B)   *Quarterion* is from the artist's third period.
    (C)   *Redemption* is sold to the private collector.
    (D)   *Redemption* is from the artist's third period.
    (E)   *Redemption* is sold to the same buyer as *Vale*.

During a certain week, an animal shelter places exactly six dogs—a greyhound, a husky, a keeshond, a Labrador retriever, a poodle, and a schnauzer—with new owners. Two are placed on Monday, two on Tuesday, and the remaining two on Wednesday, consistent with the following conditions:

The Labrador retriever is placed on the same day as the poodle.

The greyhound is not placed on the same day as the husky.

If the keeshond is placed on Monday, the greyhound is placed on Tuesday.

If the schnauzer is placed on Wednesday, the husky is placed on Tuesday.

7. Which one of the following could be a complete and accurate matching of dogs to the days on which they are placed?

 (A) Monday: greyhound, Labrador retriever
     Tuesday: husky, poodle
     Wednesday: keeshond, schnauzer
 (B) Monday: greyhound, keeshond
     Tuesday: Labrador retriever, poodle
     Wednesday: husky, schnauzer
 (C) Monday: keeshond, schnauzer
     Tuesday: greyhound, husky
     Wednesday: Labrador retriever, poodle
 (D) Monday: Labrador retriever, poodle
     Tuesday: greyhound, keeshond
     Wednesday: husky, schnauzer
 (E) Monday: Labrador retriever, poodle
     Tuesday: husky, keeshond
     Wednesday: greyhound, schnauzer

8. Which one of the following must be true?

 (A) The keeshond is not placed on the same day as the greyhound.
 (B) The keeshond is not placed on the same day as the schnauzer.
 (C) The schnauzer is not placed on the same day as the husky.
 (D) The greyhound is placed on the same day as the schnauzer.
 (E) The husky is placed on the same day as the keeshond.

9. If the poodle is placed on Tuesday, then which one of the following could be true?

 (A) The greyhound is placed on Monday.
 (B) The keeshond is placed on Monday.
 (C) The Labrador retriever is placed on Monday.
 (D) The husky is placed on Tuesday.
 (E) The schnauzer is placed on Wednesday.

10. If the greyhound is placed on the same day as the keeshond, then which one of the following must be true?

 (A) The husky is placed on Monday.
 (B) The Labrador retriever is placed on Monday.
 (C) The keeshond is placed on Tuesday.
 (D) The poodle is not placed on Wednesday.
 (E) The schnauzer is not placed on Wednesday.

11. If the husky is placed the day before the schnauzer, then which one of the following CANNOT be true?

 (A) The husky is placed on Monday.
 (B) The keeshond is placed on Monday.
 (C) The greyhound is placed on Tuesday.
 (D) The poodle is placed on Tuesday.
 (E) The poodle is placed on Wednesday.

12. If the greyhound is placed the day before the poodle, then which one of the following CANNOT be placed on Tuesday?

 (A) the husky
 (B) the keeshond
 (C) the Labrador retriever
 (D) the poodle
 (E) the schnauzer

Each day of a five-day workweek (Monday through Friday), Anastasia parks for the entire day in exactly one of three downtown parking lots—X, Y, and Z. One of the lots costs $10 for the day, another costs $12, and the other costs $15. Anastasia parks in each of the three lots at least once during her workweek. The following conditions must apply:

On Thursday, Anastasia parks in the $15 lot.
Lot X costs more than lot Z.
The lot Anastasia parks in on Wednesday costs more than the one she parks in on Friday.
Anastasia parks in lot Z on more days of the workweek than she parks in lot X.

18. Which one of the following could be a complete and accurate list of which lot Anastasia parks in each day, listed in order from Monday through Friday?

(A) Y, Z, X, Y, Z
(B) Y, Z, Z, Y, X
(C) Z, Z, X, X, Y
(D) Z, Z, X, X, Z
(E) Z, Z, X, Z, Y

19. Anastasia CANNOT park in the $15 lot on which one of the following days?

(A) Monday
(B) Tuesday
(C) Wednesday
(D) Thursday
(E) Friday

20. If lot Z is the $12 lot, then on which one of the following days must Anastasia park in lot Y?

(A) Monday
(B) Tuesday
(C) Wednesday
(D) Thursday
(E) Friday

21. Anastasia CANNOT park in lot Z on which one of the following days?

(A) Monday
(B) Tuesday
(C) Wednesday
(D) Thursday
(E) Friday

22. Which one of the following could be a complete and accurate list of the days on which Anastasia parks in the $10 lot?

(A) Monday
(B) Tuesday
(C) Monday, Tuesday
(D) Monday, Wednesday
(E) Monday, Thursday

Game #8: June 2004 Questions 18-22

Each of exactly six lunch trucks sells a different one of six kinds of food: falafel, hot dogs, ice cream, pitas, salad, or tacos. Each truck serves one or more of exactly three office buildings: X, Y, or Z. The following conditions apply:

The falafel truck, the hot dog truck, and exactly one other truck each serve Y.

The falafel truck serves exactly two of the office buildings.

The ice cream truck serves more of the office buildings than the salad truck.

The taco truck does not serve Y.

The falafel truck does not serve any office building that the pita truck serves.

The taco truck serves two office buildings that are also served by the ice cream truck.

18. Which one of the following could be a complete and accurate list of each of the office buildings that the falafel truck serves?

(A)   X
(B)   X, Z
(C)   X, Y, Z
(D)   Y, Z
(E)   Z

19. For which one of the following pairs of trucks must it be the case that at least one of the office buildings is served by both of the trucks?

(A)   the hot dog truck and the pita truck
(B)   the hot dog truck and the taco truck
(C)   the ice cream truck and the pita truck
(D)   the ice cream truck and the salad truck
(E)   the salad truck and the taco truck

20. If the ice cream truck serves fewer of the office buildings than the hot dog truck, then which one of the following is a pair of lunch trucks that must serve exactly the same buildings as each other?

(A)   the falafel truck and the hot dog truck
(B)   the falafel truck and the salad truck
(C)   the ice cream truck and the pita truck
(D)   the ice cream truck and the salad truck
(E)   the ice cream truck and the taco truck

21. Which one of the following could be a complete and accurate list of the lunch trucks, each of which serves all three of the office buildings?

(A)   the hot dog truck, the ice cream truck
(B)   the hot dog truck, the salad truck
(C)   the ice cream truck, the taco truck
(D)   the hot dog truck, the ice cream truck, the pita truck
(E)   the ice cream truck, the pita truck, the salad truck

22. Which one of the following lunch trucks CANNOT serve both X and Z?

(A)   the hot dog truck
(B)   the ice cream truck
(C)   the pita truck
(D)   the salad truck
(E)   the taco truck

CHAPTER THREE: INDIVIDUAL GAMES

81

Exactly six people—Lulu, Nam, Ofelia, Pachai, Santiago, and Tyrone—are the only contestants in a chess tournament. The tournament consists of four games, played one after the other. Exactly two people play in each game, and each person plays in at least one game. The following conditions must apply:

Tyrone does not play in the first or third game.
Lulu plays in the last game.
Nam plays in only one game and it is not against Pachai.
Santiago plays in exactly two games, one just before and one just after the only game that Ofelia plays in.

7. Which one of the following could be an accurate list of the contestants who play in each of the four games?

(A) first game: Pachai, Santiago; second game: Ofelia, Tyrone; third game: Pachai, Santiago; fourth game: Lulu, Nam
(B) first game: Lulu, Nam; second game: Pachai, Santiago; third game: Ofelia, Tyrone; fourth game: Lulu, Santiago
(C) first game: Pachai, Santiago; second game: Lulu, Tyrone; third game: Nam, Ofelia; fourth game: Lulu, Nam
(D) first game: Nam, Santiago; second game: Nam, Ofelia; third game: Pachai, Santiago; fourth game: Lulu, Tyrone
(E) first game: Lulu, Nam; second game: Santiago, Tyrone; third game: Lulu, Ofelia; fourth game: Pachai, Santiago

8. Which one of the following contestants could play in two consecutive games?

(A) Lulu
(B) Nam
(C) Ofelia
(D) Santiago
(E) Tyrone

9. If Tyrone plays in the fourth game, then which one of the following could be true?

(A) Nam plays in the second game.
(B) Ofelia plays in the third game.
(C) Santiago plays in the second game.
(D) Nam plays a game against Lulu.
(E) Pachai plays a game against Lulu.

10. Which one of the following could be true?

(A) Pachai plays against Lulu in the first game.
(B) Pachai plays against Nam in the second game.
(C) Santiago plays against Ofelia in the second game.
(D) Pachai plays against Lulu in the third game.
(E) Nam plays against Santiago in the fourth game.

11. Which one of the following is a complete and accurate list of the contestants who CANNOT play against Tyrone in any game?

(A) Lulu, Pachai
(B) Nam, Ofelia
(C) Nam, Pachai
(D) Nam, Santiago
(E) Ofelia, Pachai

12. If Ofelia plays in the third game, which one of the following must be true?

(A) Lulu plays in the third game.
(B) Nam plays in the third game.
(C) Pachai plays in the first game.
(D) Pachai plays in the third game.
(E) Tyrone plays in the second game.

For a behavioral study, a researcher will select exactly six individual animals from among three monkeys—F, G, and H—three pandas—K, L, and N—and three raccoons—T, V, and Z. The selection of animals for the study must meet the following conditions:

F and H are not both selected.
N and T are not both selected.
If H is selected, K is also selected.
If K is selected, N is also selected.

18. Which one of the following is an acceptable selection of animals for the study?

(A) F, G, K, N, T, V
(B) F, H, K, N, V, Z
(C) G, H, K, L, V, Z
(D) G, H, K, N, V, Z
(E) G, H, L, N, V, Z

19. If H and L are among the animals selected, which one of the following could be true?

(A) F is selected.
(B) T is selected.
(C) Z is selected.
(D) Exactly one panda is selected.
(E) Exactly two pandas are selected.

20. Each of the following is a pair of animals that could be selected together EXCEPT

(A) F and G
(B) H and K
(C) K and T
(D) L and N
(E) T and V

21. If all three of the raccoons are selected, which one of the following must be true?

(A) K is selected.
(B) L is selected.
(C) Exactly one monkey is selected.
(D) Exactly two pandas are selected.
(E) All three of the monkeys are selected.

22. If T is selected, which one of the following is a pair of animals that must be among the animals selected?

(A) F and G
(B) G and H
(C) K and L
(D) K and Z
(E) L and N

23. The selection of animals must include

(A) at most two of each kind of animal
(B) at least one of each kind of animal
(C) at least two pandas
(D) exactly two monkeys
(E) exactly two raccoons

This is a Linear game controlled by sequencing rules. The key to this game is to use the last rule to create the two mutually exclusive sequences that control this game.

From the game scenario, we know the following:

F G H J K L [6]

$$\underline{\quad}\ \underline{\quad}\ \underline{\quad}\ \underline{\quad}\ \underline{\quad}\ \underline{\quad}$$
$$\ \ 1\quad\ \ 2\quad\ \ 3\quad\ \ 4\quad\ \ 5\quad\ \ 6$$

Because there are no ties, this is a balanced game, wherein each of the six hotel suites is assigned to a different space.

Ultimately, the final rule controls the game , and students who begin diagramming before reading all of the rules often find themselves scrambling to re-diagram. Remember, always read the entire scenario and accompanying rules prior to starting your diagram.

For the purposes of clarity, let's review each rule individually. At the conclusion of showing the diagram for each rule, we will combine the diagrams into two super-sequences.

Rule #1. This is a basic sequential rule:

$$H > L$$

Rule #2. This is a conditional rule, and the sufficient condition is that G is more expensive than H. When that occurs, then J is more expensive than both K and L:

$$G > H \quad \longrightarrow \quad J > \begin{array}{c} K \\ \text{- - - - - -} \\ L \end{array}$$

Rule #3. This is another conditional rule, and the sufficient condition is that H is more expensive than G. When that occurs, then K is more expensive than both J and L:

$$H > G \quad \longrightarrow \quad K > \begin{array}{c} J \\ \text{- - - - - -} \\ L \end{array}$$

Rule #4. Initially this rule seems like a simple either/or rule, where F is either more expensive than G (diagrammed as F > G) or F is more expensive than H (diagrammed as F > H). However, the "but not both" portion of the rule means that F is more expensive than *only one* of G or H at a time, and since there are no ties, that means that the other variable must be more expensive than F. So, when F is more expensive than G, then H must be more expensive than F, producing the following sequence:

$$H > F > G$$

And, when F is more expensive than H, then G must be more expensive than F, producing the following sequence:

$$G > F > H$$

Every game solution must conform to one of the two sequences produced by rule #4, and thus you should take those two base sequences and create two templates for the game.

Sequence Template #1

This template is produced by the part of rule #4 that produces the H > F > G sequence. To build a super-sequence that captures the relationship between all six hotel suites, first add rule #1 to the sequence:

```
                    L
    H > - - - - - - - - -
                  F > G
```

The next step is to add rule #3 to the sequence (rule #2 does not apply to this sequence, and can be ignored). This step is more difficult than the first step above because adding the third rule creates an unwieldy diagram:

```
                    J
      K > - - - - - - - - -
      - - - - - - Ⓛ
      H > - - - - - - - - -
                  F > G
```

The relationship between K, J, and L is clear when isolated in rule #3, but when added to a sequence where L is already less expensive than another hotel suite, H, the relationship is more difficult to diagram. In the above diagram, K and H have no relationship other than both being more expensive than L, and thus they are separated by a dotted line.

The tricky part comes in analyzing the relationship between H and J, and between K and F > G. In both instances, there is no relationship. That is, J can be more or less expensive than H, and K can be more or less expensive than both F or G. Of course, this difficulty in representation and analysis is exactly what the test makers intended.

To better understand the possibilities inherent in this sequence, consider the following hypotheticals, all of which are valid:

Hypothetical 1: K - H - F - G - J - L
Hypothetical 2: K - J - H - L - F - G
Hypothetical 3: H - F - G - K - L - J
Hypothetical 4: H - F - K - J - G - L
Hypothetical 5: H - K - L - F - G - J

Also, remember to use the Sequencing Diagramming Guidelines from the *PowerScore LSAT Logic Games Bible* and consider which variables can be first and which can be last. In the sequence above, only K or H can be first, and only G, J, or L can be last.

For those of you having difficulty with the diagram of the sequence above, there is an alternate representation of the above relationships that uses arrows:

```
        ┌─► J
      K ◄───┐
            │
            L
  H > - - - - - - - - -
          F > G
```

This diagram has the same meaning as the first diagram, but may be easier for some students to use.

Sequence Template #2

This template is produced by the part of rule #4 that produces the G > F > H sequence. To build a super-sequence that captures the relationship between all six hotel suites, first add rule #1 to the sequence:

$$G > F > H > L$$

The next step is to add rule #2 to the sequence (rule #3 does not apply to this sequence, and can be ignored). This step is more difficult than the first step above because adding the second rule creates an unwieldy diagram:

```
  G > F > H > L
        J > - - -
            K
```

The relationship between K, J, and L is clear when isolated in rule #2, but when added to a sequence where L is already less expensive than three other hotel suites, the relationship is more difficult to diagram (although not as troubling as the first sequence template). The tricky part comes in analyzing the relationship between J and K and the other variables. J must be more expensive than K and L, but J has no relationship with G, F, and H. Similarly, K must be less expensive than H but otherwise K has no relationship to any other variable in the chain. Analyzing which variables can be first and which can be last, in the sequence above, only G or J can be first, and only K or L can be last.

To better understand the possibilities inherent in this sequence, consider the following hypotheticals, all of which are valid:

Hypothetical 1: G - F - H - J - L - K
Hypothetical 2: J - K - G - F - H - L
Hypothetical 3: J - G - F - H - L - K

Hypothetical 4: G - J - F - K - H - L
Hypothetical 5: G - F - J - H - K - L

For those of you having difficulty with the diagram of the sequence above, there is an alternate representation of the above relationships that uses arrows:

$$G > F > H > L$$

J ⤶

↳ K

This diagram has the same meaning as the previous diagram, but may be easier for some students to use.

Combining all of the information above leads to the following optimal setup for the game:

F G H J K L [6]

$$\underline{\quad}\;\underline{\quad}\;\underline{\quad}\;\underline{\quad}\;\underline{\quad}\;\underline{\quad}$$
1   2   3   4   5   6

H > L

                    K
G > H ⟶ J > - - - - - -
                    L

__Sequence Template #1__

                    J
K > - - - - - - - - -
- - - - - - - Ⓛ
H > - - - - - - - - -
          F > G

                    J
H > G ⟶ K > - - - - - -
                    L

H > F > G
   or
G > F > H

__Sequence Template #2__

G > F > H > L
       J > - - -
               K

Use the two sequence templates to answer the questions.

Question #6: Global, List. The correct answer choice is (B)

As with any List question, simply apply the rules to the answer choices.

Answer choice (A): This answer choice is incorrect because it violates rule #2. Specifically, when G is more expensive than H, then L cannot be more expensive than J.

Answer choice (B): This is the correct answer choice.

Answer choice (C): This answer choice is incorrect because it violates rule #3. Specifically, when H is more expensive than G, then J cannot be more expensive than K.

Answer choice (D): This answer choice is incorrect because it violates rule #4: because F is less expensive than both G and H.

Answer choice (E): This answer choice is incorrect because it violates rule #1.

Question #7: Local, Could Be True. The correct answer choice is (C)

The condition in the question stem specifies that G is the second most expensive suite. Reviewing the two sequence templates, template #1 does not allow for this possibility (at best, G can be the third most expensive suite), and thus template #2 is the only template that applies to this question. In template #2, when G is the second most expensive suite, then J must be the most expensive suite:

$$\frac{J}{1} \quad \frac{G}{2} \quad \frac{\quad}{3} \quad \frac{\quad}{4} \quad \frac{\quad}{5} \quad \frac{\quad}{6}$$

The remainder of the spaces are controlled by the following relationship:

$$F > H > L$$
$$-------$$
$$K$$

Answer choice (A): This answer choice is incorrect because H cannot be more expensive than F in template #2.

Answer choice (B): This answer choice is incorrect because H cannot be more expensive than G in template #2.

Answer choice (C): This is the correct answer choice. Under template #2, K could be more expensive than F. The following hypothetical shows one possible way: J - G - K - F - H - L.

Answer choice (D): This answer choice is incorrect because K cannot be more expensive than J in template #2.

Answer choice (E): This answer choice is incorrect because L cannot be more expensive than F in template #2.

Question #8: Global, Cannot Be True. The correct answer choice is (A)

From our analysis of the two sequence templates, we know that in template #1 only H and K can be the most expensive. This information eliminates answer choices (C) and (E). In template #2 only G and J can be the most expensive, and that eliminates answer choice (B) and (D). Thus, answer choice (A) is proven correct by process of elimination.

Alternatively, answer choice (A) can be proven correct because in template #1, F must be less expensive than H, and in template #2, F must be less expensive than G.

Answer choice (A): This is the correct answer choice.

Answer choices (B) and (D): These two answer choices are incorrect because sequence template #2 allows for G or J to be the most expensive suite.

Answer choices (C) and (E): These two answer choices are incorrect because sequence template #1 allows for H or K to be the most expensive suite.

Question #9: Local, Could Be True. The correct answer choice is (D)

If L is more expensive than F (L > F), then only Template #1 can apply to this question. Let's revisit template #1 with the addition of L > F:

$$
\begin{array}{c}
\qquad\;\; \rightarrow \text{J} \\
\text{K} \\
\text{-----} > \text{L} > \text{F} > \text{G} \\
\text{H}
\end{array}
$$

In the above diagram, both K and H are more expensive than the L > F > G chain, and J is simply less expensive than K.

Answer choice (A): This answer choice is incorrect because F cannot be more expensive than H according to the diagram above.

Answer choice (B): This answer choice is incorrect because F cannot be more expensive than K according to the diagram above.

Answer choice (C): This answer choice is incorrect because G cannot be more expensive than H according to the diagram above.

Answer choice (D): This is the correct answer choice. G can be more expensive than J.

Answer choice (E): This answer choice is incorrect because G cannot be more expensive than L according to the diagram above.

Question #10: Local, Could Be True. The correct answer choice is (D)

The question stem adds the following condition:

$$K > H > J$$

Because template #2 specifies that J > K, template #2 cannot apply, and only template #1 is applicable. Adding the question stem condition to template #1 produces the following diagram:

```
              J
          - - - - - - - -
K > H >       L
          - - - - - - - -
            F > G
```

Consequently, K is the most expensive suite and H is the second most expensive suite.

Answer choice (A): This answer choice is incorrect because F cannot be more expensive than H according to the diagram above.

Answer choice (B): This answer choice is incorrect because G cannot be more expensive than F according to the diagram above.

Answer choice (C): This answer choice is incorrect because G cannot be more expensive than H according to the diagram above.

Answer choice (D): This is the correct answer choice. J can be more expensive than L.

Answer choice (E): This answer choice is incorrect because L cannot be more expensive than K according to the diagram above.

Overall, this game is relatively easy *if* you use the last rule to create two super-sequence templates. If you do not see how the game is controlled by the templates, this game can be fairly tricky and time-consuming.

This may be the most difficult game of the section even though it is a Pure Sequencing game. Although sequencing games have traditionally been relatively easy, the rules in this game form an ungainly diagram that requires some skill to create and interpret.

The game scenario establishes that a courier delivers eight packages—G, H, J, K, L, M, N, and O—and no two packages are delivered simultaneously:

G H J K L M N O [8]

Packages: ____ ____ ____ ____ ____ ____ ____ ____
                1   2   3   4   5   6   7   8

The rules then establish a pure sequence that controls the placement of every variable. Let's first examine each rule separately, and then link them together afterward:

Rule #1. This rule can be diagrammed as:

H > L

Rule #2. This rule can be diagrammed as:

K > O

Rule #3. This rule can be diagrammed as:

H > M

Rule #4. This rule can be diagrammed as:

G > O

Rule #5. This rule can be diagrammed as:

M > G

Rule #6. This rule can be diagrammed as:

$$\begin{matrix} N \\ \text{-----} > M \\ J \end{matrix}$$

Individually, none of the rules is daunting. Linking them together into a workable diagram, however, is not easy.

To create a super-sequence, first start with the last three rules, which connect together easily:

$$
\begin{array}{l}
\text{N} \\
\text{-----} > \text{M} > \text{G} > \text{O} \\
\text{J}
\end{array}
$$

Next, add in the second and third rules, using arrows:

Finally, add in the first rule:

Note that the method of constructing this diagram worked backwards through the rules, which is another reminder that you must read all of the rules before beginning your diagram. (Note that this is not the only possible way to construct this diagram, and at the conclusion of question #22 we present two alternative diagrams that capture the same relationship in different ways).

Now that the main diagram is complete, take a moment to analyze the relationships.

Which packages can be delivered first? Only H, J, K, and N. Note how easy it is to miss K.

Which packages can be delivered last? Only L and O.

What is the earliest L can be delivered? Second, right after H.

What is the latest H can be delivered? Fourth—H can be delivered after J, K, and N.

What is the latest N can be delivered? Fifth—N can be delivered after H, J, L, and K. The same holds true for J, which can also be delivered fifth, after H, L, N, and K.

What is the earliest M can be delivered? Fourth, after H, J, and N have been delivered.

What is the latest M can be delivered? Sixth, just before G and O are delivered.

Whenever you create a complex diagram (sequencing or otherwise), always take a moment to evaluate the relationships contained within because the test makers will surely question you on any confusing relationship.

Using the setup above and keeping the relationships firmly in mind, move ahead and attack the questions.

Question #16: Global, List. The correct answer choice is (D)

To attack this List question, simply apply the rules in the given order. Although the first two rules do not eliminate any answers, there is no way to know this when you begin attacking this question.

Answer choice (A): This answer choice violates the last rule because J is not delivered earlier than M.

Answer choice (B): This answer choice violates the fifth rule because M is not delivered earlier than G.

Answer choice (C): This answer choice violates the fourth rule because O is not delivered later than G.

Answer choice (D): This is the correct answer choice.

Answer choice (E): This answer choice violates the third rule because H is not delivered earlier than M.

The presentation of answer choices by the test makers is interesting because applying the rules in the given order—which is the accepted protocol in a game where the rules are all basically similar—consumes the maximum amount of time possible. This occurs because the first two rules do not eliminate any answers, then the third rule eliminates answer choice (E), the fourth rule eliminates answer choice (C), the fifth rule eliminates answer choice (B), and the last rule eliminates answer choice (A). This presentation forces you to comb through the answers multiple times in order to eliminate all four incorrect answers. Alas, while this presentation is interesting, there is no way to reliably combat this trick—it is simply a weapon the test makers have at their disposal.

Question #17: Global, Must Be True. The correct answer choice is (C)

The only way to attack a Global question in a Pure Sequencing game is to refer to the super-sequence that controls the game.

Answer choice (A): This answer choice is incorrect because K can be delivered first, and thus it is not true that at least one parcel is delivered before K.

Answer choice (B): This answer choice is incorrect because G can be delivered seventh, and thus it is not true that at least two parcels are delivered later than G.

Answer choice (C): This is the correct answer choice. G, L, M, and O must all be delivered later than H.

Answer choice (D): This answer choice is incorrect because only three parcels must be delivered later than J (those parcels are G, M, and O).

Answer choice (E): This answer choice is incorrect because only three parcels must be delivered earlier than M (those parcels are H, J, and N).

Question #18: Local, Must Be True. The correct answer choice is (D)

The condition in the question stem indicates that M is delivered fourth. For M to be delivered fourth, *only* H, J, and N can be delivered before M (all three must be delivered before M regardless, but to allow M to be delivered fourth those can be the only three parcels delivered before M). A diagram including the new condition would appear as:

```
       H
     - - - - -              L
       N  >  M  >  - - - - - - - -
     - - - - -           G  >  O
       J        |
                |
                └──→  K  ←──┘
```

The arrows "bracketing" K indicate that K is delivered after M but before O. K has no relationship with G or L. Other than the placement of K, the diagram is relatively standard.

From a linear standpoint, this creates the following scenario:

Packages:	(H,	J,	N)	M				L/O
	1	2	3	4	5	6	7	8

Use the above information to attack the answer choices.

Answer choice (A): This answer choice is incorrect because G could be delivered fifth, sixth or seventh.

Answer choice (B): This answer choice is incorrect because O could be the eighth parcel delivered.

Answer choice (C): This answer choice is incorrect because the relationship between J and H is unfixed, and thus H could be delivered later than J.

Answer choice (D): This is the correct answer choice. N must always be one of the first three parcels delivered and K must be delivered fifth, sixth, or seventh.

Answer choice (E): This answer choice is incorrect because G and L do not have a fixed relationship, and therefore L could be delivered later than G.

Question #19: Local, Could Be True, Except. The correct answer choice is (A)

This question is similar to question #18, except that H is specified as the fourth parcel. Because J and N are already delivered before H, in order to deliver H fourth, K must be among the first three parcels delivered (leaving K, J, and N as the first three parcels, not necessarily in that order). The remaining parcels (L, M, G, O) then align behind H. A diagram including the new condition would appear as:

```
    K
  - - - - -                 L
    N  >  H  >  - - - - - - - - - - - -
  - - - - -            M  >  G  >  O
    J
```

The remainder of the question stem is a Could Be True Except question, which means that the four incorrect answers Could Be True, and the one correct answer Cannot Be True.

Answer choice (A): This is the correct answer choice. Because K must be one of the first three parcels delivered, K cannot be delivered fifth. Note how the test makers immediately examine the most difficult variable to place in this question. In this sense, the question becomes a "gut check" on whether you understand the range of possibilities inherent in K's positioning in the game itself.

Answer choice (B): This answer choice could be true, and is therefore incorrect. L could be delivered fifth, sixth, seventh, or eighth.

Answer choice (C): This answer choice could be true, and is therefore incorrect. M could be delivered fifth or sixth.

Answer choice (D): This answer choice could be true, and is therefore incorrect. G could be delivered sixth or seventh.

Answer choice (E): This answer choice could be true, and is therefore incorrect. O could be delivered seventh or eighth.

Question #20: Global, Could Be True, Except. The correct answer choice is (B)

In this Global question, simply use the main diagram to confirm or eliminate answer choices. If an answer choice Could Be True, then it is incorrect. The correct answer choice Cannot Be True.

Answer choice (A): This answer choice is incorrect because H could be delivered later than K. Remember, K could be delivered first, so even though it appears that K is at the "end" of the diagram, K can "move" forward greatly.

Answer choice (B): This is the correct answer choice. J must be delivered earlier than M, and M must be delivered earlier than G, so J can never be delivered later than G.

Answer choice (C): This answer choice is incorrect because L can be delivered last, so L can be delivered later than O.

Answer choice (D): This answer choice is incorrect. The only relationship that L and M have is that they must both be delivered later than H. However, the rules do not specify if L or M is delivered later, so M could be delivered later than L.

Answer choice (E): This answer choice is incorrect because H can be delivered first, so N can be delivered later than H.

Note that the nature of the answer choices in this question makes this a simple diagram interpretation question. If you can create a main diagram that incorporates all of the rules and also understand the relationships inherent in that diagram, then this question is easy.

Question #21: Local, Could Be True, Except. The correct answer choice is (C)

If K is the seventh parcel delivered, then O must be the eighth parcel delivered (because the second rule specifies that K > O). That leaves the remaining variables to be delivered in the first six spaces:

Answer choice (A): This answer choice is incorrect because G could be the fifth parcel delivered. The following hypothetical shows how: N-J-H-M-G-L-K-O.

Answer choice (B): This answer choice is incorrect because M could be the fifth parcel delivered. The following hypothetical shows how: N-J-H-L-M-G-K-O.

Answer choice (C): This is the correct answer choice. Because L, M, and G must all be delivered later than H, the latest that H can be delivered is third (after J and N).

Answer choice (D): This answer choice is incorrect because L could be the fourth parcel delivered. The following hypothetical shows how: N-J-H-L-M-G-K-O.

Answer choice (E): This answer choice is incorrect because J could be the third parcel delivered. The following hypothetical shows how: N-H-J-M-G-L-K-O.

Question #22: Local, False to True, Cannot Be True. The correct answer choice is (C)

When addressing this question stem, first convert the Must Be False statement into its true equivalent, Cannot Be True. Thus, the one correct answer Cannot Be True, and the four incorrect answers Could Be True.

The local condition in the question stem, L > K, is not easy to handle. The rule adds another layer of complexity to an already complex diagram. The difficulty in the L > K relationship comes from the fact that L and K are already "floating" because of their relationships with H and O, respectively. To show that the two floating variables have a relationship, and most importantly, to understand the implications of that relationship, is challenging. The diagram would appear as:

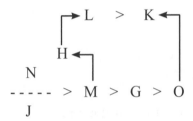

This diagram is deceptive because it makes it appear as though L must be delivered relatively early, and that K must be delivered relatively late. This is not true: L can be delivered as late as sixth (followed by K and O), and K can be delivered as early as third (preceded by H and L). When answering this question—which may be the toughest of the section—be very careful and deliberate.

Answer choice (A): This answer choice is incorrect because N could be the second parcel delivered. The following hypothetical shows how: J-N-H-L-K-M-G-O.

Answer choice (B): This answer choice is incorrect because L could be the third parcel delivered. The following hypothetical shows how: H-N-L-J-M-G-K-O.

Answer choice (C): This is the correct answer choice. Because H must all be delivered earlier than M, G, K, L, and K, the latest that H can be delivered is third (after J and N).

Answer choice (D): This answer choice is incorrect because K could be the fifth parcel delivered. The following hypothetical shows how: N-J-H-L-K-M-G-O.

Answer choice (E): This answer choice is incorrect because M could be the sixth parcel delivered. The following hypothetical shows how: J-N-H-L-K-M-G-O.

Alternate Diagrams for the Main Diagram

In sequencing games, there is sometimes more than one accepted diagram. Basing the diagram on a different starting point (emphasizing a different rule, for example) can lead to a diagram that has a different appearance, although, of course, the inherent relationships will remain identical. The following two diagrams have the same functionality as the main diagram used in attacking this game, but they look different. Some students may find a different look more beneficial, and, in any case, understanding the diagramming options is a useful learning tool.

Diagram #1: This diagram emphasizes the first and third rules as the "start" of the diagram (as a comparison, the main diagram emphasized the last rule as the starting point). Once those two rules are chosen, the other rules are then diagrammed those two:

The challenging element of this diagram is to realize that K can "move" all the way to the front of the diagram, and that N and J have no connection with L.

Diagram #2. This diagram uses the second and fourth rules as the starting point:

This may be the best diagram, but this is the most difficult diagram to construct because you have to work backwards from O. Under the time constraint of the LSAT, most students simply do not have enough time to construct a diagram such as this one. The second challenge is to realize that L is delivered later than H, but not necessarily later than N or J. Creating a diagram with this type of uncertainty is only recommended for students who are comfortable with games, and this is one reason we chose not to use this presentation as our main diagram.

This is a basic linear game featuring six groups placed in six spaces, with exactly one group per space (a Defined, Balanced game). Games of this nature—ordered with the exact number of variables for the given spaces—are considered the easiest type of Logic Game, and this is a perfect way to start a Logic Games section. The only drawback is that there are just five questions in this game; it would be preferable to see a greater number of questions attached to such a simple game scenario.

Considering just the game scenario and the rules, you should make the following basic setup for this game:

F G J M P V [6]
     *

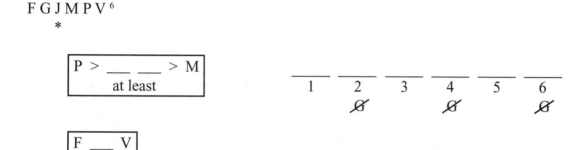

Note that the third rule, which involves G, is represented by Not Laws on groups 2, 4, and 6, and this representation indicates that G can only be in groups 1, 3, or 5.

Although the diagram above captures the basic meaning of each rule, it does not capture the inferences created by the first and second rules (such as Not Laws, etc.). In fact, you have an interesting choice at this juncture of the game: you can either show all the Not Laws that result from the two blocks or you can show templates based on the placement of the blocks. Either approach will work, although the templates approach tends to be faster. Regardless, let's show how each diagramming approach would unfold.

Approach 1: Diagram the Not Laws

Using the diagram above as a base, we can add Not Laws drawn from each of the first two rules.

Rule #1. This rule creates a large, flexible split-block involving P and M. Because there must be at least two groups between P and M, this block takes up a minimum of four spaces (leaving three options if the block is compressed as tightly as possible: groups 1-4, 2-5, or 3-6). Consequently, we can deduce that M can never appear in groups 1, 2, or 3, and we can deduce that P can never appear in groups 4, 5, or 6. Adding these Not Laws to the diagram, we arrive at:

1	2	3	4	5	6
	G̸		G̸		G̸
M̸	M̸	M̸	P̸	P̸	P̸

Rule #2. This rule creates a fixed split block involving F and V. Because V is always two groups behind F, V can never appear in groups 1 or 2; because F is always two groups ahead of V, F can never appear in groups 5 or 6. Adding these Not Laws to the prior diagram, we arrive at:

1	2	3	4	5	6
	G̶		G̶		G̶
M̶	M̶	M̶	P̶	P̶	P̶
V̶	V̶			F̶	F̶

What becomes immediately apparent from these Not Laws is that groups 2 and 6 are the most restricted, and each has only three options:

	F/J/P				J/M/V
1	2	3	4	5	6

At this point in the game, you have diagrammed and considered all of the rules, so you should head towards the questions. And, since the meaning of the third rule is completely captured by the Not Laws in the diagram, you will simply need to focus on the first two rules (as an aside, of the first two rules of the game, the first rule is more problematic because it contains a degree of uncertainty—how many other groups are between P and M—that you *must* track throughout the game).

Approach 2: Diagram the Templates

The alternative approach is to diagram the game based on templates created by the blocks. Your first choice is which block to use as the basis for the templates. In this case, the choice should be easy: use the FV block created by the second rule. This block is the better choice because it is fixed, with exactly one group between F and V. Although the PM block is larger and takes up more space, it is an inferior choice because it is flexible, and the number of groups between P and M is not fixed; this flexibility creates more options, and ultimately, more templates.

Using the FV block, we can place the block in four positions: groups 1-3, 2-4, 3-5, and 4-6. The following diagram shows each scenario:

Template	1	2	3	4	5	6
Template #4:				F		V
Template #3:			F		V	
Template #2:		F		V		
Template #1:	F		V			

Of course, the other rules can also be applied to derive more information about each template. Let's start with the third rule since it is more concrete than the first rule (thereafter, we will consider the first rule).

Rule #3. Since G must always be placed in group 1, 3, or 5, in Template #1 G must be placed in group 5 (groups 1 and 3 are already occupied by F and V). Likewise, in Template #3 G must be placed in group 1 (groups 3 and 5 are already occupied by F and V). Applying these two inferences, we can add G to Templates #1 and #3:

Template #4:
$$\underline{\quad}\ \underline{\quad}\ \underline{\quad}\ \underline{F}\ \underline{\quad}\ \underline{V}$$

Template #3:
$$\underline{G}\ \underline{\quad}\ \underline{F}\ \underline{\quad}\ \underline{V}\ \underline{\quad}$$

Template #2:
$$\underline{\quad}\ \underline{F}\ \underline{\quad}\ \underline{V}\ \underline{\quad}\ \underline{\quad}$$

Template #1:
$$\frac{\underline{F}\ \ \underline{\quad}\ \ \underline{V}\ \ \underline{\quad}\ \ \underline{G}\ \ \underline{\quad}}{1\quad 2\quad 3\quad 4\quad 5\quad 6}$$

Rule #1. Because the block created by this rule is so large, it has somewhat limited placement options around F and V, especially in the Templates #1 and #3, which are more restricted now that G has been placed in each. Let's examine the effect of the first rule on each template:

Template #1: Because P and M must be separated by at least two groups, in this template P must be placed in group 2 and M must be placed in group 6. The only remaining group is group 4, which must be filled by J, the random. Thus, this template has only one solution:

$$\frac{\underline{F}\ \ \underline{P}\ \ \underline{V}\ \ \underline{J}\ \ \underline{G}\ \ \underline{M}}{1\quad 2\quad 3\quad 4\quad 5\quad 6}$$

Template #2: The PM block has several options within Template #2. It can be placed in groups 1-5, 1-6, or 3-6. Consequently, this template will not fill in as completely as Template #1. Aside from the general position of P (group 1 or 3) and M (group 5 or 6), we can deduce that group 6 will be filled by J or M (from the initial Not Laws, group 6 cannot be filled by F, G, or P, and, in this template, group 6 cannot be filled by V, leaving only J or M). Adding all the information together, this template is still only partially complete:

$$\frac{\underline{P/}\ \ \underline{F}\ \ \underline{/P}\ \ \underline{V}\ \ \underline{M/}\ \ \underline{J/M}}{1\quad 2\quad 3\quad 4\quad 5\quad 6}$$

Note that if G marches in group 1 or 3, that will create a chain reaction forcing P into the remainder of group 1 or 3. If P is forced into group 3, then M must be in group 6 (and J must be in group 5).

Template #3: As in Template #1, the placement of the PM block is limited in this template. Because P and M must be separated by at least two groups, in this template P must be placed in group 2 and M must be placed in group 6. The only remaining group is group 4, which must be filled by J, the random. Thus, this template has only one solution:

$$\frac{G}{1} \quad \frac{P}{2} \quad \frac{F}{3} \quad \frac{J}{4} \quad \frac{V}{5} \quad \frac{M}{6}$$

Template #4: At first glance it may appear that not much can be done with this template. However, the size of the PM block again leads to a useful inference. The PM block can only be placed in groups 1-5 or 2-5. Consequently, we can infer that M must always march in group 5 in Template #4, that P can only march in group 1 or 2, and that either G or J must march in group 5:

$$\frac{P/}{1} \quad \frac{/P}{2} \quad \frac{G/J}{3} \quad \frac{F}{4} \quad \frac{M}{5} \quad \frac{V}{6}$$

Note that if P or G marches in group 1, that will create a chain reaction that, depending on which group is in group 1, either forces P into group 2 or forces G into group 3 (G, from the third rule, can only march in group 1, 3, or 5).

Compiling all four templates, we arrive at the following setup:

Template #4:	P/	/P	G/J	F	M	V
Template #3:	G	P	F	J	V	M
Template #2:	P/	F	/P	V	M/	J/M
Template #1:	F	P	V	J	G	M
	1	2	3	4	5	6

After applying all the rules, we have two very complete and powerful templates, and two other templates that contain a fair amount of information. We are now ready to attack the questions, and we will use the templates as they are more efficient that the Not Law setup.

Question #1: Global, List. The correct answer choice is (D)

As with any List question, simply apply the rules to the answer choices. Remember to apply the rules in order of the easiest to "see" within the answers. In this game, that order would be rule #3, rule #2, and then rule #1.

Answer choice (A): This answer is eliminated by the first rule. In this instance, there is only one group separating P and M.

Answer choice (B): This answer choice is eliminated by the third rule. In this answer there is no group between F and V.

Answer choice (C): This answer is eliminated by the third rule because G marches in group 4.

Answer choice (D): This is the correct answer choice.

Answer choice (E): This answer violates both the first and second rules. Interestingly, if you misdiagram the first two rules by reversing the order of the variables (for example, "V __ F"), this answer would appear correct.

One of the great benefits of this question is that we are given a free hypothetical solution to the game, in this case J-P-G-F-M-V. This could be useful in a later question.

Question #2: Local, Could Be True. The correct answer choice is (E)

This question imposes a local condition that you must address before moving to the answer choices. In this instance, the question stipulates that G and V form a block, and combining this condition with the second rule, we can form a FGV super-block where F, G, and V must appear in consecutive order. Applying our templates, the only place an FGV block can occur is in Template #2, where F is in group 2 and V is in group 4:

Template #2:

P/	F	/P	V	M/	J/M
1	2	3	4	5	6

Accordingly, G must march in group 3, which forces P to march in group 1. The only remaining uncertainty is the placement of J and M:

Question #2:

P	F	G	V	M/J	J/M
1	2	3	4	5	6

With the information above, we can quickly determine that (E) is the correct answer choice.

Answer choice (A): Under the condition in this question, G must march in group 3.

Answer choice (B): Under the condition in this question, J must march in group 5 or 6.

Answer choice (C): Under the condition in this question, M must march in group 5 or 6.

Answer choice (D): Under the condition in this question, P must march in group 1.

Answer choice (E): This is the correct answer choice.

Question #3: Local, Could Be True. The correct answer choice is (A)

If V marches immediately behind P, then, by adding the first rule we arrive at the following block:

$$\boxed{\text{P V}} > \underset{\text{at least}}{\_\_\_} > \text{M}$$

And, after adding the second rule, we arrive at the following super-block:

$$\boxed{\text{F P V}} > \underset{\text{at least}}{\_\_\_} > \text{M}$$

The question asks for which could be the second group, and a quick glance at the templates shows that Template #1 conforms to the block above. However, the group that marches second in Template #1—P—is not one of the answer choices. Hence, we must look at one of the other templates for the answer. Because Templates #3 and #4 cannot conform to the super-block above, the only possible source of the correct answer is Template #2. Because Template #2 features F as the second group, the correct answer to this problem must be F, and answer choice (A) must be correct. However, let's take a moment to examine this further.

In Template #2, F and V are in groups 2 and 4, respectively. Applying the super-block, we can create the following diagram:

Question #3:
$$\underset{1}{\_\_\_} \quad \underset{2}{\text{F}} \quad \underset{3}{\text{P}} \quad \underset{4}{\text{V}} \quad \underset{5}{\_\_\_} \quad \underset{6}{\text{M}}$$

At this juncture, the only remaining uncertainty is the placement of G and J, which can be placed in group 1 or 5:

Question #3:
$$\underset{1}{\text{G/J}} \quad \underset{2}{\text{F}} \quad \underset{3}{\text{P}} \quad \underset{4}{\text{V}} \quad \underset{5}{\text{J/G}} \quad \underset{6}{\text{M}}$$

As this hypothetical meets the rules of the game and the condition imposed in question #3, it shows that F can be in the second group.

Answer choice (A): This is the correct answer choice.

Answer choice (B): Under the condition in this question, G must march in group 1 or 5.

Answer choice (C): Under the condition in this question, J must march in group 1 or 5.

Answer choice (D): Under the condition in this question, M must march in group 6.

Answer choice (E): Under the condition in this question, V must march in group 4.

Question #4: Local, Must Be True. The correct answer choice is (E).

Within the templates, the only time J can be the fifth group is under Template #2:

Template #2: | P/ | F | /P | V | M/ | J/M |
|----|---|-----|---|-----|------|
| 1 | 2 | 3 | 4 | 5 | 6 |

If J is in group 5, them M must be in group 6:

Question #4: | P/ | F | /P | V | J | M |
|----|---|-----|---|---|---|
| 1 | 2 | 3 | 4 | 5 | 6 |

The only remaining uncertainty is the placement of G and P, which can rotate between the first and third groups:

Question #4: | G/P | F | P/G | V | J | M |
|-----|---|-----|---|---|---|
| 1 | 2 | 3 | 4 | 5 | 6 |

Because this is Must be true question, you can use the hypothetical above to quickly accelerate through the questions. In this instance, answer choice (E) is quickly proven correct.

Answer choice (A): Although P could be in the first group, P could also be in the third group, and so this answer choice does not have to be true. Note how the test makers immediately attack you on the uncertainty within this question.

Answer choice (B): F must be in the second group, not the first group.

Answer choice (C): V must be in the fourth group, not the second group.

Answer choice (D): Although G could be in the third group, G could also be in the first group, and so this answer choice does not have to be true.

Answer choice (E): This is the correct answer choice.

Question #5: Global, Cannot Be True. The correct answer choice is (B)

This question asks you to identify the group that cannot march immediately behind G. There are two ways to work out the correct answer to this question: either eliminate those variables that *can* march behind G, or find the variable that cannot march behind G. Given the considerable amount of information we have amassed in the templates, and in the hypotheticals in the answer choices, the second approach is likely to be the fastest (unless, of course, you have already deduced which variable cannot march behind G).

First, consider the templates: in Template #1, M marches immediately behind G, and thus we can eliminate M from the answer choices. In Template #3, P marches immediately behind G, and thus we can eliminate P from the answer choices.

Second, and especially important if you did not use the template approach, do not forget to consider the hypotheticals created while you answered the questions. Let's review each hypothetical:

Question #1: In this question we were given the solution J-P-G-F-M-V. This solution eliminates F from the answer choices.

Question #2: In this question we arrived at the solution P-F-G-V-M/J-J/M. This hypothetical eliminates V from the answer choices.

Question #3: In this question we arrived at the solution G/J-F-P-V-J/G-M. If G marched first, this hypothetical eliminates F from the answer choices; if G marched fifth, this hypothetical eliminates M from the answer choices.

Adding all the information together (some of it redundant), F, M, P, and V can march immediately behind G. Thus, only J cannot march immediately behind G, and therefore answer choice (B) is correct.

Answer choice (A): F can march behind G, as proven by the solution to questions #1 and #3.

Answer choice (B): This is the correct answer choice. If J marches immediately behind G, then there is not enough room to place the other blocks without violating one of the rules (try it: the GJ block would have to be placed in groups 1-2, 3-4, or 5-6; in each instance the MP block can be placed successfully, but doing so leaves no room for the FV block).

Answer choice (C): M can march behind G, as proven by Template #1 and the solution to question #3.

Answer choice (D): P can march behind G, as proven by Template #3.

Answer choice (E): V can march behind G, as proven by the solution to question #2.

Note that a question of this nature reveals that you do not have to have every piece of information about a game in order to successfully complete the game. Students often miss inferences during the setup, only to discover them during the game without negative repercussion. In this case, having the templates makes the game manageable even if you miss an inference or two.

This is a basic Linear game featuring six clients for six time slots (the gym workout can, for the most part, simply be treated as another "client," so the game is balanced as six into six). As mentioned previously, this type of basic linear game is often easy and provides a perfect starting game for an LSAT section.

A diagram of just the game scenario and rules leads to the following basic setup for this game:

R S T U Y W [6]

S > | WY | > T
     | YW |

                    ___ ___ ___ ___ ___ ___
                     1   2   3   4   5   6

U > R

We have presented the "skeleton" diagram above because this game requires you to make some diagramming choices before moving on to the questions. First, let's review the rules.

Rule #1. This is a basic sequential rule that can be diagrammed as follows:

$$S > W$$

Rule #2. This is another basic sequential rule that can be diagrammed as follows:

$$W > T$$

Rule #3. This is a standard linear rule that places W and Y in an unfixed block:

| W Y |

or

| YW |

Note that we prefer to diagram unfixed blocks with both possibilities shown because that minimizes the possibility of making a mistake under the pressure of the actual LSAT.

Of course, the first three rules can be connected together to create the following super-sequence:

S > | WY | > T
     | YW |

This sequence requires at least four spaces, and we have shown the dual-possibilities of the WY block in the middle so there is no chance of making the false assumption that one of the two is necessarily before the other.

Rule #4. This is another basic sequential rule that can be diagrammed as follows:

$$U > R$$

In a typical Linear game, we would diagram the Not Laws that follow from each of the rules above, and indeed there are plenty of Not Laws produced by the rules above. However, given the fact that we have reduced the rules to two sequences (one of which is especially powerful), and because all six variables are contained within the two sequences, the best decision would be to forgo drawing all of the Not Laws and instead to make a basic sequential analysis of which clients could be first or last, and then attack the questions with the two sequences. Using this approach, we will save the time involved in drawing the Not Laws yet not lose any knowledge or ease of attack in the game.

From the sequences, only S or U can be first in this game, and only R or T can be last in the game (more on this in question #2). These facts can be shown on the diagram as dual-options:

(more on this in question #2).

$$S > \boxed{\begin{array}{c} WY \\ YW \end{array}} > T \qquad \frac{S/U}{1} \quad \frac{}{2} \quad \frac{}{3} \quad \frac{}{4} \quad \frac{}{5} \quad \frac{R/T}{6}$$

$$U > R$$

At this point we are ready to attack the game, and we should be somewhat confident since our setup took very little time yet the sequences are easy to use and powerful.

Question #1: Global, List. The correct answer choice is (E)

As with any List question, simply apply the rules to the answer choices. In this game, the easiest approach is to apply the rules in the order given (individually, none of the rules is more complex than any other rule, so there is no reason to apply them out of order).

Answer choice (A): This answer is eliminated by the first rule because the meeting with S is not before the workout.

Answer choice (B): This answer choice is eliminated by the second rule because the meeting with T is not after the workout.

Answer choice (C): This answer violates the third rule because W and Y are not consecutive.

Answer choice (D): This answer violates the fourth rule because the meeting with U is not ahead of the meeting with R.

Answer choice (E): This is the correct answer choice.

Question #2: Global, Must Be True. The correct answer choice is (B)

As briefly mentioned in the game setup, only two of the clients can possibly meet first, at 1:00. Let's take a moment to review this inference further.

As established in the discussion of the third rule, the first three rules can be connected together to create the following chain:

$$S > \boxed{\begin{array}{c} WY \\ \hline YW \end{array}} > T$$

From this chain we can infer that T, W, and Y can never be first since each must come after S (although, for the purposes of this question, W is irrelevant since W is not an actual client).

From the fourth rule, we can infer that R can never be first since R must always meet with Patterson after U meets with Patterson. Consequently, we have eliminated R, T, and Y from meeting with Patterson at 1:00. This leaves only S and U as clients who could possibly meet with Patterson at 1:00, and thus "two" is the correct answer.

Answer choice (A), (C), (D), and (E): As discussed above, these answer choices must be incorrect because they do not state the maximum number of clients that could meet with Patterson at 1:00.

Answer choice (B): This is the correct answer choice.

Question #3: Global, Cannot Be True. The correct answer choice is (C)

This is the most difficult question of the game, and one that is not easy to answer from a quick glance at the rules.

When you encounter a Global question with no obvious answer, remember that one approach is to refer to the hypotheticals created in other questions. For example, question #1 produced a solution that placed U at 2:00. On the strength of that answer, we can eliminate answer choice (B). The discussion in question #2 indicated that U could meet at 1:00, eliminating answer choice (A). However, none of the three remaining answer choices is obviously incorrect so you have a choice: either skip the remaining answer choices and hope that future questions provide more hypotheticals so you can come back and eliminate some answers, or make a few hypotheticals right now to solve the problem.

If you choose to wait until later to answer this question, you will find that the hypothetical from question #5 eliminates answer choice (E). At that point you could simply create a hypothetical to eliminate or confirm answer choice (C) or (D).

If you choose to make hypotheticals to work your way through the final three answer choices, you would be best served by first attacking answer choice (C) or (D), and not by starting with answer choice (E). This is because (E) would seemingly be easily eliminated by the somewhat obvious hypothetical where U and R meet at 5:00 and 6:00, and the four variables in the other sequence fill in the first four hours (as in S-W-Y-T-R-U, for example). In a moment we will create hypotheticals for both answer choices (C) and (D), but before doing so, let's discuss the logic of why U is limited at all in this game.

At first glance, U appears to be a fairly unrestricted variable, with U's only limitation coming from the rule involving R. Obviously, though, 6:00 is not one of the answers to this question, so there must be some further limitation on U that has thus far gone unnoticed. In examining the two chains, the one point of concern is the WY block. The block not only requires two consecutive spaces, but it also affects S and T. Although that may not appear to be of an much issue for U, if U is placed at 3:00, there is not enough room for all the variables:

Step 1. U is placed at 3:00; R must meet at 4:00, 5:00, or 6:00:

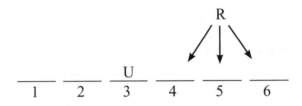

Step 2. Consider the other sequence:

Because there are three meetings after Patterson's meeting with S, normally the latest that S could meet is 3:00. But, since U already occupies the 3:00 meeting, S must be somewhere before U. Because this placement leaves only one open time slot before U, it must be that the WY block comes somewhere after U, and, of course, T is somewhere after the WY block. This chain of inferences results in a scenario where R, W, Y, and T must all come somewhere after U, but there are only three spaces for the four variables:

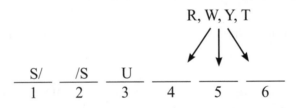

Thus, we cannot create a workable solution when U is placed third, and answer choice (C) is correct.

By the way, a similar type of logic holds for R: if R is placed in the fourth position, a workable solution to the game cannot be created.

Answer choice (A): This answer choice is incorrect. Patterson can meet with U at 1:00, as shown by the following hypothetical: U-R-S-W-Y-T.

Answer choice (B): This answer choice is incorrect. Patterson can meet with U at 2:00, as shown by the following hypothetical: S-U-W-Y-T-R.

Answer choice (C): This is the correct answer choice. Although it is proven by the previous discussion, this answer choice is difficult to arrive at without testing a few solutions.

Answer choice (D): This answer choice is incorrect. Patterson can meet with U at 4:00, as shown by the following hypothetical: S-W-Y-U-T-R.

Answer choice (E): This answer choice is incorrect. Patterson can meet with U at 5:00, as shown by the following hypothetical: S-W-Y-T-U-R.

Question #4: Local, Could Be True, Except. The correct answer choice is (D)

The condition in the question stem creates the following block and sequence:

$$\boxed{\text{S Y W}} > \text{T}$$

From this sequence, it is obvious that Patterson cannot meet with Y any later than 4:00 because Patterson must meet with W and T later than with Y. Consequently, answer choice (D) is correct.

Answer choice (A): This answer choice is incorrect. Patterson can meet with R at 2:00, as shown by the following hypothetical: U-R-S-Y-W-T.

Answer choice (B): This answer choice is incorrect. Patterson can meet with Y at 3:00, as shown by the following hypothetical: U-S-Y-W-T-R.

Answer choice (C): This answer choice is incorrect. Patterson can meet with T at 4:00, as shown by the following hypothetical: S-Y-W-T-U-R.

Answer choice (D): This is the correct answer choice.

Answer choice (E): This answer choice is incorrect. Patterson can meet with T at 6:00, as shown by the following hypothetical: U-R-S-Y-W-T.

Question #5: Local, Must Be True. The correct answer choice is (B)

When Patterson meets with T at 4:00, then from the super-sequence we know that S, W, and Y must meet with Patterson prior to 4:00, with S at 1:00, and with W and Y rotating between 2:00 and 3:00:

S	W/Y	Y/W	T		
1	2	3	4	5	6

Placing S, T, W, and Y forces U and R into the final two meetings, with U at 5:00 and R at 6:00:

S	W/Y	Y/W	T	U	R
1	2	3	4	5	6

Since this is a Must be true question, you should look for answer choices containing fixed variables (such as S, T, U, and R) and avoid answer choices that contain variables with uncertainty (W and Y).

Answer choice (A): This answer choice is incorrect because R must meet with Patterson at 6:00.

Answer choice (B): This is the correct answer choice.

Answer choice (C): This answer choice is incorrect because Patterson can meet with Y at 2:00 or 3:00.

Answer choice (D): This answer choice is incorrect because Patterson can meet with Y at 2:00 or 3:00.

Answer choice (E): This answer choice is incorrect because Patterson can workout at 2:00 or 3:00.

Question #6: Global, List. The correct answer choice is (E)

This question is identical to question #1, with the exception that W has been dropped from the ordering (but, of course, the rules involving W are still active). Thus, you should approach this question in the same fashion as any List question.

Answer choice (A): This answer specifies that Patterson meets with Y before S, but, as we know from the combination of the first and second rule, Patterson cannot meet with Y before S, and thus this answer choice is incorrect.

Answer choice (B): This answer specifies that Patterson meets with T before Y, but, as we know from the combination of the second and third rule, Patterson cannot meet with T before Y, and thus this answer choice is incorrect.

Answer choice (C): This answer violates the fourth rule because the meeting with U is not ahead of the meeting with R.

Answer choice (D): Like answer choice (B), this answer specifies that Patterson meets with T before Y, but since Patterson cannot meet with T before Y, this answer choice is incorrect.

Answer choice (E): This is the correct answer choice.

This Advanced Linear game is about equal in difficulty to the previous two games. Like the previous two games, this game has only six variables and three rules, and so creating the diagram is not an especially lengthy process.

From the game scenario, we know that there are two purchasers: a private collector and a museum. There are three different periods (periods 1, 2, and 3, from earliest to latest) and that suggests a linear setup with two stacks, one for the private collector and one for the museum:

$$Q\ R\ S\ T\ V\ Z^6$$
*

Private: _____   _____   _____

Museum: _____   _____   _____
     1   2   3

The first rule can be diagrammed as :

$$S_P > Z_M$$

This rule indicates that Z cannot be from the first period (and thus must be from the second or third period), and that S cannot be from the third period (and thus must be from the first or second period). The rule also indicates that S cannot be sold to the museum and that Z cannot be sold to the private collector:

Private: S/   /S   _____ $\cancel{Z}$

Museum: _____   Z/   /Z $\cancel{S}$
      1   2   3
     $\cancel{Z}$ $\cancel{S}$

Because there are only three periods, if S is from the second period, then Z must be from the third period. Conversely, if Z is from the second period, then S must be from the first period:

$$S_2 \longrightarrow Z_3$$

$$Z_2 \longrightarrow S_1$$

The second rule can be a bit tricky to diagram. The rule states that Q is *not from an earlier period* than T. Many students interpret this rule to mean that T must be from an *earlier* period than Q; that is not correct. Although Q cannot be from an earlier period than T, Q could be from the *same* period as T (remember, always read the rules closely!). Consequently, this rule is best diagrammed as:

$$T \geq Q$$

Because T and Q could be from the same period, no Not Laws can be drawn from this rule. However, if T is from the third period, then Q must also be from the third period, and if Q is from the first period, T must also be from the first period.

The third rule indicates that V is from the second period, and that consequently V cannot be from the first or third periods:

Private: ___ $\underline{V/}$ ___

Museum: ___ $\underline{/V}$ ___
          1   2   3
          ✗   ✗

The actions of V clearly impact the first rule. If V is sold to the private collector, then S must be from the first period; if V is sold to the museum, then Z must be from the third period:

$$V_{2P} \longrightarrow S_1$$

$$V_{2M} \longrightarrow Z_3$$

Combining all the rules and inferences together, we arrive at the following diagram for the game:

Q R S T V Z [6]
  *

$S_P > Z_M$ Private: $\underline{S/}$ $\underline{V/S/}$ ___   ✗

$T \geq Q$ Museum: ___ $\underline{Z/V/}$ $\underline{/Z}$ ✗
                             1   2   3
                             ✗   ✗
                             ✗   ✗

$Z = 2$

$$S_2 \longrightarrow Z_3$$

$$Z_2 \longrightarrow S_1$$

$$V_{2P} \longrightarrow S_1$$

$$V_{2M} \longrightarrow Z_3$$

Given the amount of information in the diagram, some students ask if it would be wise to make four templates based on the position of S, V, and Z (when V is sold to the private collector, S must be from the first period and Z can be from the second or third period; when V is sold to the museum, Z must be from the third period and S can be from the first or second period). Although at first glance this may seem like a powerful strategy, it only places S, V, and Z in four arrangements, and none of those arrangements definitively place Q, R, or T. Hence, the templates provide little additional insight into the placement of the variables, and it is better to attack the game with a straightforward setup.

Question #13: Global, List. The correct answer choice is (B)

As usual, use the rules to attack a List question. The best order to apply the rules is to apply the third rule, then the first rule, and finally the second rule.

Note that the physical formatting of this question is a good example of how Law Services can make things harder for test takers by neglecting to present the information clearly. If this question was formatted so the paintings in each answer choice were indented to the same point to the right of the private collector and museum, it would be much easier to compare the order of the paintings. Instead, test takers are forced to waste valuable time examining which paintings are from which period.

Answer choice (A): This answer choice violates the second rule because Q is from an earlier period than T. Therefore this answer is incorrect.

Answer choice (B): This is the correct answer choice.

Answer choice (C): This answer is incorrect because it violates the first rule by selling S to the museum.

Answer choice (D): V must always be from the artist's second period, but in this answer V is from the artist's third period. Thus, this answer choice is incorrect.

Answer choice (E): According to the first rule S is from an earlier period than Z. Thus, this answer choice is incorrect because it places S and Z in the same period.

Question #14: Local, Could Be True. The correct answer choice is (B)

This is an unusually easy question. The first rule of the game establishes that Z must be purchased by the museum. Thus, any answer choice in this question featuring Z must be incorrect. Using that logic, we can eliminate answer choices (A), (D), and (E).

The question stem places S in the artist's second period, which, from our initial discussion of the rules, forces Z into the artist's third period. V, which must also be from the artist's second period, has to be purchased by the museum:

```
Private:    _____        S        _____


Museum:     _____        V         Z
              1           2         3
```

At this point, we have established that V must be purchased by the museum, and consequently answer choice (C) can be eliminated.

Answer choice (B): This is the correct answer choice.

Question #15: Global, List. The correct answer choice is (D)

Through the Not Laws we have established that neither V nor Z can be paintings from the artist's first period that are sold to the private collector. Consequently, most students correctly surmise that the remaining four paintings could be the first period paintings sold to the private collector. However, let's systematically prove that assertion.

First, any answer choice containing V or Z can be eliminated. This process removes answer choice (E) from consideration. Second, from question #13, we know that S can be a first period painting sold to the private collector, and since answer choice (A) does not contain S, we can eliminate (A). Third, using the base diagram created in question #14, we can deduce that any of Q, R, and T can be a first period painting sold to the private collector, and thus the correct answer choice must contain those paintings as well.

Answer choice (D): This is the correct answer choice. The deduction above eliminates every answer choice except answer choice (D).

Question #16: Local, Could Be True. The correct answer choice is (B)

From question #14, we know the following diagram is produced when S is from the artist's second period:

Private:	_____	S	_____
Museum:	_____	V	Z
	1	2	3

The wording of the question stem also provides a clue into the placement of Q: by referencing the period "immediately preceding Q's period," it is clear that Q will not be first in this scenario (there is no period that precedes the first period). Consequently, because the second period is already occupied, Q must be from the third period in this question, and since the museum's third period painting is already occupied by Z, Q must be the third period painting of the private collector (and R and T rotate in the first period):

Private:	R/T	S	Q
Museum:	T/R	V	Z
	1	2	3

Answer choices (A), (C), and (E): None of these answer choices contain a painting that can be from a period immediately preceding Q's period. Thus, each of these answer choices is incorrect.

Answer choice (B): This is the correct answer choice. From the diagram, we can determine that S can be the painting from the same buyer in the period immediately preceding Q.

Answer choice (D): Although V can be a painting from the period immediately preceding Q's period, V is sold to a different buyer than Q, and thus this answer choice is incorrect.

Question #17: Local, Must Be True. The correct answer choice is (B)

The conditions in the question stem establish a horizontal ZT block:

$$\boxed{Z\ T}$$

Because we have already established that Z can only be sold to the museum as either the second or third period piece, the block *must* be placed so that Z is from the second period and T is from the third period:

Private: ____   ____   ____

Museum: ____ $\dfrac{Z}{2}$ $\dfrac{T}{3}$
        1

At this point, we can apply the first rule and third rules, which serve to establish that S is from the first period and that V is sold to the private collector:

Private: $\dfrac{S}{}$ $\dfrac{V}{}$ ____

Museum: $\dfrac{}{1}$ $\dfrac{Z}{2}$ $\dfrac{T}{3}$

The only remaining variables yet to be placed are Q and R. From the second rule we know that $T \geq Q$, and thus Q must be from the third period (otherwise it would violate the second rule). Consequently, Q must be sold to the private collector, and R, the random, occupies the museum's first period:

Private: $\dfrac{S}{}$ $\dfrac{V}{}$ $\dfrac{Q}{}$

Museum: $\dfrac{R}{1}$ $\dfrac{Z}{2}$ $\dfrac{T}{3}$

Using this analysis, the problem is easy.

Answer choices (A), (C), (D), and (E): Each of these answer choices cannot occur, and therefore each is incorrect.

Answer choice (B): This is the correct answer choice.

This game has a Linear structure paired with four Grouping rules. Because there are two dogs placed each day, our diagram will feature the days as the base, with two spaces per day:

G H K L P S [6]

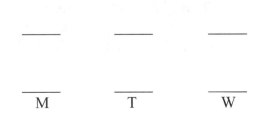

The first two rules include one block and one not-block:

Since these two rules address four of the six dogs in the game, what is the relationship between the two dogs—S and K—not included in these two rules? To determine this relationship, first analyze what happens when the blocks are placed (in this analysis, disregard the linear aspect of the game and just consider the groups).

1. L and P must occupy one entire day:

2. G and H cannot be placed on the same day, and since there are only two days open, G and H must form a dual-option that occupies one space on each day:

L   ____   ____

P   G/H   H/G
Day   Day   Day

3. By Hurdling the Uncertainty, we can infer that the two remaining variables, K and S, can never be placed on the same day:

L	K/S	S/K

| P | G/H | H/G |
| Day | Day | Day |

Consequently, we can infer that S and K form a not-block:

This inference is directly tested in question #8.

There are also two powerful conditional rules in the game:

The third rule: $K_M \longrightarrow G_T$

The fourth rule: $S_W \longrightarrow H_T$

Because these rules involve two separate days and they both involve the second rule, they ultimately result in a single solution to the game:

The third rule. When K is placed on Monday, then G must be placed on Tuesday. The LP block must then be placed on Wednesday. Consequently, because G is on Tuesday, H must be placed on Monday. The last remaining dog, S, must then be placed on Tuesday. Thus, when K is placed on Monday, there is only one solution to the game:

H	S	L

| K | G | P |
| M | T | W |

The fourth rule. When S is placed on Wednesday, then H must be placed on Tuesday. The LP block must then be placed on Monday. Consequently, because H is on Tuesday, G must be placed on Wednesday. The last remaining dog, K, must then be placed on Tuesday. Thus, when S is placed on Wednesday, there is only one solution to the game:

L	K	G

| P | H | S |
| M | T | W |

The information above provides more than sufficient information to attack the questions, but a savvy test taker might suspect that given the powerful rules in this game, and the fact that there are no randoms, that there might be a limited number of solutions to this game. In fact, there are only eight solutions to the game, and these eight solutions can be captured using five templates. One option for attacking this game would be to show the templates, and in the interest of absolute clarity we will discuss how to make each template.

The basis for the templates is the placement of the LP block. Since the LP block can go on any of the three days, there are three basic avenues that lead to the templates:

LP on Monday:

When the LP block is placed on Monday, H and G must be split between Tuesday and Wednesday. However, the placement of S and K has an impact on G and H because of the action of the fourth rule. This ultimately creates two templates:

<table>
<tr><td>

Template #1:
LP on Monday
S on Tuesday, K on Wednesday

</td><td>

Template #2:
LP on Monday
S on Tuesday, K on Wednesday

</td></tr>
<tr><td>

L	G/H	H/G
P	S	K
M	T	W

</td><td>

L	H	G
P	K	S
M	T	W

</td></tr>
</table>

Template #1 contains two solutions; template #2 contains only one solution.

LP on Tuesday:

When the LP block is placed on Tuesday, both the third and fourth rules are affected: K cannot be placed on Monday, and S cannot be placed on Wednesday. Consequently, K must be placed on Wednesday and S must be placed on Monday. G and H form a dual-option that rotates between Monday and Wednesday:

Template #3:
LP on Monday

G/H	L	H/G
S	P	K
M	T	W

This template contains two solutions.

LP on Wednesday:

When the LP block is placed on Wednesday, H and G must be split between Monday and Tuesday. However, the placement of S and K has an impact on G and H because of the action of the third rule. This ultimately creates two templates:

Template #4:
LP on Wednesday
S on Monday, K on Tuesday

Template #5:
LP on Wednesday
S on Tuesday, K on Monday

G/H	H/G	L		H	G	L

S	K	P		K	S	P
M	T	W		M	T	W

Template #4 contains two solutions; template #5 contains only one solution.

Either a regular setup or the template approach will effectively solve this game. In our explanations of the questions we will use the regular setup because more people attack the game using that method, and the template method still leaves several possible solutions undefined.

Question #7: Global, List. The correct answer choice is (E)

As with any List question, simply apply the rules to the answer choices. In this game, the best order to apply the rules is: rule #1, rule #2, rule #3, and then rule #4.

Answer choice (A): This answer choice violates the first rule and is therefore incorrect.

Answer choice (B): This answer choice violates the third rule and is therefore incorrect.

Answer choice (C): This answer choice violates the second rule and is therefore incorrect.

Answer choice (D): This answer choice violates the fourth rule and is therefore incorrect.

Answer choice (E): This is the correct answer choice.

Question #8: Global, Must Be True. The correct answer choice is (B)

As discussed in the setup to this game, because of the interaction of the first two rules, we can deduce that K and S can never be placed on the same day. Consequently, answer choice (B) is correct.

Answer choices (A), (C), (D), and (E): Each of these answer choices could be true, but none of them must be true, and therefore each is incorrect.

Answer choice (B): This is the correct answer choice.

Question #9: Local, Could Be True. The correct answer choice is (A)

When the L is placed on Tuesday, then from the first rule we know that P is also placed on Tuesday. With Tuesday occupied, both the third and fourth rules are affected: K cannot be placed on Monday (because G cannot be placed on Tuesday), and S cannot be placed on Wednesday (because H cannot be placed on Tuesday). Consequently, K must be placed on Wednesday and S must be placed on Monday. G and H form a dual-option that rotates between Monday and Wednesday:

G/H   L   H/G

S   P   K

M   T   W

Answer choice (A): This is the correct answer choice.

Answer choice (B): This answer choice violates the third rule. K cannot be placed on Monday because there is no space for G to be placed on Tuesday.

Answer choice (C): The question stem stipulates that P must be placed on Tuesday, and from the first rule L must also be placed on Tuesday. Therefore, this answer choice cannot occur and it is incorrect.

Answer choice (D): Since L and P occupy the two spaces on Tuesday, no other dog can be placed on Tuesday, and thus this answer choice is incorrect.

Answer choice (E): This answer choice violates the fourth rule. S cannot be placed on Wednesday because there is no space for H to be placed on Tuesday.

Question #10: Local, Must Be True. The correct answer choice is (E)

The question stem places G and K in a block:

┌───┐
│ G │
│ K │
└───┘

Since L and P are also aligned in a block, two of three days must be completely filled by those two blocks:

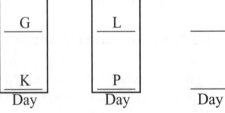

Thus, because the only two remaining spaces are on the same day, the two remaining dogs—H and S—must also be in a block, and the key to this question is to determine the days on which each block can be placed. Let's examine each block in closer detail:

The GK block: The only rule applicable to this block is the third rule, which states that if K is placed on Monday then G must be placed on Tuesday. Consequently, we can infer that the GK block cannot be placed on Monday since that placement would violate this rule.

The LP block: The LP block could be placed on any one of the three days.

The HS block: The only rule applicable to this block is the fourth rule, which states that if S is placed on Wednesday then H must be placed on Tuesday. Consequently, we can infer that the HS block cannot be placed on Wednesday since that placement would violate this rule.

With the information above, we are ready to attack the answer choices.

Answer choice (A): Although H could be placed on Monday, H does not have to be placed on Monday and so this answer choice is incorrect.

Answer choice (B): Although L could be placed on Monday, L does not have to be placed on Monday and so this answer choice is incorrect.

Answer choice (C): Although K could be placed on Tuesday, K does not have to be placed on Tuesday and so this answer choice is incorrect.

Answer choice (D): This answer choice, like answer choice (E), slips a "not" into the middle of the answer (remember, read carefully!). Because P could be placed on Wednesday, this answer choice is incorrect.

Answer choice (E): This is the correct answer choice. As discussed above, the HS block cannot be placed on Wednesday because doing so would violate the fourth rule.

Question #11: Local, Cannot Be True. The correct answer choice is (D)

The question stem creates a horizontal HS block:

| H S |

This block must be placed on either Monday and Tuesday, or Tuesday and Wednesday. Consequently, the LP vertical block must be placed on Monday or Wednesday. This deduction is sufficient to show that P cannot be placed on Tuesday, and so answer choice (D) is correct. However, in the interests of fully understanding the relationships at work in this question, let's continue our analysis. So far we have two blocks, and since HS is a horizontal block, we will show the other spaces with H and S:

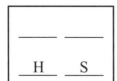

The remaining two variables are G and K. Because the second rule specifies that G and H cannot be placed on the same day, we can infer that G must placed with S. K must then be placed with H:

```
┌─────────────┐        ┌─────────┐
│  K    G     │        │   L     │
│             │        │         │
│  H    S     │        │   P     │
└─────────────┘        └─────────┘
```

Because of the fortuitous arrangement of the variables, the blocks can be placed in any order.
Answer choices (A), (B), (C) and (E): Each of these answer choices could be true, as proven by the following hypothetical:

$$
\frac{\text{K}}{} \qquad \frac{\text{G}}{} \qquad \frac{\text{L}}{}
$$

$$
\frac{\text{H}}{\text{M}} \qquad \frac{\text{S}}{\text{T}} \qquad \frac{\text{P}}{\text{W}}
$$

Answer choice (D): This is the correct answer choice. As discussed above, the LP vertical block must be placed on either Monday or Wednesday.

Question #12: Local, Cannot Be True. The correct answer choice is (A)

One approach to attacking this question is to use the hypotheticals from the previous three questions. Each contains scenarios that match the condition in this question stem, and collectively that information can be used to eliminate every incorrect answer choice. If you do not choose that approach, this question can still be done easily by making hypotheticals.

The condition in the question stem, in combination with the first rule, creates a powerful GLP block:

```
┌───────────┐
│      L    │
│           │
│  G    P   │
└───────────┘
```

This block can only be placed on Monday-Tuesday or Tuesday-Wednesday:

Hypothetical #1:   Hypothetical #2:
GLP on Monday-Tuesday   GLP on Tuesday-Wednesday

$$
\frac{}{} \quad \frac{\text{L}}{} \quad \frac{}{} \qquad\qquad \frac{}{} \quad \frac{}{} \quad \frac{\text{L}}{}
$$

$$
\frac{\text{G}}{\text{M}} \quad \frac{\text{P}}{\text{T}} \quad \frac{\text{H}}{\text{W}} \qquad\qquad \frac{\text{H}}{\text{M}} \quad \frac{\text{G}}{\text{T}} \quad \frac{\text{P}}{\text{W}}
$$

Of course, due to the second rule, H cannot be placed on the same day as G, so H must be placed on

Wednesday in the first hypothetical and on Monday in the second hypothetical.

In addition, because of the fourth rule, in the first hypothetical S must be placed on Monday (otherwise, if it were placed on Wednesday, then H could not be placed on Monday), and therefore K is placed on Monday in the first hypothetical. In the second hypothetical K and S form a dual option:

Hypothetical #1:
GLP on Monday-Tuesday

$\underline{\text{S}}$	$\underline{\text{L}}$	$\underline{\text{K}}$

$\dfrac{\text{G}}{\text{M}}$	$\dfrac{\text{P}}{\text{T}}$	$\dfrac{\text{H}}{\text{W}}$

Hypothetical #2:
GLP on Tuesday-Wednesday

$\underline{\text{S/K}}$	$\underline{\text{K/S}}$	$\underline{\text{L}}$

$\dfrac{\text{H}}{\text{M}}$	$\dfrac{\text{G}}{\text{T}}$	$\dfrac{\text{P}}{\text{W}}$

Answer choice (A): This is the correct answer choice.

Answer choices (B), (C), (D), and (E): As shown in the two hypotheticals, G, K, L, P, and S could be placed on Tuesday. Thus, each of these answer choices is incorrect.

Like the third game, this is an Advanced Linear game. While there are three variable sets presented in the game scenario, the days of the week should be chosen as the base. Remember, when days of the week appear in a game, they should almost always be used as the base of the game.

With the days of the week as the base, two stacks can be created—one for the parking lots and one for the prices (again, leave ample vertical space between the two stacks for individual Not Laws):

Lots: X Y Z ³
Cost: 10 12 15 ³

Cost: ____ ____ ____ ____ ____

Lot: ____ ____ ____ ____ ____
     M   T   W   Th   F

Unlike the third game, the setup for this game will not conclude with most of the spaces occupied. However, the rules still yield a fair amount of information, and several of the rules in particular require more than a surface analysis.

Rule #1. This simple rule results in a "15" being placed on Thursday in the Cost stack.

Rule #2. To capture the literal meaning of this rule, diagram it as follows:

$$\$X > \$Z$$

If X costs more than Z, then we can conclude that X cannot cost \$10 and that Z cannot cost \$15. Hence, X must cost \$12 or \$15, and Z must cost \$10 or \$12:

$$X \longrightarrow 12/15$$

$$Z \longrightarrow 10/12$$

The connection between X and Z is such that if X is \$12, then Z must be \$10, and if Z is \$12, then X must be \$15:

$$X_{12} \longrightarrow Z_{10}$$

$$Z_{12} \longrightarrow X_{15}$$

At this point, since the first rule has already established that the Thursday lot costs $15, we can infer that Anastasia cannot park in lot Z on Thursday, and that she must park in lot X or Y. That inference can be shown with a dual-option on Thursday:

Cost: _____ _____ _____ $\underset{}{15}$ _____

Lot: $\underset{\text{M}}{\_\_\_\_}$ $\underset{\text{T}}{\_\_\_\_}$ $\underset{\text{W}}{\_\_\_\_}$ $\underset{\underset{\cancel{Z}}{\text{Th}}}{\text{X/Y}}$ $\underset{\text{F}}{\_\_\_\_}$

Rule #3. This rule establishes a connection between the cost of the Wednesday and Friday lots, namely that the Wednesday lot must cost more than the Friday lot. The literal meaning of this rule can be diagrammed as:

$$\$W > \$F$$

Functionally, we can conclude that the Wednesday lot cannot cost $10 and that the Friday lot cannot cost $15. Hence, the Wednesday lot must cost $12 or $15, and the Friday lot must cost $10 or $12:

Wednesday $\longrightarrow$ 12/15

Friday $\longrightarrow$ 10/12

These inferences can be shown with by dual-options in the Cost row on Wednesday and Friday:

Cost: _____ _____ $\underset{\cancel{10}}{\text{12/15}}$ $\underset{}{15}$ $\underset{\cancel{15}}{\text{10/12}}$

Lot: $\underset{\text{M}}{\_\_\_\_}$ $\underset{\text{T}}{\_\_\_\_}$ $\underset{\text{W}}{\_\_\_\_}$ $\underset{\underset{\cancel{Z}}{\text{Th}}}{\text{X/Y}}$ $\underset{\text{F}}{\_\_\_\_}$

The connection between Wednesday and Friday is such that if the Wednesday lot is $12, then the Friday lot must be $10, and if the Friday lot is $12, then the Wednesday lot must be $15:

Wednesday$_{12}$ $\longrightarrow$ Friday$_{10}$

Friday$_{12}$ $\longrightarrow$ Wednesday$_{15}$

Rule #4. This rule establishes a numerical distribution for the lots. Like the prior two rules there is a simple diagram for this rule, but the relationships that follow from the rule prove more useful than the diagram of the rule itself. The rule can be diagrammed as:

$$\#Z > \#X$$

Numerically, then, there must be more than one day on which Anastasia parks in lot Z. And, because the game scenario establishes that Anastasia parks in each lot at least once, we can infer that she cannot park in Z more than three times (parking in X and Y one time each leaves a maximum of three days to park in Z). Thus, Anastasia must park in lot Z either two or three times, leading to the following two distributions:

> If Anastasia parks in lot Z three times, then she must park in lot X once and in lot Y once, creating the following fixed 3-1-1 distribution (Anastasia cannot park in lot X twice because then there would not be a day for her to park in lot Y):

> Z Z Z   X   Y

> If Anastasia parks in lot Z two times, then she can only park in lot X once, and the remaining two times she must park in lot Y, creating the following fixed 2-1-2 distribution:

> Z Z   X   Y Y

The two scenarios above are the only two possible distributions of the parking lots to the five days. Note that regardless of the scenario, Anastasia can only park in lot X a single time.

Because the fourth rule establishes fixed numerical distribution but does not allow us to place any of the variables within the diagram, the linear diagram created during the discussion of rule #3 is the final diagram for the game (excluding the diagramming of each of the rules, of course). In reviewing this diagram, you should note that Monday and Tuesday are completely open, and thus, when attacking the questions you should not initially look to Monday or Tuesday to solve a question. Wednesday, Thursday, and Friday are much better starting points for your analysis. And, although the linear diagram of the five days has a number of open spaces, the second, third, and fourth rules provide a wealth of information with which to attack the questions.

Question #18: Global, List. The correct answer choice is (A)

Because this List question includes only the parking lots and not the costs, at first you may not think you have enough information to eliminate each of the four incorrect answer choices. However, two of the answer choices can be eliminated by the numerical distribution, and the other two answer choices can be eliminated by combining the rules.

Answer choice (A): This is the correct answer choice.

Answer choice (B): This is probably the most difficult answer choice to eliminate, and it relies on an inference that is very difficult to make during the setup.

In this answer choice, lot Z is listed on Wednesday. According to our analysis of Wednesday costs, this lot must cost either $12 or $15. In this game answer, lot X is listed on Friday, and from our analysis of Friday costs, this lot must cost either $10 or $12. This combination presents a problem because the second rule indicates that lot X must cost more than lot Z. If the most that lot X can cost is $12, and the least that lot Z can cost is $12, then there is no way to conform to the second rule, and this answer choice must be incorrect.

This relationship reveals the inference that Z cannot be the Wednesday lot and X cannot be the Friday lot *in the same solution* (Z could be the Wednesday lot if X is not the Friday lot, and X could be the Friday lot if Z is not the Wednesday lot).

Answer choice (C): Because this answer choice has an equal number of X and Z lots, it violates the last rule and is therefore incorrect.

Answer choice (D): The game scenario stipulates that Anastasia parks in each of three lots at least once during the week. This answer choice does not include lot Y, and therefore it is incorrect. Note that, whenever you have a distribution in a game, there is often a List question answer choice that will attempt to drop one of the variables that must be present.

Answer choice (E): As discussed in the setup, the combination of the first two rules yields the inference that Anastasia must park in lot X or Y on Thursday. Because this answer specifies that she parks in lot Z on Thursday, this answer is incorrect.

Question #19: Global, Cannot Be True. The correct answer choice is (E)

This is the second easiest question of the entire section (#21 is the easiest). As detailed in the setup, the third rule states that the Wednesday lot must cost more than the Friday lot, and that consequently the Wednesday lot cannot cost $10 and that the Friday lot cannot cost $15. Hence, answer choice (E) is correct in this Cannot be true question.

Answer choices (A), (B), (C), and (D): Any of the days listed in these answer choices could be the $15 lot, and hence each one of these answers is incorrect.

Answer choice (E): This is the correct answer choice.

Question #20: Local, Must Be True. The correct answer choice is (E)

This is an extremely challenging question if you do not understand the distribution of lots in this game. Remember, Anastasia can only park in lot X a single time.

If lot Z is the $12 lot, then from the second rule we can infer that lot X is the $15 lot. With the cost of X and Z established, we can infer that lot Y must be the $10 lot.

Because X is the $15 lot, Anastasia must park in lot X on Thursday. And, because Anastasia can only park in lot X a single time, she cannot park in X on any of the other days. This fact has a direct impact on Wednesday and Friday. Wednesday's lot, which must cost either $12 or $15, cannot cost $15 because that would mean X was Wednesday's lot. Consequently, Anastasia must park in lot Z on

Wednesday. And, since according to the third rule the Wednesday lot costs more than the Friday lot, we can conclude that Anastasia must park in lot Y, the $10 lot, on Friday. Hence, answer choice (E) must be correct.

Answer choices (A) and (B): Neither of the days listed in these answer choices must be a day on which Anastasia parks in lot Y, and hence both of these answers are incorrect.

Answer choices (C) and (D): Neither of these answers could be a day on which Anastasia parks in lot Y, and hence both of these answers are incorrect.

Answer choice (E): This is the correct answer choice.

Question #21: Global, Cannot Be True. The correct answer choice is (D)

This is the easiest question of the entire section. As detailed in the setup, the combination of the first two rules yields the inference that Anastasia cannot park in lot Z on Thursday because doing so would lead to a violation of the second rule. Hence, answer choice (D) is correct.

Answer choices (A), (B), (C), and (E): Any of the days listed in these answer choices could days on which Anastasia parks in lot Z, and hence each one of these answers is incorrect.

Answer choice (D): This is the correct answer choice.

Question #22: Global, List. The correct answer choice is (C)

Please note that this question asks for the list of days on which Anastasia could park in the $10 lot in a *single solution* to the game, not the complete list of *all possible* days on which Anastasia could park in the $10 lot. Thus, the correct answer choice must be part of a single workable solution.

From our initial diagram we know that neither Wednesday nor Thursday can be a day on which Anastasia parks in the $10 lot. This information eliminates answer choices (D) and (E) from contention.

The remaining three answer choices involve Monday or Tuesday or both, and as discussed in the setup, there are no rules regarding Monday or Tuesday. Thus, at first it may appear that any of the three remaining answer choices could be the correct answer. At this point, if you were running out of time you should guess (C) because it is "different" than the other two answers in that it contains two days whereas the other two answers only contain one day. Answer choice (C) does turn out to be correct, but obviously it is better to select that answer based on facts as opposed to an educated guess. With that in mind, let's use answer choice (A) to show why both answer choices (A) and (B) are incorrect.

Answer choice (A): If Monday is the *only* day on which Anastasia parks in the $10 lot, then from the numerical distribution, the $10 lot cannot be Z and it must be X or Y (lot Z must appear more than once in the five days). But, of course, from the second rule we know that lot X costs more than lot Z, and thus the $10 lot cannot be X, and therefore the lot that Anastasia parks in on Monday must be lot Y.

We can also infer that Friday will be a $12 lot (remember, there can be only one $10 lot, and Friday must be $10 or $12), and that therefore Wednesday will be a $15 lot (because the third rule stipulates that Wednesday's lot costs more than Friday's lot).

Further, because we have inferred that lot Y is the $10 lot, we know that Thursday's $15 lot, which could only have been lot X or Y, must in fact be lot X. This deduction leads to the further deduction that lot Z is the $12 lot. This establishes the following relationship of lots to cost:

Lot X = $15
Lot Y = $10
Lot Z = $12

These deductions lead to the following setup:

Cost:	10	12/15	____	15	15	12

Lot:	Y	Z/X	X	X	Z
	M	T	W	Th	F

However, astute test takers may have already noticed a problem—lot X has appeared twice in our setup and we have already established that X can only appear once in this game. Thus, assigning Monday as the only $10 lot does not allow for a viable solution to the game.

Answer choice (B): The reasoning used to eliminate answer choice (A) also applies to (B); simply shift the $10 lot to Tuesday and proceed with the same logic.

Answer choice (C): This is the correct answer choice.

Answer choice (D): Because Wednesday cannot be a $10 lot, this answer choice can be eliminated.

Answer choice (E): Because Thursday must be a $15 lot, this answer choice can be eliminated.

This game was widely considered the most difficult of the June 2004 exam. After three linear-based games, the test makers saved a Partially Defined Grouping game for last, but test takers do get a break because this game has only five questions.

At first, this game appears to be a straight defined Grouping game: six lunch trucks serve three office buildings. However, the game scenario does not specify that each truck serves only one building, and in fact the second rule explicitly indicates that a truck can serve more than one building (by itself, this fact opens up the game to many more possible solutions). If each lunch truck served only one building, the game would be considerably easier because the assignment of a truck to a building would eliminate that truck from further consideration. Thus, one reason test takers felt this game was more difficult was because there is much more to consider within the setup of this game compared to the prior three games (there are also twice as many rules in this game as in any of the other games on this test).

The first decision in this game is what variable set to choose as the base. Either the lunch trucks or the buildings could serve as the base, but we will use the buildings since there are fewer buildings and each of the rules references the trucks going to the buildings. There is also an intuitive element here as it is easier to see the trucks going to the buildings; if the buildings were assigned to the trucks it would be counter to how things work in the real world (trucks move, buildings don't).

With that in mind, we can create the following basic representation of the variable sets:

F H I P S T[6]

$$\underline{\hspace{3em}}\qquad\underline{\hspace{3em}}\qquad\underline{\hspace{3em}}$$
$$\quad\text{X}\qquad\qquad\text{Y}\qquad\qquad\text{Z}$$

Now, let's examine each rule.

Rule #1. The first rule establishes that Y is served by exactly three lunch trucks, two of which are F and H:

$$\begin{array}{ccc} & 3 & \\ & \underline{\hspace{2em}} & \\ & \text{H} & \\ & \underline{\text{F}} & \\ \underline{\hspace{2em}} & \underline{\hspace{2em}} & \underline{\hspace{2em}} \\ \text{X} & \text{Y} & \text{Z} \end{array}$$

Rule #2. This rule indicates that F serves two buildings, one of which is Y, and the other is X or Z:

$$\begin{array}{ccc} & 3 & \\ & \underline{\hspace{2em}} & \\ & \text{H} & \\ \underline{\text{F/}} & \underline{\text{F}} & \underline{\text{/F}} \\ \text{X} & \text{Y} & \text{Z} \end{array}$$

Rule #3. Like the first two rules, this rule addresses a numerical relationship within the game. Given the open-ended nature of the truck assignments in the game scenario, you *must* look for rules that establish exact numbers, and, hopefully, a complete Numerical Distribution of trucks to buildings. More on this point later.

According to this rule, I must serve more buildings than S:

$$\#I > \#S$$

So, at this point, I must serve either two or three buildings, and S must serve either one or two buildings (note that it *is* possible for I and S to serve the same building). This rule is worth tracking since other rules can (and will) impact these possibilities.

Rule #4. This rule, which states that T does not serve Y, can be added as a Not Law to our setup:

3

F/	H	/F
X	F	Z
	Y	
	T̶	

Rule #5. This is a powerful rule, and one whose implications can be easily overlooked. First, the diagram for this rule is as follows:

F
P

If F and P do not serve the same building, the obvious deduction is that P does not serve building Y. However, we already know from the second rule that F serves exactly two buildings. Since P cannot serve those two buildings and there are only three buildings, we can infer that P can serve only one building and that it must be the building *not* served by F. Thus, for example, if F is assigned to building X, then P would have to be assigned to building Z. There are several variations on this rule, but the gist in each case is the same: when one of F or P is assigned to building X, the other is assigned to building Z, when one of F or P is assigned to building Z, the other is assigned to building X. We can represent this with a dual F/P option on buildings X and Z:

3

F/P	H	P/F
X	F	Z
	Y	
	T̶	
	P̶	

Thus, numerically we have now established that P can serve only one building, and from the second rule we know that F serves exactly two buildings.

With this rule we have also eliminated several lunch trucks from serving building Y. With two trucks assigned to Y (trucks F and H), and two trucks eliminated from serving Y (trucks T and P), only two trucks remain to fill the third space at Y: truck I or S. This can also be diagrammed with a dual-option:

$$3$$

$$
\begin{array}{ccc}
 & \dfrac{\text{I/S}}{\dfrac{\text{H}}{\dfrac{\text{F}}{\text{Y}}}} & \\
\dfrac{\text{F/P}}{\text{X}} & \begin{array}{c}\cancel{T}\\\cancel{P}\end{array} & \dfrac{\text{P/F}}{\text{Z}}
\end{array}
$$

Rule #6. This rule can be diagrammed as:

$$
\text{I} \longleftrightarrow \text{T}
$$
$$2$$

The first part of this rule indicates that T serves two buildings. Since from rule #4 we know that T cannot serve building Y, we can infer that T serves buildings X and Z. The second part of this rule indicates that T and I serve two of the same buildings, and this means that I must also serve buildings X and Z. I could also serve building Y, but does not have to. With the information above, the diagram is:

$$3$$

$$
\begin{array}{ccc}
\dfrac{\text{F/P}}{\dfrac{\text{I}}{\dfrac{\text{T}}{\text{X}}}} & \dfrac{\text{I/S}}{\dfrac{\text{H}}{\dfrac{\text{F}}{\text{Y}}}} & \dfrac{\text{P/F}}{\dfrac{\text{I}}{\dfrac{\text{T}}{\text{Z}}}} \\
 & \begin{array}{c}\cancel{T}\\\cancel{P}\end{array} &
\end{array}
$$

Note that I can still serve the remaining building, building Y. This rule only specifies that T serves two buildings also served by I; I could serve all three buildings without violating this rule (or any other).

The setup above is the final setup for the game, but given all of the numerical rules in this game, you must examine the numerical possibilities for each variable before proceeding to the questions (remember, always examine rules about numbers!). Let's examine the options for each lunch truck:

F: As specified in the second rule, F serves exactly two buildings, one of which is Y.

H: H is somewhat of a wild card in this game. H must serve at least building Y, but there is no other rule limiting how many buildings H must serve. Consequently, H could serve one, two, or three buildings.

I: I must serve at least two buildings (X and Z), and possibly all three buildings.

P: Because of the interaction of the second and fifth rules, P can only serve one building (X or Z).

S: From the third rule we know that S is limited to serving either one or two buildings, but which buildings those are is undetermined.

T: From the third and sixth rules we know that T serves exactly two buildings, and those buildings are X and Z.

This distribution is critical, and having command of the numerical possibilities will allow you to easily solve several of the questions.

Reviewing the game, there are three elements of uncertainty that must be tracked throughout the questions:

    1. The F/P dual-option.
    2. How many buildings H serves.
    3. The relationship between I and S.

Question #18: Global, List. The correct answer choice is (D)

This is one of the easiest LSAT games questions ever (proving that even if you miss the setup completely, you can still answer some questions correctly in a game just by applying the rules). From the first rule we know that F must serve building Y. Since answer choices (A), (B), and (E) fail to include Y, they are incorrect. From the second rule we know that F must serve exactly two buildings. Since answer choice (C) contains three buildings, it is incorrect.

Answer choice (D): This is the correct answer choice.

Question #19: Global, Must Be True. The correct answer choice is (C)

This question asks you to identify two trucks that must serve the same building (although they could serve other buildings as well). There are several pairs that should immediately jump to mind—including F and H, and I and T—but none of the obvious pairs is listed as a possible answer. Consequently, you should consider each answer choice on its own merits.

Answer choice (A): Although H and P could serve the same building, they do not *have* to serve the same building. For example, H could serve just building Y, and P could serve just building Z. Thus, this answer choice is incorrect.

Answer choice (B): Although T must serve both buildings X and Z, it is possible that H serves only building Y. Thus, H and T do not have to serve the same building and this answer choice is incorrect.

Answer choice (C): This is the correct answer choice. I must serve both buildings X and Z. From our discussion of the F/P dual-option, we know that P must serve either building X or Z, and thus there must be one building that both I and P serve together.

Answer choice (D): This answer choice is incorrect because it is possible for I to serve just buildings X and Z, and for S to serve just building Y. Thus, I and S do not have to serve the same building.

Answer choice (E): Although T must serve both buildings X and Z, it is possible that S serves only building Y. Thus, S and T do not have to serve the same building and this answer choice is incorrect.

Question #20: Local, Must Be True. The correct answer choice is (E)

The condition in the question stem affects the Numerical Distribution discussed in the setup analysis. From the discussion of the distribution we know that I serves either two or three buildings. If, as stipulated in this question, I is to serve fewer office buildings than H, then I cannot serve all three office buildings and we can deduce that I serves exactly two office buildings. This also allows us to deduce that H must serve all three buildings. In addition, from the third rule, we know that I serves more office buildings than S, so S must serve exactly one building.

With the above numerical information, we know that I serves only buildings X and Z, and that therefore S must serve building Y:

3

F/P		P/F
H	S	H
I	H	I
T	F	T
X	Y	Z

From this diagram it is apparent that I and T serve exactly the same buildings, and therefore answer choice (E) is correct.

Answer choice (A): Because F always serves two buildings and H serves three buildings in this question, this answer choice cannot be correct.

Answer choice (B): In this question S serves only one building but F always serves two buildings. Thus, this answer choice is incorrect.

Answer choice (C): Because P always serves one buildings and I serves two buildings in this question, this answer choice cannot be correct.

Answer choice (D): From the third rule we know that I always serves more buildings than S, so the two trucks could never serve exactly the same buildings, and this answer choice must be wrong.

Answer choice (E): This is the correct answer choice.

Question #21: Global, List. The correct answer choice is (A)

This question also trades on the Numerical Distribution established by the rules, so let's take a moment to revisit that Numerical Distribution:

F: F serves exactly two buildings.
H: H could serve one, two, or three buildings.
I: I must serve at least two buildings, and possibly all three buildings.
P: P can only serve one building.
S: S is limited to serving either one or two buildings.
T: T serves exactly two buildings.

The distribution proves that only H and I can serve all three buildings, and thus answer choice (A) is correct.

Answer choice (A): This is the correct answer choice.

Answer choice (B): Because S can serve only one or two buildings, this answer choice is incorrect.

Answer choice (C): Because T serves exactly two buildings, this answer choice is incorrect.

Answer choice (D): Because P serves exactly one building, this answer choice is incorrect.

Answer choice (E): Because P serves exactly one building, and S can serve only one or two buildings, this answer choice is incorrect.

Question #22: Global, Cannot Be True. The correct answer choice is (C)

Again, we can use the distribution to quickly and easily destroy this question.

As we have previously established, lunch truck P can serve only one building. Hence, P could never serve both buildings X and Z, and therefore (C) is the correct answer choice.

Answer choice (A): Because H could serve all three buildings, H could serve both X and Z. Therefore, this answer choice could be true and it is incorrect.

Answer choice (B): As established in the setup of this game, I serves both X and Z. Therefore, this answer choice must be true and it is incorrect.

Answer choice (C): This is the correct answer choice.

Answer choice (D): If I served all three buildings, then S could serve buildings X and Z. Hence, this answer choice could be true and it is incorrect.

Answer choice (E): As established in the setup of this game, T serves both X and Z. Therefore, this answer choice must be true and it is incorrect.

This Grouping and Linear combination game features six players who must form four groups of two players each. The Linear aspect of this game is that the four games are played consecutively. However, one benefit for test takers is that no individual seat assignments are made within each game, and this limits the complexity of the game. The Grouping element results from the rules governing the formation of acceptable two-person games. From the game scenario it is immediately evident that some players will play multiple times, and you should actively seek a Numerical Distribution while working with the rules.

Our initial diagram references the six people, and represents the four games:

L N O P S T [6]

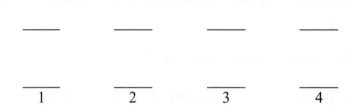

Rules #1 and #2. The first two rules can be added to the diagram easily. The first rule is reflected by T split-option on the second and fourth games (plus the Not Laws on the first and third games), and the second rule is represented by placing L in one of the spaces of the fourth game (it does not matter which space L occupies since the game does not assign seat positions):

	T/		T/
			L
1	2	3	4
T̶		T̶	

Note that T could play in *both* the second and fourth games.

Rule #3. This rule establishes that N and P do not play in the same game, and it additionally establishes that N plays in one and only one game. The Grouping aspect of this rule can be diagrammed as:

We will discuss the numerical aspect of this rule during the discussion of rule #4.

Rule #4. With six players for eight spots, and with each player playing in at least one game, there are initially only two Numerical Distributions of the eight positions to the six players: 3-1-1-1-1- or 2-2-1-1-1-1. The first three rules do not provide us with any numerically useful information aside from the fact that T cannot be a player who plays in three games and that N must be a player who plays exactly one game, but the fourth rule is more useful because it eliminates one of the distributions. By establishing that S plays in exactly two games, this rule eliminates the possibility that a 3-1-1-1-1-1 distribution could exist. Hence, the eight positions must be distributed to the six players in a 2-2-1-1-1-1 relationship:

2: S   (from the fourth rule, S plays in two games)
2:
1:
1:
1: O   (from the third rule, O plays in one game)
1: N   (from the fourth rule, N plays in one game)

Consequently, the three players not assigned above—L, P, and T—must be distributed in a 2-1-1 relationship, where one of the three must play twice and the other two play just once.

The fourth rule also creates a powerful horizontal block:

$$\boxed{\text{S O S}}$$

Because this SOS block requires so much space, it can only be placed in two positions: games 1-2-3 or games 2-3-4. Because this block is limited, and because there are several other powerful rules, you should make the decision to diagram both of the templates created by the SOS block:

<u>Template #1</u>: SOS in games 1-2-3.

With the assignment of the SOS block to games 1-2-3, and with the placement of L in game 4 (from the second rule), we now have one player assigned to each game:

N, P, L/P/T ⟶ _____   T/_____   _____   T/_____

_S_   _O_   _S_   _L_
1   2   3   4
X̸   X̸

Because each player must play in at least one game, we must still assign N, P, and T to games. However, assigning N, P, and T would only fill three of the remaining four spaces, and so, from the distribution discussed previously, we know that the remaining space must be filled by one of L, P, or T (that is, one of those three people plays in two games).

At this point in the template, we have placed the SOS block and determined which players must still be assigned. Since there is only one open space in each game, we can ignore the NP not-block rule since N and P cannot now be placed together. We have also fully addressed the second and fourth rules, and so the only concerns still present in this template is which game(s) T will play in and who, aside from S, will be assigned to play twice (L, P, or T).

<u>Template #2</u>: SOS in games 2-3-4.

When the SOS block is assigned to games 2-3-4, the fourth game is now fully assigned to L and S. This placement affects T, who can only play in the second and fourth games. Thus, T must play in the second game:

	T		L
	S	O	S
1	2	3	4
X̶		X̶	

The remaining three spaces must be occupied by N and P (who have thus far not been assigned to a game), and the apparent choice L, P, or T to play in a second game (someone must play twice and fill the final space). But, look closely at L, P, and T as possible two-game players: T can be eliminated because the remaining spaces are in the first and third games; P can be eliminated because selecting P would create the group of N, P, and P to fill in the final three spaces, and since two of the spaces are in the same game, the result would be that either N and P would play together (a violation of the third rule) or P would play both positions in one game (a violation of the stipulations in the game scenario). Consequently, we can conclude that L must be the player that plays two games, and that the group that fills the final three open spaces in this template is L, N, and P.

As if the determining the remaining players were not powerful enough, because two of the spaces are in the same game, we can also use the third rule to infer that one of N or P must play in the first game, and the other must play in the third game (if one of N and P does not play in the third game, then both play in the first game, a violation of the third rule). This forces L into the first game, resulting in a template with only two solutions:

L	T	P/N	L
N/P	S	O	S
1	2	3	4

The two templates give us an excellent overview of the general formations within this game, but because the first template has so many solutions, they do not give us complete information.

Question #7: Global, List. The correct answer choice is (A)

As with any List question, simply apply the rules to the answer choices. Given the presentation of the answer choices in this problem (the test makers have made them somewhat difficult to read), the easiest order of attack is to apply the second rule, then the first rule, then the third rule, and finally the last rule.

Answer choice (A): This is the correct answer choice.

Answer choice (B): This answer choice is incorrect because the first rule specifies that T cannot play in the third game.

Answer choice (C): This answer choice is incorrect because it violates both the third and fourth rules. The third rule is violated because N appears in two games; the fourth rule is violated because there is no SOS block.

Answer choice (D): This answer choice is incorrect because N can only play in one game, yet the answer features N in two games.

Answer choice (E): This answer choice is incorrect because L must play in the fourth game.

Question #8: Global, Could Be True. The correct answer choice is (A)

There are two ways to answer this question. The first way is to use the rules to eliminate each of the incorrect answer choices. The second is to use the templates to see which player could possibly play in two consecutive games. Let's examine both approaches:

Use the Rules

This is the easiest and fastest approach. The third and fourth rules tell us that N and O play in exactly one game, and so answer choices (B) and (C) can be eliminated. The fourth rule also indicates that while S plays in two games, those two games cannot be consecutive, so answer choice (D) can be eliminated. The first rule states that T cannot play in the first or third games, and so T could not play in consecutive games, and answer choice (E) can be eliminated. Thus, answer choice (A) is proven correct by process of elimination.

Use the Templates

When examining the templates, always look at Template #2 first because it contains more specific information. In Template #2, none of the variables could play in consecutive games, so we automatically know that the variable that plays consecutively does so under the parameters of Template #1.

Template #1 immediately eliminates all players except L, P, or T, because only L, P, or T could play twice and could conceivably be consecutive (although S plays twice, the template shows that S is not consecutive and is thus eliminated). However, P is not one of the answer choices, so the answer must be L or T. Of course, as shown on the template, T cannot be consecutive, and so L is the player who could play consecutively and answer choice (A) is the correct answer.

Answer choice (A): This is the correct answer choice.

Answer choices (B), (C), (D), and (E): The players in each of these answer cannot play in consecutive games, and thus each one of these answers is incorrect.

Question #9: Local, Could Be True. The correct answer choice is (A)

If T plays in the fourth game, then only Template #1 can apply to this question. Let's revisit template #1 with the addition of T in the fourth game:

N, P, L/P/T $\longrightarrow$
$$\underline{\quad\quad}\quad\quad \underline{\quad\quad}\quad\quad \underline{\quad\quad}\quad\quad \underline{\quad T\quad}$$

$$\underline{\quad S\quad}\quad \underline{\quad O\quad}\quad \underline{\quad S\quad}\quad \underline{\quad L\quad}$$
$$\quad 1 \qquad\quad 2 \qquad\quad 3 \qquad\quad 4$$

The variables yet to be placed include N, P, and the choice of L, P, or T, but there is no way to place those remaining variables exactly. So, although you might wish you could derive more information as a consequence of the placement of T, there are still a number of possibilities and you must move forward and attack the answer choices without getting bogged down trying to assign every player.

Answer choice (A): This is the correct answer choice. N could play in the second game as proven in the following hypothetical:

$$\underline{\quad P\quad}\quad \underline{\quad N\quad}\quad \underline{\quad L\quad}\quad \underline{\quad T\quad}$$

$$\underline{\quad S\quad}\quad \underline{\quad O\quad}\quad \underline{\quad S\quad}\quad \underline{\quad L\quad}$$
$$\quad 1 \qquad\quad 2 \qquad\quad 3 \qquad\quad 4$$

Answer choice (B): This answer choice cannot be true because O plays only once, in the second game.

Answer choice (C): This answer choice is incorrect because S must play in the first and third games, not the second game.

Answer choice (D): This answer choice is incorrect. N can only play in one game, and N's choices for playing partners are S or O (that is, the only open spaces in the diagram are paired with S or O). Thus, N cannot play with L.

Answer choice (E): This answer choice is similar to answer choice (D). Although P can play in more than one game, there is no possibility of P playing with L. As with (D), the only open spaces in the diagram are paired with S or O. Thus, P cannot play with L, and this answer is incorrect.

Question #10: Global, Could Be True. The correct answer choice is (A)

A Global question is made for the templates, and so you should immediately refer to the templates as you attack each answer choice.

Answer choice (A): This is the correct answer choice. P could play L in the first game as proven by the following hypothetical from Template #1:

L	T	N	L
P	S	O	S
1	2	3	4

Answer choice (B): As shown by the two templates, either O or S always plays in the second game. Thus, P cannot play N in the second game, and this answer choice is incorrect.

Answer choice (C): The fourth rule specifies that O plays exactly one game, and that S plays two games, one just before O and one just after O. Hence, O and S can never play in a game together.

Answer choice (D): As shown by the two templates, either O or S always plays in the third game. Thus, P cannot play L in the third game, and this answer choice is incorrect.

Answer choice (E): The second rule indicates that L must play in the fourth game, and hence N cannot play S in the fourth game.

Question #11: Global, List. The correct answer choice is (C)

This Global question asks for who cannot be paired with T. As with question #8, there are two ways to answer this question. The first way is to use previously created hypotheticals to eliminate each of the incorrect answer choices. The second is to use the templates to see who cannot play against T. Let's examine both approaches:

<u>Use Hypotheticals</u>

This approach has the benefit of eliminating several answer choices quickly. From question #7, answer choice (A), we know that T can play against O. Hence, any answer choice that contains O can be eliminated, and answer choices (B) and (E) can be removed from consideration.

The question stem of #9 places T in the last game. From the second rule, we know L plays in the last game, and thus T can play against L. Answer choice (A), which contains L, can therefore be eliminated.

At this juncture, answer choices (C) and (D) remain in contention, and both contain N. Thus, we need not concern ourselves with N and we can focus on the other variables in each answer: P and S, respectively. There are two different paths to the correct answer from this point:

1. Analyze the possibilities without writing them down. From a logical point of view, it is likely that T can play against S since S plays twice, and S can be placed in such a way as to conform to T's requirements (T must play in the second or fourth game). T and P, on the other hand, present a problem since they form a vertical block, and in order to make room for the horizontal SOS block, the TP vertical block would have to be placed in the fourth game. However, since L already plays in the fourth game, this cannot occur, and thus there is no way to reach a viable solution when T plays with P. Hence, answer choice (C) is correct.

2. Create a new hypothetical. Once you are down to two answer choices, you can simply power through the problem by creating a hypothetical to match one of the remaining answer choices. This hypothetical, for instance, shows that S can play against T, and that therefore answer choice (D) is incorrect:

L	T	N	L
P	S	O	S
1	2	3	4

The Hypothetical approach has the advantage of eliminating several answers quickly, and then it is not too difficult to eliminate the final answer choice.

Use the Templates

This approach is somewhat more logically attractive because it relies completely on work you did during the setup. In creating the templates, Template #2 paired T and S. Thus, we can eliminate any answer choice that contains S, and answer choice (D) can be removed from consideration.

Template #1 allows T to play against L or O, the players in the second and fourth games, respectively. Since there no limitations on variable placement in that template, both L and O can play against T, and any answer choice containing L or O is incorrect. That inference eliminates answer choices (A), (B), and (E), and thus answer choice (C) is correct.

Regardless of which method you use to arrive at the correct answer, the reasoning that underlies the answer is the same: placing T with either N or P creates a placement issue with the SOS block. The only way to successfully place the SOS block and a TN or TP vertical block forces the T block into the fourth game, which cannot occur since L already is there.

Answer choice (A): T can play against L, and so this answer choice is incorrect.

Answer choice (B): T can play against O, and so this answer choice is incorrect.

Answer choice (C): This is the correct answer choice.

Answer choice (D): T can play against S, and so this answer choice is incorrect.

Answer choice (E): T can play against O, and so this answer choice is incorrect.

Question #12: Local, Must Be True. The correct answer choice is (E)

If O plays in the third game, this enacts the scenario in Template #2:

L	T	P/N	L
N/P	S	O	S
1	2	3	4

Consequently, T must play in the second game, and answer choice (E) is correct.

Answer choice (A): This answer choice is incorrect because L plays in the first and last games.

Answer choice (B): This answer choice is incorrect because although N could play in the third game, N does not have to play in the third game.

Answer choice (C): This answer choice is incorrect because although P could play in the first game, P does not have to play in the first game.

Answer choice (D): This answer choice is incorrect because although P could play in the third game, P does not have to play in the third game.

Answer choice (E): This is the correct answer choice. If you are looking for the reasoning of how we arrived at the diagram above, please go back to the discussion of Template #2 in the setup analysis.

This is a Defined-Fixed, Unbalanced: Overloaded Grouping game.

Monkeys: F G H
           *

Pandas: K L N   Six Animals
        *

Raccoons: T V Z   ____ ____ ____ ____ ____ ____
          * *

9 ⟶ 6

<u>Inferences</u>

F ⟷ H   K ⟷ T

N ⟷ T   H ⟷ T

H ⟶ K ⟶ N   Either 1 or 2 monkeys must be selected.

In the setup, some students create a second row within the group to show the type of animal—monkey, panda, or raccoon. While there is nothing wrong with this decision, operationally it has little effect as the questions focus more on the individual animals than on their type, and also, the questions can easily be answered without adding that second row.

There are more inferences in this game than might appear at first. Let us take a moment to examine the few inferences that can be drawn.

First, at the group level, we can deduce from the first rule that if two monkeys are selected, then G must be one of those monkeys (we know this by Hurdling the Uncertainty—since F and H can never be selected together, if two monkeys are selected then G must always be selected). As a corollary, we can conclude that at most two monkeys will ever be selected (and, from the second rule, we can conclude that at least one monkey must be selected: since N and T cannot be selected together, we cannot form a viable group from just the six pandas and raccoons, and therefore at least one monkey will always be selected).

Second, at the variable level, several more inferences can be drawn. By connecting the second and fourth rules we can infer that K and T can never be selected together. By recycling that inference and combining it with the third rule, we can also infer that H and T can never be selected together.

The last two rules form a chain linking H, K, and N. Consequently, H is an important variable because if H is selected then K and N must also be selected, and once H, K, and N are selected we can conclude from the first two rules that F and T would not be selected. At that point, any of the remaining animals could be selected because all four rules in the scenario would have been satisfied (and, as you might expect, the remaining variables—G, L, V, and Z—are randoms). Hence, the selection of H yields a number of ready-made hypothetical solutions:

$$\underline{\quad H \quad} \ \underline{\quad K \quad} \ \underline{\quad N \quad} \ \underline{(G, \ \underline{\ L,}\ \ V, \ Z)}$$

As with any conditional chain sequence, you should also consider what occurs if the final necessary condition is not selected. In this case, if N is not selected, via the contrapositive you know that K and H cannot be selected. At first, this may appear unremarkable, but remember that this is a "9 into 6" grouping scenario, and if H, K, and N are all eliminated, then there are no "extra" variables, and all the remaining variables must be used. This creates the following hypothetical:

$$\underline{\quad F \quad} \ \underline{\quad G \quad} \ \underline{\quad L \quad} \ \underline{\quad T \quad} \ \underline{\quad V \quad} \ \underline{\quad Z \quad}$$

Note that you should not just simply assume that such a hypothetical is valid; instead, quickly check the rules to make sure there are no violations (in the above hypothetical, there are no violations). If there was a violation, you would then know that the necessary condition—in this case, N—would have to be selected in every scenario and you would have gained a valuable piece of information (as it stands, since the hypothetical scenario above is workable, N does not have to be selected).

The other variable of note is T. Because T and N cannot be selected together, when T is selected there can be only one solution to the game (because N will not be selected, leading to the hypothetical discussed above).

Question #18: Global, Could Be True, List. The correct answer choice is (D)

Answer choice (A) is incorrect because N and T cannot be selected together.

Answer choice (B) is incorrect because F and H cannot be selected together.

Answer choice (C) is incorrect because if K is selected then N must be selected.

Answer choice (D) is the correct answer.

Answer choice (E) is incorrect because if H is selected then K must be selected.

Question #19: Local, Could Be True. The correct answer choice is (C)

According to the question stem, H and L are selected. From our discussion, we know that once H is selected, then K and N are also selected and F and T are not selected. This leaves the following situation:

$$\underline{\quad H \quad} \ \underline{\quad K \quad} \ \underline{\quad N \quad} \ \underline{\quad L \quad} \ \underline{(G, \ V, \ Z)}$$

Answer choices (A) and (B) are eliminated due to the Not Laws. Answer choices (D) and (E) are eliminated because all three pandas must be selected. Consequently, answer choice (C) is correct.

Question #20: Global, Could Be True, Except. The correct answer choice is (C)

From our discussion of inferences, we know that K and T cannot be selected together (the combination of the third, fourth, and second rules makes it impossible). Consequently, answer choice (C) is correct.

Question #21: Local, Must Be True. The correct answer choice is (B)

This is the only question stem to contain a reference to the animal groups. If all three raccoons are selected, then T, V, and Z must be selected. Since T is selected, from the rules and inferences we know that N, K, and H cannot be selected, and therefore F, G, and L must be selected (see the discussion of inferences if this does not make sense):

$$\underline{T_R} \quad \underline{V_R} \quad \underline{Z_R} \quad \underline{F_M} \quad \underline{G_M} \quad \underline{L_P}$$

$$\cancel{N}$$
$$\cancel{K}$$
$$\cancel{H}$$

Answer choices (A), (C), (D), and (E) can never be true. Answer choice (B) must be true, and is therefore correct.

Question #22: Local, Must Be True. The correct answer choice is (A)

Similar to question #21, when T is selected, from the rules and inferences we know that N, K, and H cannot be selected, and therefore F, G, and L must be selected:

$$\underline{T} \quad \underline{V} \quad \underline{Z} \quad \underline{F} \quad \underline{G} \quad \underline{L}$$

$$\cancel{N}$$
$$\cancel{K}$$
$$\cancel{H}$$

Answer choice (A) is therefore correct.

Another way of attacking this question is to eliminate answers that contain a variable that cannot be selected with T: use the rule that N and T cannot be selected together to eliminate answer choice (E); then use the inference that K and T cannot be selected together to eliminate answer choices (C) and (D); then use the inference that K and H cannot be selected together to eliminate answer choice (B).

Question #23: Global, Must Be True. The correct answer choice is (B)

At first glance, this appears to be a difficult Global question. Remember, if you do not have a ready inference to apply to this type of question, prepare to use hypotheticals and previous information.

Answer choice (A) can be eliminated by the question stem to #21.

Answer choice (C) can be eliminated by the hypothetical produced in #21 (and in our discussion of what occurs when N is not selected).

Answer choice (D) can be eliminated by the hypothetical array we produced when discussing the selection of H, K, and N (when H, K, and N are selected, then any three of G, L, V, and Z can be selected, allowing for a hypothetical with only one monkey).

Answer choice (E) can be eliminated by the question stem to #21.

Answer Choice (B) is correct.

INDIVIDUAL GAMES

CHAPTER FOUR: COMPLETE GAMES SECTIONS

Chapter Notes ▮▮▮▮▮▮▮▮▮▮▮▮▮▮▮▮▮▮▮▮▮▮▮▮▮▮▮▮▮▮▮▮▮▮▮▮▮▮

This chapter contains five complete LSAT Logic Games sections drawn from actual LSATs. We recommend taking each complete section as a timed exercise by allotting yourself 35 minutes to complete the section. Then, check your work against the answer key that immediately follows each section, and compare your setup to the setup and explanations provided.

To identify each game section and the corresponding explanations, use the black sidebars as a reference. As different games sections are presented, the sidebar will identify the year and month of the LSAT the section is drawn from. Explanations sections are appended with an "Explanations" identifier in the black bar.

As you begin each section, remember to consider your overall time and pacing strategy, and to remember that you are not required to complete the games in the order they are presented to you. Take control of your performance and be aggressive yet calm, and you will perform optimally. Good luck!

DECEMBER 2002
LOGIC GAMES SECTION

SECTION I
Time—35 minutes
23 Questions

Directions: Each group of questions in this section is based on a set of conditions. In answering some of the questions, it may be useful to draw a rough diagram. Choose the response that most accurately and completely answers each question and blacken the corresponding space on your answer sheet.

Questions 1-5

Eight files will be ordered from first to eighth. Each file falls into exactly one of three categories: red files (H, M, O), green files (P, V, X), or yellow files (T, Z). The files must be ordered according to the following conditions:

H must be placed into some position before O, but H cannot immediately precede O.

X must be placed into some position before V.

X and V must be separated by the same number of files as separate H and O.

Z must immediately precede M.

The first file cannot be a red file.

1. Which one of the following is an acceptable ordering of the files from first to eighth?

	1	2	3	4	5	6	7	8
(A)	H	X	O	V	Z	M	P	T
(B)	P	M	Z	H	X	O	V	T
(C)	P	Z	M	H	O	T	X	V
(D)	X	Z	M	V	H	T	P	O
(E)	Z	M	H	P	O	X	V	T

2. The largest possible number of files that can separate Z from H is

(A) two
(B) three
(C) four
(D) five
(E) six

3. If each of the three red files is immediately followed by a green file, which one of the following must be a yellow file?

(A) the first
(B) the second
(C) the third
(D) the fourth
(E) the fifth

4. The largest possible number of files that can separate X from V is

(A) three
(B) four
(C) five
(D) six
(E) seven

5. If Z is placed in the fifth position, then which one of the following is a complete and accurate list of the positions, anyone of which could be H's position?

(A) first, third, fourth
(B) first, second, third
(C) second, third, fourth
(D) second, third, fourth, sixth
(E) third, fourth, sixth, seventh

GO ON TO THE NEXT PAGE.

Questions 6-11

Exactly three employees of Capital Enterprises—Maria, Suki, and Tate—attend a three-day conference together. Each day, there are exactly three sessions on the three topics of the conference—one on hiring, one on investing, and one on regulations. The following rules govern the conference:

Each conference participant attends exactly two sessions, which are on different topics and on different days.

Neither Maria nor Suki attends any session on investing.

Tate does not attend any session on the third day.

At most two Capital employees attend any given session together.

6. What is the maximum number of sessions attended by at least one Capital employee?

(A) three
(B) four
(C) five
(D) six
(E) seven

7. Which one of the following must be false?

(A) Maria attends sessions only on the first two days.
(B) Suki attends sessions only on the last two days.
(C) Exactly two Capital employees attend a session together on the second day.
(D) Exactly one session is attended by one or more Capital employees on the second day.
(E) Exactly three sessions are attended by one or more Capital employees on the third day.

8. If exactly two sessions on the third day are attended by one or more Capital employees, then which one of the following must be true?

(A) Exactly two sessions on the first day are attended by one or more Capital employees.
(B) Exactly two sessions on the second day are attended by one or more Capital employees.
(C) Maria and Suki do not attend any session together.
(D) Maria and Tate do not attend any session together.
(E) Tate attends a session on investing.

9. Each of the following is possible EXCEPT:

(A) Every session attended by at least one Capital employee is attended by exactly one Capital employee.
(B) Every session attended by at least one Capital employee is attended by exactly two Capital employees.
(C) Every session attended by Maria is also attended by Suki.
(D) Every session attended by Suki is also attended by Tate.
(E) Every session attended by Tate is also attended by Maria.

10. If all three sessions on the first day are attended by one or more Capital employees, then which one of the following must be false?

(A) Maria and Suki attend a session together on the third day.
(B) Suki and Tate attend a session together on the second day.
(C) Maria attends a session on hiring on the second day.
(D) Suki attends a session on regulations on the third day.
(E) Tate attends a session on investing on the first day.

11. If Maria and Tate are the only Capital employees to attend a session on the first day, then each of the following could be true EXCEPT:

(A) Maria and Suki attend exactly two sessions together.
(B) Maria and Tate attend exactly two sessions together.
(C) Suki and Tate attend exactly one session together.
(D) Maria attends a session on regulations on the second day.
(E) Tate attends a session on hiring on the second day.

GO ON TO THE NEXT PAGE.

Questions 12-18

Of the five Pohl children—Sara, Theo, Uma, Will, and Zoe—three are left-handed and two are right-handed. Each of the five children was born in a different one of seven calendar years, 1990 through 1996. The following conditions apply:

No two left-handed children were born in consecutive years.

No two right-handed children were born in consecutive years.

Sara, who is left-handed, was born before Uma.

Zoe was born before both Theo and Will.

A left-handed child was born in 1991.

Uma, who is right-handed, was born in 1993.

12. Which one of the following could be an accurate matching of each Pohl child with the year in which that child was born?

    (A)   Sara: 1990; Zoe: 1992; Uma: 1993; Will: 1994; and Theo: 1995

    (B)   Sara: 1991; Uma: 1993; Theo: 1994; Zoe: 1995; and Will: 1996

    (C)   Zoe: 1990; Sara: 1991; Uma: 1992; Theo: 1994; and Will: 1995

    (D)   Zoe: 1990; Sara: 1991; Uma: 1993; Theo: 1994; and Will: 1995

    (E)   Zoe: 1990; Sara: 1991; Uma: 1993; Theo: 1994; and Will: 1996

13. If Sara was born before Zoe was born, then which one of the following statements CANNOT be true?

    (A)   Will is left-handed.

    (B)   Zoe is left-handed.

    (C)   Theo was born after Will was born.

    (D)   Uma was born after Zoe was born.

    (E)   No child was born in 1990.

14. Which one of the following must be false?

    (A)   None of the children was born in 1990, nor was a child born in 1992.

    (B)   None of the children was born in 1992, nor was a child born in 1995.

    (C)   None of the children was born in 1994, nor was a child born in 1996.

    (D)   One of the children was born in 1990, and another in 1993.

    (E)   One of the children was born in 1993, and another in 1995.

15. If Theo was born after Will was born, then how many sequential orderings of the children, from firstborn to lastborn, are possible?

    (A)   one

    (B)   two

    (C)   three

    (D)   four

    (E)   five

16. If none of the children was born in 1995, then which one of the following statements must be true?

    (A)   Theo was born in 1994.

    (B)   Will was born in 1994.

    (C)   Will was born in 1996.

    (D)   Zoe was born in 1990.

    (E)   Zoe was born in 1994.

17. If Theo is right-handed, then each of the following statements must be false EXCEPT:

    (A)   Theo was born in 1996.

    (B)   Will was born in 1995.

    (C)   Uma was born exactly three years before Theo was born.

    (D)   Zoe was born exactly one year before Theo was born.

    (E)   Will is right-handed.

18. If Zoe was born before Uma was born, then which one of the following statements must be false?

    (A)   No child was born in 1992.

    (B)   No child was born in 1995.

    (C)   Theo is left-handed.

    (D)   Zoe is left-handed.

    (E)   Will is left-handed.

GO ON TO THE NEXT PAGE.

Questions 19-23

Barbara is shopping at a pet store to select fish for her new aquarium from among the following species: J, K, L, M, N, O, and P. For each of the seven species, the store has several fish available. Barbara makes her selection in a manner consistent with the following conditions:

If she selects one or more K, then she does not select any O.

If she selects one or more M, then she does not select any N.

If she selects one or more M, then she selects at least one O.

If she selects one or more N, then she selects at least one O.

If she selects one or more O, then she selects at least one P.

If she selects one or more P, then she selects at least one O.

If she selects any O at all, then she selects at least two O.

19. Which one of the following could be a complete and accurate list of the fish Barbara selects for her aquarium?

(A) three J, one K, two M
(B) one J, one K, one M, three O
(C) one J, one M, two O, one P
(D) one J, one N, one O, two P
(E) one M, one N, two O, one P

20. If Barbara does not select any fish of species P, then it could be true that she selects fish of species

(A) J and of species K
(B) J and of species M
(C) K and of species M
(D) K and of species N
(E) L and of species O

21. If Barbara selects fish of as many species as possible, then she cannot select any fish of which one of the following species?

(A) K
(B) L
(C) M
(D) N
(E) P

22. Which one of the following statements must be false?

(A) Barbara selects exactly four fish, at least one of which is a J.
(B) Barbara selects exactly four fish, at least one of which is an L.
(C) Barbara selects exactly three fish, at least one of which is an M.
(D) Barbara selects exactly three fish, at least one of which is an O.
(E) Barbara selects exactly three fish, at least one of which is a P.

23. If Barbara selects at least one fish for her aquarium, then which one of the following lists the minimum and maximum possible numbers, respectively, of different species of fish that Barbara selects?

(A) 1, 4
(B) 1, 5
(C) 1, 6
(D) 2, 5
(E) 2, 6

S T O P

IF YOU FINISH BEFORE TIME IS CALLED, YOU MAY CHECK YOUR WORK ON THIS SECTION ONLY.
DO NOT WORK ON ANY OTHER SECTION IN THE TEST.

DECEMBER 2002 LOGIC GAMES SECTION

1.	D	8.	C	15.	B	22.	C
2.	C	9.	B	16.	D	23.	B
3.	A	10.	A	17.	D		
4.	C	11.	A	18.	D		
5.	C	12.	E	19.	C		
6.	D	13.	D	20.	A		
7.	E	14.	C	21.	A		

This is a Balanced Advanced Linear game.

Red: H M O ³

Green: P V X ³
    *

Yellow: T Z ²
    *

H > O

H̶/̶O̶

X > V

H > O = X > V

Z M

G/Y							
X̶							
1	2	3	4	5	6	7	8
H̶	Ø̶	Ø̶				H̶	H̶
M̶	X̶					X̶	X̶
Ø̶							Z̶
X̶							

This game is standard, except for the third rule, which is unusual. There are a number of different possible representations of this rule, but we have chosen a diagram that features blocks around the sequences in order to make sure the rule is clear. In our estimation, this representation:

$$H > O = X > V$$

is clearer than:

$$H > O = X > V$$

There are several inferences that can be drawn from this rule, namely:

1. Because the file separation must be equal for both pairs, if X is placed first, V cannot be placed eighth, and if V is placed eighth, then X cannot be placed first. The same relationship applies to H and O (although the last rule already established that H cannot be placed first). Also, V cannot be placed second (since H and O must always be separated by at least one space, therefore if X was first the earliest V could be placed would be third).

2.   Because H̶/̶O̶ , we can infer that X̶/̶V̶ .

There are also some interesting Not Laws within the diagram:

1. <u>O cannot be placed second</u>. Because H cannot be placed first, and O must be placed in some position after H, we can infer that O cannot be placed second.

2. <u>O cannot be placed third.</u> The earliest that H can be placed is second. But, because O cannot immediately follow H, we can infer that O cannot be placed third.

3. <u>H cannot be placed seventh</u>. If H is placed seventh, then O must be placed eighth, and that would cause a violation of the rule that states that H cannot immediately precede O.

Question #1: Global, Could Be True, List. The correct answer choice is (D)

Answer choice (A) is incorrect because H cannot be placed first.

Answer choice (B) is incorrect because Z must immediately precede M.

Answer choice (C) is incorrect because H cannot immediately precede O.

Answer choice (D) is the correct answer.

Answer choice (E) is incorrect because X and V must be separated by the same number of files as separate H and O.

Question #2: Global, Must Be True, Maximum. The correct answer choice is (C)

This is a perfect question to attack with a hypothetical. Either of the following two hypotheticals of the files only prove answer choice (C) correct:

Hypothetical #2:	X	H	V	O	P	T	Z	M
Hypothetical #1:	Z	M	X	P	V	H	T	O
	1	2	3	4	5	6	7	8

Question #3: Local, Must Be True. The correct answer choice is (A)

The condition in the question stem produces three red-green blocks:

$$\boxed{RG} \qquad \boxed{RG} \qquad \boxed{RG}$$

Consequently, a green file can never be placed first. This inference, in combination with the last rule, proves answer choice (A).

Question #4: Global, Must Be True, Maximum. The correct answer choice is (C)

From our initial analysis of the third rule, we know that if X is placed first, then V cannot be placed eighth. However, if X is placed first, perhaps V could be placed seventh. The following hypothetical template proves this is possible:

Hypothetical #1:	X	H	(	P,	T,	ZM)		V	O
	1	2	3	4	5	6	7	8

This hypothetical, one of several possible, proves answer choice (C) correct.

Question #5: Local, Could Be True, List. The correct answer choice is (C)

This question is quite easy. From the Not Laws, we know that H cannot be placed first or seventh, and this information eliminates answer choices (A), (B), and (E). Next, the local condition in the question stem establishes that Z is in the fifth position. From the fourth rule, if Z is in the fifth position, them M must be in the sixth position. This information eliminates answer choice (D), and thus answer choice (C) is correct.

As you review the game, closely examine questions #2 and #5 as they both can be effectively attacked by using hypotheticals.

December 2002 Questions 6-11 *6. D 7. E 8. C 9. B 10. A 11. A*

This is a Partially Defined Grouping game.

M S T³

min 3 E's

2 sessions per employee

max 2 employees together

R: ___ ___ ___

I: ___ ___ E ~~M S~~

H: ___ ___ ___
    1   2   3
         ~~T~~

At first, this game appears to be fairly standard: nine sessions are being filled, and three employees are available to fill those sessions. The first rule then establishes that each employee can attend only two of the sessions. This rule makes the game appear Underfunded, which is not a concern because we can create three empty spaces to balance out the game. But, the final rule reveals that employees can attend sessions together, and this leaves the number of sessions attended by the employees uncertain. Because we know the employees can attend a maximum of six different sessions or a minimum of four sessions, this game is Partially Defined.

Because the employees can attend a maximum of six different sessions, at least three of the nine sessions will be "empty" for our purposes. These can be designated with "E."

Question #6: Global, Must Be True, Maximum. The correct answer choice is (D)

As mentioned in the discussion above, six is the maximum number of sessions that the Capital employees can attend. Thus, answer choice (D) is correct. Here is one hypothetical that proves the point:

R: E   S   M

I: E   T   E

H: T   M   S
      1   2   3

Question #7: Global, Cannot Be True, FTT. The correct answer choice is (E)

Because M and S can never attend an investing session, and T cannot attend a session on the third day, we were able to deduce in the setup that investing on the third day is empty. Answer choice (E) is impossible and therefore correct.

Question #8: Local, Must Be True. The correct answer choice is (C)

Because T cannot attend a session on the third day, for employees to attend two sessions on the third day then M and S must separately attend the hiring and regulations sessions:

```
R:  ____  ____  M/S

I:  ____  ____   E

H:  ____  ____  S/M
     1     2     3
```

This inference allows us to prove that answer choice (C) is correct. For example, if M attends the regulations session on day three and S attends the hiring session on day three, then M cannot attend another regulation session and S cannot attend another hiring session. So, if M and S were to attend a session together, they would have to do so at an investing session. But we know from the second rule that M and S cannot attend an investing session. Thus, we can infer that M and S do not attend any session together.

This discussion allows us to make an inference that will be useful later in the game, on question #10: when M and S attend different session topics, i.e. one attends a hiring session and one attends a regulations session (regardless of the day attended), they cannot attend a session together at any point in the game.

Question #9: Global, Could Be True, Except. The correct answer choice is (B)

Like the other Global questions in this game (#6, #7, and #8), this question can be time-consuming. Remember, on many Global questions using hypotheticals is a fast and effective method of attack.

Answer choice (A) is proven incorrect by the hypothetical provided in question #6.

Answer choice (B) is the correct answer choice. If the condition in the answer choice is true, then only three sessions would be attended by the employees (two sessions per employee and two employees at each session equals three sessions of two employees each). However, there is no acceptable scenario where this can occur because none of the employees can repeat a session topic.

Answer choice (C) is proven incorrect by the hypothetical

```
R:   T    MS    E

I:   E    T     E

H:   MS   E     E
     1    2     3
```

Answer choices (D) and (E) are functionally identical, and therefore both are incorrect. M and S are basically interchangeable, and these two answers simply pair S with T, and then M with T. If S can pair with T, then logically M can pair with T. According to the Uniqueness Theory of Answer Choices, each correct answer choice is identifiably unique, and so any pair of functionally identical answer choices must be incorrect.

Question #10: Local, Cannot Be True, FTT. The correct answer choice is (A)

The condition in the question stem leads to the following basic scenario:

R: M/S ____ ____

I: T ____ E

H: S/M ____ ____
    1   2   3

As discussed in question #8, when M and S attend different session topics (as on the first day in this question), they cannot attend a session together at any point in the game. Hence, answer choice (A) is correct.

Question #11. Local, Could Be True, Except. The correct answer choice is (A)

If M and T are the only employees to attend a session on the first day, we can infer that S must attend sessions on both the second day and the third day. And because T cannot attend a session on the third day, T must attend a session on the second day. Thus, M and T attend a session on the first day, S and T attend a session on the second day, and S attends a session on the third day. This information is sufficient to prove answer choice (A) correct.

This is an Advanced Linear Game: Unbalanced, Identify the Templates.

S T U W Z⁵ E E

L L L R R⁵ E E

Because there are seven years and only five children, this linear game is Unbalanced. However, this imbalance is easily corrected by creating two empty years, designated by the "E's" above. Since an E in either the L/R row or the child row means that the entire year is empty, we can show the two empty years as:

This game requires a series of related steps to create the complete setup above:

Step 1. The combination of the first rule and the fifth rule allows us to infer that a left-handed child was not born in 1990 or 1992.

Step 2. U, a right-handed child, was born in 1993. Thus, a right-handed child was not born in 1992 or 1994. Further, from the third rule we can infer that S, a left-handed child, was born in 1990, 1991, or 1992. However, when this inference is combined with step 1, we can infer that S was born in 1991.

Step 3. Since neither a left-handed or a right-handed child can be born in 1992, 1992 must be an empty year. Since a left-handed child cannot be born in 1990, 1990 must be either an empty or a right-handed year.

Step 4. From the first three steps above, we have placed one right-handed child, one left-handed child, and one empty year. Further, 1990 has been established as either an empty or a right-handed year.

Consequently, two left-handed children must be born in the years 1994, 1995, and 1996. Because of the first rule, we can therefore infer that the two left-handed children are born in 1994 and 1996. From that inference we can deduce that 1995 is the remainder of the right-handed/empty dual-option from 1990. At this point, the entire L/R row is complete, and the only uncertainty is in 1990 and 1995.

Step 5. Due to steps 1 though 4 above, all the rules are "dead" except the fourth rule. The fourth rule is the only remaining active rule, and even then there are limitations, as shown by the dual- and triple-options in the child row of the diagram.

The discussion above reveals the deep restrictions in this game. In fact, there are only two basic templates that exist:

Template #1: Z born in 1990

L/R:	R	L	E	R	L	E	L
Child:	Z	S	E	U	T/W	E	W/T
	90	91	92	93	94	95	96

Template #2: Z born in 1994

L/R:	E	L	E	R	L	R	L
Child:	E	S	E	U	Z	T/W	W/T
	90	91	92	93	94	95	96

Either the original diagram or these two templates can be used to effectively attack this game.

Question #12: Global, Could Be True, List question. The correct answer choice is (E)

Answer choice (A) is incorrect because S was born in 1991, not 1990. (A) is also incorrect because no one was born in 1992.

Answer choice (B) is incorrect because Z was born before both T and W.

Answer choice (C) is incorrect because U was born in 1993, not 1992.

Answer choice (D) is incorrect because one of 1990 or 1995 was an empty year.

Answer choice (E) is the correct answer.

Question #13: Local, Cannot Be True. The correct answer choice is (D)

If S was born before Z, then Z must have been born in 1994, as in Template #2:

L/R:	E	L	E	R	L	R	L
Child:	E	S	E	U	Z	T/W	W/T
	90	91	92	93	94	95	96

Consequently, answer choice (D) is proven correct. Also, please note that in this template, the E in the 1990 child row forces a corresponding E in the L/R row, and in turn you can infer that in 1995 a right-handed child was born.

Question #14: Global, Cannot Be True, FTT. The correct answer choice is (C)

Our original diagram proves answer choice (C) correct. If your setup was incomplete, please be aware that you could have used the answer to question #12 to eliminate answer choices (B) and (D).

Question #15: Local, Must Be True, Maximum. The correct answer choice is (B)

The question is specific in requesting the number of different sequential orderings, not the number of different orders of children and years. If $W > T$, there are two possible sequential orderings:

Order #1: $Z > S > U > W > T$

Order #2: $S > U > Z > W > T$

Hence, answer choice (B) is correct.

Question #16: Local, Must Be True. The correct answer choice is (D)

The condition in the question stem creates the following scenario, identical to template #1:

L/R:	R	L	E	R	L	E	L
Child:	Z	S	E	U	T/W	E	W/T
	90	91	92	93	94	95	96

Therefore, answer choice (D) is correct.

Again, if you had difficulty creating the scenario above, the solution from question #12 can be used to eliminate answer choices (B) and (E).

Question #17: Local, Cannot Be True, Except, FTT. The correct answer choice is (D)

If T is right-handed, then the only year T could have been born is 1995. If 1995 is a right-handed year, then 1990 is an empty year, and we can conclude that Z was born in 1994:

L/R:	E	L	E	R	L	R	L

Child:	E	S	E	U	Z	T	W
	90	91	92	93	94	95	96

Thus, answer choice (D) is proven correct.

Question #18: Local, Cannot Be True, FTT. The correct answer choice is (D)

If Z > U, then Z was born in 1990, as in Template #1:

L/R:	R	L	E	R	L	E	L

Child:	Z	S	E	U	T/W	E	W/T
	90	91	92	93	94	95	96

Hence, answer choice (D) is correct.

Once again, if you had difficulty creating the scenario above, the solution from question #12 can be used to eliminate answer choices (A) and (B).

This game is a model example of an Advanced Linear game. Our organized attack features two key pieces: first, we created two "E" placeholders to compensate for the Unbalanced aspect of the game; second, we attacked the rules by linkage, and we kept a close watch on the two not-blocks, especially the LL not-block as the game contained three L's. These two steps reduced the game to a simple exercise in tracking the fourth rule, the only remaining active rule (a quick survey of the questions reveals that every Local question references either T, W, or Z). Students able to recognize the restriction inherent in the fourth rule can then create two templates to attack the game.

This is an Undefined Grouping game.

J K L M N O P[7]
*   *

Rules	Inferences
K $\longleftarrow\!\!\mid\!\!\longrightarrow$ O	M $\longleftarrow\!\!\mid\!\!\longrightarrow$ K
M $\longleftarrow\!\!\mid\!\!\longrightarrow$ N	N $\longleftarrow\!\!\mid\!\!\longrightarrow$ K
M $\longrightarrow$ O	M $\longrightarrow$ P
N $\longrightarrow$ O	N $\longrightarrow$ P
O $\longleftarrow\!\!\longrightarrow$ P	P $\longleftarrow\!\!\mid\!\!\longrightarrow$ K
$O_1 \longrightarrow O_2$	M $\longrightarrow O_2$
	N $\longrightarrow O_2$
	P $\longrightarrow O_2$

At first this game appears to be a fairly standard Grouping game, but the test makers throw a slight twist into the mix with the last rule that specifies the number of Os selected. Fortunately, this is the only numerical rule, and thus it is easy to remember throughout the game.

Because of the large number of rules, there are also a large number of inferences:

1. M $\longleftarrow\!\!\mid\!\!\longrightarrow$ K. This inference is produced by the combination of the first and third rules.

2. M $\longleftarrow\!\!\mid\!\!\longrightarrow$ N. This inference is produced by the combination of the first and fourth rules.

3. M $\longrightarrow$ P. This inference is produced by the combination of the third and fifth rules.

4. N $\longrightarrow$ P. This inference is produced by the combination of the fourth and fifth rules.

5. P $\longleftarrow\!\!\mid\!\!\longrightarrow$ K. This inference is produced by the combination of the first and sixth rules.

6. M $\longrightarrow O_2$. This inference is produced by the combination of the third and last rules.

7. N $\longrightarrow O_2$. This inference is produced by the combination of the fourth and last rules.

8. P $\longrightarrow O_2$. This inference is produced by the combination of the sixth and last rules.

Two further notes:

1. In the rule diagrams, the fifth and sixth rules were combined to create the double-arrow representation, which perfectly captures the relationship between O and P.

2. J and L are both randoms, and in an Undefined Grouping game randoms are very unlikely to have any power at all. Hence, your focus in this game should be almost entirely on K, M, N, O and P.

Question #19: Global, Could Be True, List. The correct answer choice is (C)

Answer choice (A) is incorrect because M and K cannot be selected together; alternately, if M is selected, than at least two Os must be selected.

Answer choice (B) is incorrect because K and O cannot be selected together.

Answer choice (C) is the correct answer.

Answer choice (D) is incorrect because if one O is selected, than at least two Os must be selected.

Answer choice (E) is incorrect because M and N cannot be selected together

Question #20: Local, Could Be True. The correct answer choice is (A)

If P is not selected, then O cannot be selected. Via the contrapositive, if O is not selected, then N and M cannot be selected. This information is sufficient to eliminate answer choices (B), (C), (D), and (E). Thus, by process of elimination, answer choice (A) is proven correct.

Question #21: Local, Cannot Be True. The correct answer choice is (A)

To solve this question, we must first determine which fish species should be included; that is, which fish species are necessary to allow other fish species to be chosen. In this game, one fish species stands out as the strongest candidate: O. Because O is a necessary condition for M, N, and P, if O is not selected, then via the contrapositive M, N, and P cannot be selected, a loss of four fish species (O, M, N, P). On the other hand, if O is selected, then O, P, and the choice of M or N can be selected, a total of three selected fish species (O, P, M/N). Clearly, the selection of O has a dramatic positive effect on the maximum number of fish species selected. Hence, if we accept that O should be one of the selected fish species, then from the first rule we can establish that K cannot be selected. Answer choice (A) is therefore correct.

Question #22: Global, Cannot Be True, FTT. The correct answer choice is (C)

Answer choice (A) is proven incorrect by the following hypothetical: J J J J.

Answer choice (B) is proven incorrect by the following hypothetical: L L L L.

Answer choice (C) is the correct answer. If M is selected, then O must be selected, and if O is selected, then two Os must be selected. Also, if O is selected then P must be selected. So, at a minimum, if M is selected, then at least four fish must be selected.

Answer choice (D) is proven incorrect by the following hypothetical: O O P.

Answer choice (E) proven incorrect by the following hypothetical: P O O.

Please note that answer choices (A) and (B) are functionally identical since they both hinge on a random. Thus, answer choices (A) and (B) are both incorrect. A similar, but slightly different relationship exists between answer choices (D) and (E). The same hypothetical eliminates each answer choice, so once you determine one answer choice is incorrect, you can eliminate the other answer choice.

Question #23: Local, Must Be True, Maximum-Minimum. The correct answer choice is (B)

If Barbara selects at least one fish species for her aquarium, the minimum number of fish species she can select is one—she can select either J or L (again, the randoms). Because answer choices (D) and (E) indicate that the minimum number of fish selected is two, both answer choices can be eliminated.

From our discussion in question #21, we know that O is a fish species that should be selected. If O is selected, we must then also select P. We can also select M or N, but not both. In addition, since J and L are both randoms, we can also select those two species. However, we cannot select K. Thus, the maximum number of fish species Barbara can select is five:

O   P   M/N   J   L

Therefore, answer choice (B) is proven correct.

OCTOBER 2005
LOGIC GAMES SECTION

SECTION II
Time—35 minutes
22 Questions

Directions: Each group of questions in this section is based on a set of conditions. In answering some of the questions, it may be useful to draw a rough diagram. Choose the response that most accurately and completely answers each question and blacken the corresponding space on your answer sheet.

Questions 1-5

Exactly seven products—P, Q, R, S, T, W, and X—are each to be advertised exactly once in a section of a catalog. The order in which they will be displayed is governed by the following conditions:

Q must be displayed in some position before W.
R must be displayed immediately before X.
T cannot be displayed immediately before or
  immediately after W.
S must be displayed either first or seventh.
Either Q or T must be displayed fourth.

1. Which one of the following CANNOT be the product that is displayed first?

    (A)   P
    (B)   Q
    (C)   R
    (D)   T
    (E)   X

2. If X is displayed immediately before Q, then which one of the following could be true?

    (A)   T is displayed first.
    (B)   R is displayed fifth.
    (C)   Q is displayed last.
    (D)   Q is displayed second.
    (E)   P is displayed second.

3. If P is displayed second, then which one of the following could be displayed third?

    (A)   R
    (B)   S
    (C)   T
    (D)   W
    (E)   X

4. Which one of the following could be true?

    (A)   Q is displayed fifth.
    (B)   Q is displayed seventh.
    (C)   R is displayed third.
    (D)   W is displayed third.
    (E)   X is displayed fifth.

5. If R is displayed sixth, then which one of the following must be displayed fifth?

    (A)   P
    (B)   Q
    (C)   T
    (D)   W
    (E)   X

GO ON TO THE NEXT PAGE.

Questions 6–11

A lighting control panel has exactly seven switches, numbered from 1 to 7. Each switch is either in the on position or in the off position. The circuit load of the panel is the total number of its switches that are on. The control panel must be configured in accordance with the following conditions:

If switch 1 is on, then switch 3 and switch 5 are off.
If switch 4 is on, then switch 2 and switch 5 are off.
The switch whose number corresponds to the circuit load of the panel is itself on.

6. Which one of the following could be a complete and accurate list of the switches that are on?

(A)   switch 2, switch 3, switch 4, switch 7
(B)   switch 3, switch 6, switch 7
(C)   switch 2, switch 5, switch 6
(D)   switch 1, switch 3, switch 4
(E)   switch 1, switch 5

7. If switch 1 and switch 3 are both off, then which one of the following could be two switches that are both on?

(A)   switch 2 and switch 7
(B)   switch 4 and switch 6
(C)   switch 4 and switch 7
(D)   switch 5 and switch 6
(E)   switch 6 and switch 7

8. If exactly two of the switches are on, then which one of the following switches must be off?

(A)   switch 3
(B)   switch 4
(C)   switch 5
(D)   switch 6
(E)   switch 7

9. If switch 6 and switch 7 are both off, then what is the maximum circuit load of the panel?

(A)   one
(B)   two
(C)   three
(D)   four
(E)   five

10. If switch 5 and switch 6 are both on, then which one of the following switches must be on?

(A)   switch 1
(B)   switch 2
(C)   switch 3
(D)   switch 4
(E)   switch 7

11. What is the maximum circuit load of the panel?

(A)   three
(B)   four
(C)   five
(D)   six
(E)   seven

GO ON TO THE NEXT PAGE.

Questions 12–17

In Crescentville there are exactly five record stores, whose names are abbreviated S, T, V, X, and Z. Each of the five stores carries at least one of four distinct types of music: folk, jazz, opera, and rock. None of the stores carries any other type of music. The following conditions must hold:

Exactly two of the five stores carry jazz.
T carries rock and opera but no other type of music.
S carries more types of music than T carries.
X carries more types of music than any other store in Crescentville carries.
Jazz is among the types of music S carries.
V does not carry any type of music that Z carries.

12. Which one of the following could be true?

    (A) S carries folk and rock but neither jazz nor opera.
    (B) T carries jazz but neither opera nor rock.
    (C) V carries folk, rock, and opera, but not jazz.
    (D) X carries folk, rock, and jazz, but not opera.
    (E) Z carries folk and opera but neither rock nor jazz.

13. Which one of the following could be true?

    (A) S, V, and Z all carry folk.
    (B) S, X, and Z all carry jazz.
    (C) Of the five stores, only S and V carry jazz.
    (D) Of the five stores, only T and X carry rock.
    (E) Of the five stores, only S, T, and V carry opera.

14. If exactly one of the stores carries folk, then which one of the following could be true?

    (A) S and V carry exactly two types of music in common.
    (B) T and S carry exactly two types of music in common.
    (C) T and V carry exactly two types of music in common.
    (D) V and X carry exactly two types of music in common.
    (E) X and Z carry exactly two types of music in common.

15. Which one of the following must be true?

    (A) T carries exactly the same number of types of music as V carries.
    (B) V carries exactly the same number of types of music as Z carries.
    (C) S carries at least one more type of music than Z carries.
    (D) Z carries at least one more type of music than T carries.
    (E) X carries exactly two more types of music than S carries.

16. If V is one of exactly three stores that carry rock, then which one of the following must be true?

    (A) S and Z carry no types of music in common.
    (B) S and V carry at least one type of music in common.
    (C) S and Z carry at least one type of music in common.
    (D) T and Z carry at least one type of music in common.
    (E) T and V carry at least two types of music in common.

17. If S and V both carry folk, then which one of the following could be true?

    (A) S and T carry no types of music in common.
    (B) S and Z carry no types of music in common.
    (C) T and Z carry no types of music in common.
    (D) S and Z carry two types of music in common.
    (E) T and V carry two types of music in common.

GO ON TO THE NEXT PAGE.

Questions 18-22

Maggie's Deli is open exactly five days every week: Monday through Friday. Its staff, each of whom works on at least one day each week, consists of exactly six people—Janice, Kevin, Nan, Ophelia, Paul, and Seymour. Exactly three of them—Janice, Nan, and Paul—are supervisors. The deli's staffing is consistent with the following:

Each day's staff consists of exactly two people, at least one of whom is a supervisor.
Tuesday's and Wednesday's staffs both include Ophelia.
Of the days Nan works each week, at least two are consecutive.
Seymour does not work on any day before the first day Paul works that week.
Any day on which Kevin works is the first day during the week that some other staff member works.

18. Which one of the following could be an accurate staffing schedule?

(A) Monday: Janice, Kevin
Tuesday: Nan, Ophelia
Wednesday: Nan, Paul
Thursday: Kevin, Paul
Friday: Janice, Seymour
(B) Monday: Paul, Seymour
Tuesday: Ophelia, Paul
Wednesday: Nan, Ophelia
Thursday: Kevin, Nan
Friday: Janice, Seymour
(C) Monday: Janice, Kevin
Tuesday: Nan, Ophelia
Wednesday: Nan, Ophelia
Thursday: Kevin, Paul
Friday: Paul, Seymour
(D) Monday: Janice, Kevin
Tuesday: Janice, Ophelia
Wednesday: Nan, Ophelia
Thursday: Nan, Seymour
Friday: Kevin, Paul
(E) Monday: Paul, Seymour
Tuesday: Ophelia, Paul
Wednesday: Nan, Ophelia
Thursday: Janice, Kevin
Friday: Nan, Paul

19. If Kevin and Paul work Thursday, who must work Friday?

(A) Janice
(B) Kevin
(C) Nan
(D) Paul
(E) Seymour

20. Each of the following could be true EXCEPT:

(A) Janice works Monday and Tuesday.
(B) Kevin and Paul work Friday.
(C) Seymour works Monday and Friday.
(D) Janice and Kevin work Thursday.
(E) Paul works Monday and Friday.

21. Which one of the following CANNOT be the pair of staff that works Monday?

(A) Janice and Seymour
(B) Kevin and Paul
(C) Paul and Seymour
(D) Nan and Ophelia
(E) Janice and Nan

22. Which one of the following could be true?

(A) Nan works Wednesday and Friday only.
(B) Seymour works Monday and Paul works Tuesday.
(C) Kevin works Monday, Wednesday, and Friday.
(D) Nan works Wednesday with Ophelia and Thursday with Kevin.
(E) Ophelia and Kevin work Tuesday.

S T O P

IF YOU FINISH BEFORE TIME IS CALLED, YOU MAY CHECK YOUR WORK ON THIS SECTION ONLY.
DO NOT WORK ON ANY OTHER SECTION IN THE TEST.

OCTOBER 2005 LOGIC GAMES SECTION

1.	E	8.	B	15.	C	22.	B
2.	A	9.	C	16.	C		
3.	C	10.	C	17.	B		
4.	A	11.	C	18.	C		
5.	D	12.	E	19.	E		
6.	B	13.	D	20.	B		
7.	A	14.	B	21.	A		

This is a Basic Linear Game: Balanced.

P Q R S T W X [7]
*

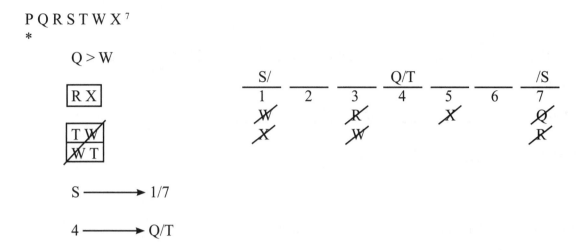

The rules in this game are straightforward and most students find them easy to diagram.

The first two rules generate some easy Not Laws:

The first rule creates two Not Laws: because Q is displayed before W, Q cannot be displayed last and W cannot be displayed first.

The second rule creates two Not Laws: because R is displayed immediately before X, R cannot be displayed last and X cannot be displayed first. The last Not Law is directly tested in the first question.

The combination of the second and last rules generates two more Not Laws:

Because Q or T is always displayed fourth, and R and X are consecutive, R cannot be displayed third and X cannot be displayed fifth.

Finally, the combination of the first, third, and last rules leads to a very difficult Not Law:

When W is displayed third an untenable situation results: Q cannot be displayed fourth because it must be displayed ahead of W, leaving T in the fourth position next to W. Because that scenario violates the third rule, W can never be displayed third.

Question #1: Global, Cannot Be True. The correct answer choice is (E)

As explained in the discussion of Not Laws above, X can never be displayed first, and answer choice (E) is correct.

Question #2: Local, Could Be True. The correct answer choice is (A)

The condition in the question stem creates the following configuration:

$$\boxed{R\ X\ Q} > W$$

Due to the operation of the last rule, this configuration can only be placed in two positions:

R in first: R   X   Q   T   ___   ___   ___

R in second: ___   R   X   Q   ___   ___   ___
            1   2   3   4   5   6   7

These two partial templates eliminate the four incorrect answer choices:

Answer choice (B) can be eliminated because R must be displayed first or second.

Answer choice (C) can be eliminated because Q must be displayed third or fourth.

Answer choice (D) can be eliminated because Q must be displayed third or fourth.

Answer choice (E) can be eliminated because X or R must be displayed second.

Answer choice (A) is thus proven correct by process of elimination.

Note that in the top template, the other variables can be filled in as well. Because S must be first or last, S must be last, and because W cannot be consecutive with T, W must be sixth, leaving P to be displayed fifth:

R in first: R   X   Q   T   P   W   S
            1   2   3   4   5   6   7

Question #3: Local, Could Be True. The correct answer choice is (C)

When P is displayed second, the RX block is pushed behind Q/T and must be displayed fifth and sixth, or sixth and seventh:

    ___   P   ___   Q/T   ___   R/X   ___
       1   2   3   4   5   6   7

Answer choice (A) can be eliminated because from the original Not Laws R can never be displayed third.

Answer choice (B) can be eliminated because S must be displayed first or last.

Answer choice (D) can be eliminated because from the original Not Laws W can never be displayed third.

Answer choice (E) can be eliminated because X must be displayed sixth or seventh.

Answer choice (C) is thus proven correct by process of elimination.

Question #4: Global, Could Be True. The correct answer choice is (A)

The Not Laws eliminate every incorrect answer choice in this question. Remember, when you are asked a Global Could Be True question, immediately look at your Not Laws to eliminate some or all of the answer choices.

Answer choice (B) can be eliminated because from the first rule Q can never be displayed last.

Answer choice (C) can be eliminated because from the interaction of the second and last rules R can never be displayed third.

Answer choice (D) can be eliminated because as discussed previously W can never be displayed third.

Answer choice (E) can be eliminated because from the interaction of the second and last rules X can never be displayed fifth.

Answer choice (A) is thus proven correct by process of elimination.

Question #5: Local, Must Be True. The correct answer choice is (D)

If R is displayed sixth, then X must be displayed seventh, and S must be displayed first:

$$\frac{\text{S}}{1} \quad \frac{\quad}{2} \quad \frac{\quad}{3} \quad \frac{\quad}{4} \quad \frac{\quad}{5} \quad \frac{\text{R}}{6} \quad \frac{\text{X}}{7}$$

With Q, T, W, and the random P still in play, you should look at the interaction of Q, T, and W and consider the possibilities. If T is displayed fourth, then the Q > W ultimately forces W to be displayed next to T, a violation of the third rule. Consequently, Q must be displayed fourth, and then W is displayed fifth, leaving P and T to rotate between the second and third positions:

$$\frac{\text{S}}{1} \quad \frac{\text{P/T}}{2} \quad \frac{\text{T/P}}{3} \quad \frac{\text{Q}}{4} \quad \frac{\text{W}}{5} \quad \frac{\text{R}}{6} \quad \frac{\text{X}}{7}$$

Accordingly, answer choice (D) is correct.

This is a Partially Defined Grouping game.

This Game was considered to be fairly difficult by test takers, in part because they struggled to appropriately show the "on" and "off" designations, and also because the last rule was seen by many as confusing. To represent "on" and "off," simply use a slash through the number when that light is off.

1 2 3 4 5 6 7

Rule 1:

1 ←——|——→ 3
1 ←——|——→ 5

Rule 2:

4 ←——|——→ 2
4 ←——|——→ 5

Rule 3:

Number Switches On = Switch # On

When combined with the first two rules, the last rule can be fairly restrictive. Consider the hypothetical where five switches are on. That means that switch number 5 must be on. If 5 is on, then 1 and 4 are off, so the five switches that are on must be 2, 3, 5, 6, and 7.

Note too that you must always have at least two switches off, since 1 cannot be on with either 3 or 5, and 4 cannot be on with either 2 or 5. If 1 and 4 are off, then the other five can be on, and if either 1 or 4 are on then the maximum number of switches that can be on is four. For instance, if 1 is on, then 3 and 5 are off, and either 2 or 4 must also be off since they cannot be on together (that is three switches off: 3, 5, and 2/4).

Question #6: Global, Could Be True, List. The correct answer choice is (B)

Answer choice (A) is incorrect because 2 and 4 cannot both be on.

Answer choice (B) is the correct answer choice.

Answer choice (C) is incorrect because if three switches are on switch 3 must be on.

Answer choice (D) is incorrect because 1 and 3 cannot both be on.

Answer choice (E) is incorrect because if two switches are on switch 2 must be on.

Question #7: Local, Could Be True. The correct answer choice is (A)

Since 1 and 3 are both off, and since either 2 or 4 must also be off (cannot both be on), the maximum number of on switches here is four. Also, you cannot have only one switch on because it would have to be switch 1 (rule 3), and you cannot have three switches on because switch 3 would have to be one of them (rule 3). Further, if you try to have four switches on, those switches would have to be 4, 6, 7 and then either 2 or 5. But 4 cannot go with 2 or 5 (rule 2), so it is impossible to have four switches on, as well. That means there must be only two switches on:

Two switches on: 2 and either 5, 6, or 7.

So the correct answer choice must come from one of those possible combinations. Answer choice (A) is correct as 2 and 7 can both be on.

Question #8: Local, Must Be True. The correct answer choice is (B)

If two switches are on, then switch 2 must be on. And if switch 2 is on then switch 4 must be off (rule 2), so answer choice (B) is correct.

Question #9: Local, Must Be True, Maximum. The correct answer choice is (C)

If 6 and 7 are both off, then there are only five switches remaining. All five cannot be on because then 1 and 3, 1 and 5, 2 and 4, and 2 and 5 would all be on together. Four switches cannot be on because switch 4 would be on, meaning 2 and 5 would both be off, and either 1 or 3 would also be off, for a total of five switches off (1/3, 2, 5, 6, and 7). Three switches on is possible: 2, 3, and 5. Thus the correct answer is (C).

Question #10: Local, Must Be True. The correct answer choice is (C)

If 5 and 6 are both on, then you cannot have four switches on (since 4 and 5 cannot be on together). So you must have either three switches on (5, 6, and 3) or five switches on (2, 3, 5, 6, and 7). Either way switch 3 must be on so the correct answer is (C).

Question #11: Global, Must Be True, Maximum. The correct answer choice is (C)

As discussed previously, the maximum number of switches that can be on at once is five: 2, 3, 5, 6, and 7. The correct answer is (C).

This is a Partially Defined Grouping game.

Stores: S T V X Z [5]
Music: F J O R [4]

You should use the stores as the base and try to determine both what type of music, and how many types of music they carry (the distribution).

Rule 1:

$J = 2$

Rule 2:

$T = R + O$

This means that T is locked.

Rule 3:

$\#S > \#T$

Thus, S can either carry 3 or 4 types of music.

Rule 4:

$X = F J O R$ (all 4 types)

Since X has more than any other store, that means that S must carry 3 types of music (more than T but less that S).

Rule 5:

$S = J + 2$

So you know the two stores that carry J are S and X. This means that V and Z cannot carry J.

Rule 6:

V ◄———┼———► Z

Since V and Z could only carry at most 3 types (no J), and they cannot have any in common, V and Z must carry either 1 or 2 types each.

The rules combine to create the setup for this game:
Stores: S T V X Z [5]
Music: F J O R [4]

$J = 2 (S + X)$

$T = R + O$

$\#S > \#T$

$X = F J O R$ (all 4 types)

$S = J + 2$

$V \longleftrightarrow Z$

③   ②   ⑴/2   ④   ⑴/2

```
                                F
                                ‾
                                J
              ___       R       ‾
   ___        J    O    R
   J     O              O
   S     T    V    X    Z
              𝗑         𝗑
```

Question #12: Global, Could Be True. The correct answer choice is (E)

Answer choice (A) is incorrect because S carries J.

Answer choice (B) is incorrect because T carries R and O.

Answer choice (C) is incorrect because V carries either 1 or 2 types.

Answer choice (D) is incorrect because X carries all 4 types.

Answer choice (E) is the correct answer choice.

Question #13: Global, Could Be True. The correct answer choice is (D)

Answer choice (A) is incorrect because V and Z do not have any types in common.

Answer choice (B) is incorrect because Z cannot carry J.

Answer choice (C) is incorrect because V cannot carry J.

Answer choice (D) is the correct answer choice.

Answer choice (E) is incorrect because X carries O.

Question #14: Local, Could Be True. The correct answer choice is (B)

If only one store carries F that store must be X. That means that S carries J, O, and R. Also, V and Z must carry R and O, with R/O split between them (1 type each).

Answer choice (A) is incorrect because V carries only 1 type.

Answer choice (B) is the correct answer choice. S and T both carry R and O.

Answer choice (C) is incorrect because V carries only 1 type.

Answer choice (D) is incorrect because V carries only 1 type.

Answer choice (E) is incorrect because Z carries only 1 type.

Question #15: Global, Must Be True. The correct answer choice is (C)

This question is based purely on the distribution possibilities.

Answer choice (A) is incorrect because V could carry only 1 type, and T carries 2 types.

Answer choice (B) is incorrect because V or Z could carry 2 types while the other carries only 1.

Answer choice (C) is the correct answer choice.

Answer choice (D) is incorrect because T carries 2 types and Z cannot carry more than 2 types.

Answer choice (E) is incorrect because X carries exactly one more type than S carries.

Question #16: Local, Must Be True. The correct answer choice is (C)

If V is one of three stores that carry R, then those three stores must be T, X, and V. So S must carry J, O, and F. And Z must carry O, F, or both.

Answer choice (A) is incorrect because S and Z must have at least O or F in common.

Answer choice (B) is incorrect because V could carry only R.

Answer choice (C) is the correct answer choice. S and Z have at least O or F in common (possibly both).

Answer choice (D) is incorrect because Z could carry only F.

Answer choice (E) is incorrect because V could carry only R.

Question #17: Local, Could Be True. The correct answer choice is (B)

If S and V both carry F, then the other type that S carries is either R or O. That also means that Z must carry either R, O, or both.

Answer choice (A) is incorrect because S must carry either R or O.

Answer choice (B) is the correct answer choice. Z could carry O, while S carries R.

Answer choice (C) is incorrect because Z must carry either R or O.

Answer choice (D) is incorrect because if Z has 2 types they are R and O, and S cannot carry both R and O (only one of the two).

Answer choice (E) is incorrect because V can only carry 2 types, and one of those types must be F in this question. So V cannot have 2 types in common with T (R and O).

This is an Unbalanced: Underfunded Advanced Linear game.

J K N O P S [6]
Supervisors: J N P

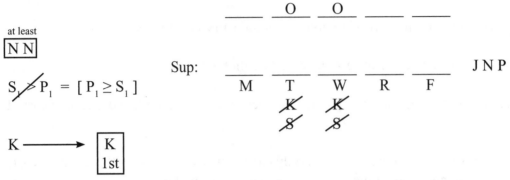

* Note that the first rule states that "at least" one of the people working each day is a supervisor. This wording leaves open the possibility that two supervisors work on a given day, and thus the second stack is *not* labeled as the "non-supervisor" stack.

* The second rule establishes that O works on Tuesday and Wednesday, and because O is not a supervisor, automatically K and S are precluded from working on Tuesday and Wednesday.

* The third rule also feature the qualifier "at least," establishing that when N works, at a minimum there is a double-N block, but leaving open the possibility that the block could be larger. The rule also leaves open the possibility that N could work three (or more times), but only two of the days might be consecutive (which would satisfy the wording of the rule).

* The fourth rule is another odd rule, one that requires careful tracking throughout the game. Note that while P and S can work on the *same* day, S cannot work earlier in the week than P's *first day*.

* The last rule is also unusual (and, in fact, every rule in this game is somewhat non-standard, which increases the difficulty). Because every rule is unusual, you should expect the test makers to repeatedly test your knowledge of how the rules apply. This is what occurs, and ultimately this game is more about rote rule application than any powerful inferences.

Question #18: Global, Could Be True, List. The correct answer choice is (C)

Answer choice (A) is incorrect because O does not work on Wednesday.

Answer choice (B) is incorrect because K works with N, but Thursday is not N's first work day, a violation of the last rule.

Answer choice (D) is incorrect because S works earlier than P's first day, a violation of the fourth rule.

Answer choice (E) is incorrect because N works, but N does not work at least two consecutive days. Thus, answer choice (C) is correct.

Question #19: Local, Must Be True. The correct answer choice is (E)

If K and P work on Thursday, then from the last rule Thursday must be P's first day. Combining that information with the fourth rule, we can deduce that S must work on Friday. Hence, answer choice (E) is correct.

Question #20: Global, Could Be True, Except. The correct answer choice is (B)

If you answered question #19 correctly, question #20 should make sense. In answer choice (B), if K and P work on Friday, then from the last rule Friday must be P's first day. However, this would create a violation of the fourth rule because S could not work during the week. Hence, answer choice (B) cannot be true and is correct.

Question #21: Global, Cannot Be True. The correct answer choice is (A)

Monday is only a problem for workers controlled by sequencing rules such as the fourth rule. Hence, P and S are a prime target for analysis in this question.

If S works on Monday, then from the fourth rule P would have to work on Monday. However, answer choice (A) states that J would work with S on Monday. As this is impossible, answer choice (A) cannot occur and is correct.

Question #22: Global, Could Be True. The correct answer choice is (B)

Answer choice (A) is incorrect because it violates the third rule.

Answer choice (C) is incorrect because it K cannot work on Wednesday (O is already there).

Answer choice (D) is incorrect because it violates the last rule.

Answer choice (E) is incorrect because no supervisor would be assigned to Tuesday.

Thus, answer choice (B) is correct (and, in answer choice (B), P would also have to work on Monday).

DECEMBER 2005
LOGIC GAMES SECTION

SECTION III
Time—35 minutes
22 Questions

Directions: Each group of questions in this section is based on a set of conditions. In answering some of the questions, it may be useful to draw a rough diagram. Choose the response that most accurately and completely answers each question and blacken the corresponding space on your answer sheet.

Questions 1–6

Henri has exactly five electrical appliances in his dormitory room: a hairdryer, a microwave oven, a razor, a television, and a vacuum. As a consequence of fire department regulations, Henri can use these appliances only in accordance with the following conditions:

    Henri cannot use both the hairdryer and the razor simultaneously.

    Henri cannot use both the hairdryer and the television simultaneously.

    When Henri uses the vacuum, he cannot at the same time use any of the following: the hairdryer, the razor, and the television.

1. Which one of the following is a pair of appliances Henri could be using simultaneously?

    (A) the hairdryer and the razor
    (B) the hairdryer and the television
    (C) the razor and the television
    (D) the razor and the vacuum
    (E) the television and the vacuum

2. Assume that Henri is using exactly two appliances and is not using the microwave oven. Which one of the following is a list of all the appliances, other than the microwave oven, that Henri CANNOT be using?

    (A) hairdryer
    (B) razor
    (C) vacuum
    (D) hairdryer, razor
    (E) hairdryer, vacuum

3. Which one of the following CANNOT be true?

    (A) Henri uses the hairdryer while using the microwave oven.
    (B) Henri uses the microwave oven while using the razor.
    (C) Henri uses the microwave oven while using two other appliances.
    (D) Henri uses the television while using two other appliances.
    (E) Henri uses the vacuum while using two other appliances.

4. If Henri were to use exactly three appliances, then what is the total number of different groups of three appliances any one of which could be the group of appliances he is using?

    (A) one
    (B) two
    (C) three
    (D) four
    (E) five

5. Which one of the following statements, if true, guarantees that Henri is using no more than one of the following: the hairdryer, the razor, the television?

    (A) Henri is using the hairdryer.
    (B) Henri is using the television.
    (C) Henri is not using the hairdryer.
    (D) Henri is not using the microwave oven.
    (E) Henri is not using the vacuum.

6. Which one of the following must be true?

    (A) Henri uses at most three appliances simultaneously.
    (B) Henri uses at most four appliances simultaneously.
    (C) Henri uses at most one other appliance while using the microwave oven.
    (D) Henri uses at most one other appliance while using the razor.
    (E) Henri uses at least two other appliances while using the hairdryer.

GO ON TO THE NEXT PAGE.

Questions 7-12

A farmer harvests eight separate fields—G, H, J, K, L, M, P, and T. Each field is harvested exactly once, and no two fields are harvested simultaneously. Once the harvesting of a field begins, no other fields are harvested until the harvesting of that field is complete. The farmer harvests the fields in an order consistent with the following conditions:

Both P and G are harvested at some time before K.
Both H and L are harvested at some time before J.
K is harvested at some time before M but after L.
T is harvested at some time before M.

7. Which one of the following could be true?

(A) J is the first field harvested.
(B) K is the second field harvested.
(C) M is the sixth field harvested.
(D) G is the seventh field harvested.
(E) T is the eighth field harvested.

8. If M is the seventh field harvested, then anyone of the following could be the fifth field harvested EXCEPT:

(A) H
(B) J
(C) K
(D) L
(E) P

9. Which one of the following CANNOT be the field that is harvested fifth?

(A) G
(B) J
(C) M
(D) P
(E) T

10. If J is the third field harvested, then which one of the following must be true?

(A) L is the first field harvested.
(B) H is the second field harvested.
(C) T is the fourth field harvested.
(D) K is the seventh field harvested.
(E) M is the eighth field harvested.

11. If H is the sixth field harvested, then which one of the following must be true?

(A) G is harvested at some time before T.
(B) H is harvested at some time before K.
(C) J is harvested at some time before M.
(D) K is harvested at some time before J.
(E) T is harvested at some time before K.

12. If L is the fifth field harvested, then which one of the following could be true?

(A) J is harvested at some time before G.
(B) J is harvested at some time before T.
(C) K is harvested at some time before T.
(D) M is harvested at some time before H.
(E) M is harvested at some time before J.

GO ON TO THE NEXT PAGE.

In a repair facility there are exactly six technicians: Stacy, Urma, Wim, Xena, Yolanda, and Zane. Each technician repairs machines of at least one of the following three types—radios, televisions, and VCRs—and no other types. The following conditions apply:

Xena and exactly three other technicians repair radios.
Yolanda repairs both televisions and VCRs.
Stacy does not repair any type of machine that Yolanda repairs.
Zane repairs more types of machines than Yolanda repairs.
Wim does not repair any type of machine that Stacy repairs.
Urma repairs exactly two types of machines.

13. For exactly how many of the six technicians is it possible to determine exactly which of the three types of machines each repairs?

(A) one
(B) two
(C) three
(D) four
(E) five

14. Which one of the following must be true?

(A) Of the types of machines repaired by Stacy there is exactly one type that Urma also repairs.
(B) Of the types of machines repaired by Yolanda there is exactly one type that Xena also repairs.
(C) Of the types of machines repaired by Wim there is exactly one type that Xena also repairs.
(D) There is more than one type of machine that both Wim and Yolanda repair.
(E) There is more than one type of machine that both Urma and Wim repair.

15. Which one of the following must be false?

(A) Exactly one of the six technicians repairs exactly one type of machine.
(B) Exactly two of the six technicians repair exactly one type of machine each.
(C) Exactly three of the six technicians repair exactly one type of machine each.
(D) Exactly one of the six technicians repairs exactly two types of machines.
(E) Exactly three of the six technicians repair exactly two types of machines each.

16. Which one of the following pairs of technicians could repair all and only the same types of machines as each other?

(A) Stacy and Urma
(B) Urma and Yolanda
(C) Urma and Xena
(D) Wim and Xena
(E) Xena and Yolanda

17. Which one of the following must be true?

(A) There is exactly one type of machine that both Urma and Wim repair.
(B) There is exactly one type of machine that both Urma and Xena repair.
(C) There is exactly one type of machine that both Urma and Yolanda repair.
(D) There is exactly one type of machine that both Wim and Yolanda repair.
(E) There is exactly one type of machine that both Xena and Yolanda repair.

GO ON TO THE NEXT PAGE.

Three folk groups—Glenside, Hilltopper, Levon—and three rock groups—Peasant, Query, Tinhead—each perform on one of two stages, north or south. Each stage has three two-hour performances: north at 6, 8, and 10; south at 8, 10, and 12. Each group performs individually and exactly once, consistent with the following conditions:

Peasant performs at 6 or 12.
Glenside performs at some time before Hilltopper.
If any rock group performs at 10, no folk group does.
Levon and Tinhead perform on different stages.
Query performs immediately after a folk group, though not necessarily on the same stage.

18. Which one of the following could be a complete and accurate ordering of performances on the north stage, from first to last?

(A) Glenside, Levon, Query
(B) Glenside, Query, Hilltopper
(C) Hilltopper, Query, Peasant
(D) Peasant, Levon, Tinhead
(E) Peasant, Query, Levon

19. Which one of the following groups must perform earlier than 10?

(A) Glenside
(B) Hilltopper
(C) Levon
(D) Peasant
(E) Tinhead

20. Which one of the following groups could perform at 6?

(A) Glenside
(B) Hilltopper
(C) Levon
(D) Query
(E) Tinhead

21. If Query performs at 12, then which one of the following could be an accurate ordering of the performances on the north stage, from first to last?

(A) Glenside, Levon, Query
(B) Peasant, Hilltopper, Tinhead
(C) Peasant, Tinhead, Glenside
(D) Peasant, Tinhead, Hilltopper
(E) Peasant, Tinhead, Levon

22. If a rock group performs at 10, then which one of the following must be true?

(A) A folk group performs at 6.
(B) A folk group performs at 8.
(C) A folk group performs at 12.
(D) A rock group performs at 8.
(E) A rock group performs at 12.

S T O P

IF YOU FINISH BEFORE TIME IS CALLED, YOU MAY CHECK YOUR WORK ON THIS SECTION ONLY.
DO NOT WORK ON ANY OTHER SECTION IN THE TEST.

DECEMBER 2005 LOGIC GAMES SECTION

1.	C	8.	B	15.	D	22.	B
2.	E	9.	C	16.	C		
3.	E	10.	E	17.	C		
4.	A	11.	D	18.	A		
5.	A	12.	E	19.	A		
6.	A	13.	C	20.	A		
7.	C	14.	A	21.	D		

This is an Undefined game with a selection pool of Uniform Variables. It is Undefined because the number of variables chosen (i.e., the number of appliances chosen) is not fixed. The selection pool is comprised of Uniform Variables because the variables are all equal members of the same basic group, not subdivided into categories. Since this is a pure grouping game, the setup will be comprised solely of conditional statements. We should note that M is a random in this game—it is the only variable not directly constrained by any of the rules.

The first rule tells us that if Henri uses the hairdryer, he cannot use the razor, and vice-versa. This can be characterized as follows:

$$H \longleftarrow\!\!\!\!|\!\!\!\!\longrightarrow R$$

The second rule can be shown as:

$$H \longleftarrow\!\!\!\!|\!\!\!\!\longrightarrow T$$

The final rule provides us with the following conditional statement:

$$V \longleftarrow\!\!\!\!|\!\!\!\!\longrightarrow \begin{array}{c} H \\ + \\ R \\ + \\ T \end{array}$$

With the conditional statements above, we have all three rules represented. It is valuable to note that H and V are the variables subject to the most constraints. In addition, there is value in showing the set of appliances that each individual appliance cannot be used with:

$$H \longrightarrow \cancel{R}, \cancel{T}, \cancel{V}$$

$$R \longrightarrow \cancel{H}, \cancel{V}$$

$$T \longrightarrow \cancel{H}, \cancel{V}$$

$$V \longrightarrow \cancel{H}, \cancel{R}, \cancel{T}$$

$$M \longrightarrow \text{none}$$

Question #1: Global, Could Be True. The correct answer choice is (C)

Answer choice (A) is incorrect based on the first rule. Answer choice (B) is proved incorrect by the second rule, and answer choices (D) and (E) are ruled out by the third rule. This leaves answer choice (C), which is the correct answer choice.

Question #2: Local, Must Be True, List. The correct answer choice is (E)

This local question dictates that Henri cannot use the microwave. This leaves variables H, R, T, and V. Henri cannot use the V because of the third rule: using V would rule out H, R and T, so there would be no way for Henri to use exactly two appliances.

If Henri were to use H, the rules would dictate that he not use the R or the T (from the first two rules) or the V (from the third rule). This would leave no other appliances, precluding his ability to use exactly two.

Henri could use the T and the R, so the only ones precluded would be the V and the H, so (E) is the correct answer choice.

Question #3: Global, Cannot Be True. The correct answer choice is (E)

The correct answer choice is (E), because if Henri uses the V, he cannot, according to the third rule, use the H, the R, or the T. This leaves only the M, making answer choice (E) impossible, and thus correct.

Question #4: Local, Must Be True. The correct answer choice is (A)

As we have noted in the questions above, V precludes three of the other variables (H, R, and T), and the use of H also prohibits the use of three other variables (R, T, and V). Thus, if Henri is to use exactly three appliances, he must avoid both V and H. This leaves M, R, and T, so there is only one group of three appliances Henri can use. Thus, the correct answer choice is (A).

Question #5: Local, Must Be True. The correct answer choice is (A)

Answer choice (A) is correct, because if Henri uses the H, the first two rules dictate that he cannot use the R or the T. None of the other answer choices dictate that only one of the three listed variables is used.

Question #6: Global, Must Be True. The correct answer choice is (A)

As noted in the explanation of question #4, Henri's use of H or V precludes his use of three other variables, so if either H or V is used, there can only be a maximum of two appliances used. Even if Henri avoids both H and V, this leaves M, R, and T. If he uses all three, that is the greatest number of appliances he can ever use at once, so the correct answer choice is (A).

This is a Pure Sequencing Game.

Variables: G H J K L M P T [8]

$$
\begin{array}{c}
T \\
\end{array}
$$

```
              T ←┐
   P             │
  - - -          │
   G   > K > M ──┘
  - - -
   Ⓛ
  - - -  > J
   H
```

* This is an extremely difficult chain to diagram. L links to both K and J, but do not make the mistake of linking J to K, linking J to P or G, or linking H to K.
* H, L, P, G, or T can be harvested first.
* Only M or J can be harvested last.

Question #7: Global, Could Be True. The correct answer choice is (C)

Answer choice (A) is incorrect because only H, L, P, G, or T can be harvested first.

Answer choice (B) is incorrect because the earliest K can be harvested is fourth.

Answer choice (D) is incorrect because the latest G can be harvested is sixth.

Answer choice (E) is incorrect because only M or J can be harvested last.

Question #8: Local, Could Be True, Except. The correct answer choice is (B)

If M is the seventh field harvested, then J must be the eighth field harvested (only M or J can be harvested last). Thus, answer choice (B) must be correct in this Except question.

Question #9: Global, Cannot Be True. The correct answer choice is (C)

The earliest M can be harvested is sixth, and thus answer choice (C) is correct.

Answer choice (A) is proven incorrect by the following hypothetical solution: P-L-H-J-G-K-T-M.

Answer choice (B) is proven incorrect by the following hypothetical solution: P-L-H-G-J-K-T-M.

Answer choice (D) is proven incorrect by the following hypothetical solution: G-L-H-J-P-K-T-M.

Answer choice (E) is proven incorrect by the following hypothetical solution: P-L-H-G-T-K-M-J.

Question #10: Local, Must Be True. The correct answer choice is (E)

If J is the third field harvested, then automatically M must be the last field harvested because only J or M can be harvested last. Thus, answer choice (E) is correct.

Question #11: Local, Must Be True. The correct answer choice is (D)

If H is the sixth field harvested, then according to the second rule J must be harvested seventh or eighth, and then only M is available to fill the remainder of the seventh or eighth space (this is because all the other fields must be harvested before other fields, for example, K must be harvested before M, and L must be harvested before K):

$$\underline{\quad}\ \underline{\quad}\ \underline{\quad}\ \underline{\quad}\ \underline{\quad}\ \underline{\text{H}}\ \underline{\text{J/M}}\ \underline{\text{M/J}}$$
$$\quad 1 \qquad 2 \qquad 3 \qquad 4 \qquad 5 \qquad 6 \qquad 7 \qquad 8$$

Consequently, answer choice (D) is correct.

Question #12: Local, Could Be True. The correct answer choice is (E)

When L is harvested, then according to the second and third rules J, K, and M must all be harvested after L, with no restriction on the placement of J in the last three spaces:

$$\underline{\quad}\ \underline{\quad}\ \underline{\quad}\ \underline{\quad}\ \underline{\text{L}}\ \underline{\quad}\ (\ \text{J}\ ,\ \text{K} > \text{M}\ )$$
$$\quad 1 \qquad 2 \qquad 3 \qquad 4 \qquad 5 \qquad 6 \qquad 7 \qquad 8$$

Accordingly, answer choice (E) is correct.

This is a Grouping Game: Partially Defined.

The scenario in this game lists six technicians, each one of which is repairing between one and three types of machines. Thus, each technician is a separate "group," and one of the tasks of the game is to attempt to determine how many machines each technician repairs.

The rules contain a great deal of numerical information, which is not surprising given the uncertainty in the scenario about group sizes. We know from the scenario that each technician repairs at least one type of machine, so let's look at each of the six rules and see what other information we can gather about group sizes:

Rule #1:

   This rule establishes that exactly four technicians (including X) must repair R.

Rule #2:

   This rule establishes that Y repairs at least two types of machines, T and V.

Rule #3:

   This rule starts off a run of four rules that all address the size of the groups in the game. In this case, S and Y cannot repair the same type of machine. Because each technician must repair at least one type of machine, this rule effectively eliminates S and Y from each repairing all three types of machines. When combined with the second rule, then, we can deduce that Y repairs exactly two types of machines, and those machines are T and V. Of course, if Y repairs T and V, then S cannot repair T and V, and thus S must repair exactly one machine, R.

The first three rules thus establish the following setup:

R T V ^{3}

$$R \longrightarrow X, S + 2$$

$$S \longleftrightarrow\!\!\!| \longrightarrow Y$$

①

②

			V		
R			R	T	
S	U	W	X	Y	Z

Note that the circled numbers above S and Y indicate that those technicians are fixed at those group sizes. Of course, this is only a partial setup based on the first three rules. Let's continue on by examining the remaining rules:

Rule #4:

This rule establishes that Z repairs more types of machines than Y. Because we have already established that Y repairs exactly two types of machines, we can now infer that Z repairs three types of machines, and since there are only three types of machines in total, Z must repair R, T, and V:

```
R T V ³

R ————> X, S, Z + 1          ①              ② ③
                                                    V
S ◄——┼——► Y                                   V    T
                             R        R        T    R
                           ——— ——— ——— ——— ——— ———
                            S   U   W   X    Y    Z
```

Rule #5:

This rule is similar to the third rule, but in this instance W and S do not repair any of the same types of machines. We can thus infer that W does not repair R, and that W repairs either one or two machines (either T or V or both):

```
R T V ³

R ————> X, S, Z + 1          ①        1/2        ② ③
                                                        V
S ◄——┼——► Y                                       V    T
                             R       T/V   R       T    R
                           ——— ——— ——— ——— ——— ———
                            S   U    W    X    Y    Z
                                     R̸
```

Rule #6:

The final rule establishes that U repairs exactly two types of machines. And, due to the constraints created by the first rule, we can determine that U must repair R, and that the second machine U repairs is then T or V. The only remaining point of indeterminacy in the game is X. We know X must repair R, but it is also possible (but not necessary) that X repairs one or two additional machines. This uncertainty is identified with a 1/2/3 notation above X:

```
R T V ³

R ————> X, S, Z, U       ①   ②   1/2   1/2/3   ② ③
                                                      V
S ◄——┼——► Y                   T/V                V    T
                         R    R   T/V    R        T    R
                       ——— ——— ——— ——— ——— ———
                        S   U   W    X     Y    Z
                                R̸
```

COMPLETE GAMES SECTIONS
DECEMBER 2005 EXPLANATIONS

This last setup is our final setup, and note how much information the rules have provided. Although the game scenario did not establish individual group sizes, the rules provided enough information so that every group is defined except for W and X, and only the machines in U, W, and X are not perfectly determined. Thus, the game is Partially Defined, and we know that we must keep a close watch on U, W, and X in the game as these are the only points of uncertainty.

Question #13: Global, Must Be True. The correct answer choice is (C)

In our discussion of the rules, we were able to ascertain the exact types of machines repaired by three of the technicians—S, Y, and Z. Accordingly, answer choice (C) is correct.

Note that although we were able to determine that U repairs exactly two machines, we do not know exactly which machines U repairs.

Question #14: Global, Must Be True. The correct answer choice is (A)

The final setup indicates that both S and U repair R, and that S repairs no other machine. Thus, answer choice (A) is correct.

Answer choice (B) is incorrect because it does not have to be true that X and Y share exactly one type of machine. They could have no machines in common, or one or two machines in common. Note that any answer choice that specifies an "exact" number of machines and that includes X will be suspect since X has so many options.

Answer choice (C) is incorrect because it does not have to be true that W and X share exactly one type of machine. They could have no machines in common, or one or two machines in common. Aside from the fact that this answer choice contains X and specifies an "exact" number of machines, it also contains W, which is also suspect in an "exact" question since W is also uncertain.

Answer choice (D) is incorrect because although this answer choice could be true, it does not have to be true (W could repair only one type of machine).

Note that the wording on the last two answer choices switches to "more than one" from the "exact" specification in answer choices (A), (B), and (C).

Answer choice (E) is incorrect because although this answer choice could be true, it does not have to be true (W could repair only one type of machine).

Question #15: Global, Cannot Be True, FTT. The correct answer choice is (D)

In this Cannot Be True question, each of the four incorrect answer choices could be true. Answer choice (D) cannot be true because U and Y must each repair exactly two machines.

Answer choice (A) could be true and is thus incorrect because S could be the only technician to repair one machine.

Answer choice (B) could be true and is thus incorrect because S and W, or S and X, could be the only two technicians to repair exactly one machine.

Answer choice (C) could be true and is thus incorrect because S, W, and X could be the only technicians to repair exactly one machine.

Answer choice (E) could be true and is thus incorrect because U, Y, and W, or U, Y and X could be the only two technicians to repair exactly two machines.

Question #16: Global, Could Be True. The correct answer choice is (C)

Answer choice (C) is correct because U and X could both repair R and T, or R and V. In each of the other four answer choices the pairs can never repair the exact same types (or numbers) of machines.

Answer choice (A) is incorrect because S repairs one machine and Y must repair two machines.

Answer choice (B) is incorrect because although U and Y can repair the same number of machines, U repairs R whereas Y does not.

Answer choice (D) is incorrect because although W and X can repair the same number of machines, X repairs R whereas W does not.

Answer choice (E) is incorrect because although X and Y can repair the same number of machines, X repairs R whereas Y does not.

Question #17: Global, Must Be True. The correct answer choice is (C)

This is another "similarity of repair" question, and our diagram establishes that U and Y must share exactly one machine, namely T or V. Thus, answer choice (C) is correct.

Answer choice (A) can be a bit tricky, but, for example, U could repair T, and W could repair V, making answer choice (A) not necessarily true and thus incorrect.

Answer choice (B) is incorrect because U and X could repair two types of machines (R and T, or R and V).

Answer choice (D) is incorrect because W and Y could both repair T and V.

Answer choice (E) is incorrect because X and Y could both repair T and V.

One note of interest about this game is that all five of the questions are Global. This likely occurs because the rules contain so much information.

This is a Grouping/Linear Combination Game.

This is an extremely challenging game, with a unique game setup and a disparate set of rules. The two stages and the performance times should be shown in an Advanced Linear format, with separate rows for each stage. The unavailable times for each stage should be shown with an X in those spaces. Here is the base diagram, with the first rule represented:

F: G H L ^{3}
R: P Q T ^{3}

North: ___P/___ _____ _____ ___X___

South: ___X___ _____ _____ ___/P___
           6   8   10   12

The remaining rules require further analysis.

Rule #2:

This rule establishes that G performs before H, which can be represented as:

$$G_F > H_R$$

The immediate consequence of this rule is that H cannot perform on the north stage at 6, and G cannot perform on the south stage at 12. These two inferences can be shown as Not Laws on the diagram.

This rule ultimately plays a powerful role in the game, but only in conjunction with other rules.

Rule #3:

This rule indicates that if any rock group performs at 10, then no folk group performs at 10. Thus, if a rock group performs at 10, the other group playing at 10 must also be a rock band. By the contrapositive, if a folk band plays at 10, then the other band playing must be a folk band. This rule, then, leads to two blocks:

| R | or | F |
| R |₁₀ | F |₁₀

Thus, the two 10 slots must be performed by bands of the same type.

Rule #4:

According to this rule, L and T must perform on different stages:

The rule does not generate a simple not-block; instead the rule applies to each entire stage and the order of the variables is not important (and thus a TL not-block would also be valid, but unnecessary because of the "Stage" subscript on the block). The operating effect of this rule is that L and T cannot perform on the same stage, and thus exactly one of L or T is always performing on the north stage, and the other performs on the south stage.

Rule #5:

This rule also creates a horizontal block, but not one tied to a particular stage. If Q must follow a folk band playing in the prior time slot, the best representation is:

$$\boxed{\text{G/H/L}_F \quad \text{Q}_R}$$

Like other rules, this one has a degree of uncertainty to it because Q and the folk band prior to Q can perform on the same stage, or on different stages.

Because this is a fixed block (e.g. the two variables are fixed in consecutive order), Q can never perform in the 6 slot on the north stage, creating another Not Law. There are further implications to this rule as well, such as that if P plays at 6, Q cannot play at 8 (and, via the contrapositive, if Q plays at 8, P cannot play at 6 and must play at 12).

Because of the unusual nature of the rules, there are more inferences in this game, but let's use the questions to discuss those inferences, and then at the end we'll provide a complete setup.

Question #18: Global, Could Be True, List. The correct answer choice is (A)

This List question can be solved by applying the proper List question technique of applying one rule to all contending answer choices until the four incorrect answers are eliminated.

Answer choice (B) is incorrect because if neither L or T perform on the north stage, then they must both perform on the south stage, a violation of the fourth rule.

Answer choice (C) is incorrect because if H performs at 6, the second rule is violated.

Answer choice (D) is incorrect because both L and T perform on the same stage, a violation of the fourth rule.

Answer choice (E) is incorrect because the PQ ordering violates the last rule.

Thus, answer choice (A) is proven correct by process of elimination.

Question #19: Global, Must Be True. The correct answer choice is (A)

This is a very difficult question, and it trades on one of the inferences we referenced would be discussed in the questions. Note that the question stem wording is important—"must perform *earlier* than 10" means that we need to identify the group that can only perform at 6 or 8.

As discussed in the setup, from the second rule G cannot work at 12. Thus, G is a strong candidate to also be unable to perform at 10. During the test, the best approach would be to make a hypothetical with G performing at 10 and observe the consequences.

When G performs at 10, then from the second rule H must perform at 12, and from the first rule P must perform at 6:

North: P _____ G/ X

South: X _____ /G H
       6   8   10   12

The remaining groups to perform are L, Q, and T. Q cannot perform at 8 when P performs at 6 due to the actions of the last rule, and thus Q must perform at 10. However, G and Q cannot both perform at 10 due to the third rule. Thus, G cannot perform at 10 (and can only perform at 6 or 8), and answer choice (A) is correct.

Question #20: Global, Could Be True. The correct answer choice is (A)

The easiest guess for both questions #19 and #20 is G, because G is a variable that would prefer to perform earlier based on the second rule. However, during the game we would prefer you not to have to guess.

As discussed briefly at the end of question #19, G can perform at 6, and thus answer choice (A) is correct. Answer choice (B) can be eliminated because H in 6 violates the second rule. Answer choice (D) can be eliminated because Q in 6 violates the last rule. Answer choices (C) and (E) require further analysis.

Answer choices (C) and (E) involve two variables that are identical except for the fact that L is a folk band and T is a rock band. Otherwise, they operate in identical fashion. This basic similarity ultimately explains why neither can perform at 6.

If L or T performs at 6, then P must perform at 12. This leaves a set of four variables—G, H, Q, and the remainder of T/L—to fill all four of the performances at 8 and 10. If L performs at 6, the following scenario results:

North:	L	G/	H/	X

South:	X	/G	/H	P
	6	8	10	12

Because of the second rule, G and H cannot perform at the same time, and thus G performs at 8 and H performs at 10. This leads to a violation of the third rule because only rock groups are available to perform with H, a folk group. Thus, L cannot perform at 6, and answer choice (C) is incorrect.

A similar result occurs when T performs at 6:

North:	T	G/	H/Q	X

South:	X	/G	Q/H	P
	6	8	10	12

In this scenario, G works at 8 and H works at 10. Because T, a rock band, works at 6, from the last rule Q cannot work at 8, and Q must work at 10. However, if Q works with H a violation of the third rule occurs. Thus, T cannot work at 6, and answer choice (E) can be eliminated.

This inference works in the reverse as well: if L or T performs at 12, then P performs at 6, and the same variable set is available to fill the 8 and 10 performances. As this group cannot create a viable hypothetical, L and T also cannot perform at 12.

Question #21: Local, Could Be True, List. The correct answer choice is (D)

If Q performs at 12, then P must perform at 6. In addition, from the actions of the last rule, a folk group must play at 10, and from the third rule we can then deduce that two folk groups play at 10, leading to the following setup:

North:	P		F	X

South:	X		F	Q
	6	8	10	12

G, H, L, and T are the remaining groups that must still perform. From the second rule, G must perform earlier than H, and so G performs at 8 and H performs at 10. In order to conform to the third rule, L, the only other folk group, must then also perform at 10, and T is left to perform at 8. These inferences lead to the following setup:

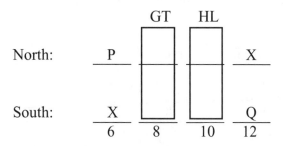

North: P   X

South: X   Q

Thus, although we cannot determine the stages that G, H, L, and T perform on, we can determine the times that they perform.

Answer choice (A) is incorrect because P must perform first on the north stage.

Answer choice (B) is incorrect because H cannot perform at 8, and T cannot perform at 10.

Answer choice (C) is incorrect because G cannot perform at 10.

Answer choice (E) is incorrect because from the fourth rule L and T cannot perform on the same stage.

Answer choice (D) is thus proven correct.

Question #22: Local, Must Be True. The correct answer choice is (B)

If a rock group performs at 10, then from the third rule the other group performing at 10 must also be a rock group. This immediately affects Q, because according to the last rule Q must perform after a folk group. Thus, Q cannot perform at 12 (or at 6 from that same rule). Therefore, it *appears* that Q must perform at 8 or 10. However, Q cannot perform at 8 due to the following reasoning:

> If Q, a rock group, performs at 8, then according to the last rule the group that performs at 6 must be a folk group. P, which is a rock group, therefore cannot perform at 6 and must instead perform at 12. However, this presents a problem because only one rock group remains unassigned—group T—yet two rock groups are still needed to play at 10. Thus, if Q performs at 8 under the conditions of this question, no viable solution can be produced. Hence, Q cannot perform at 8, and Q must instead perform at 10.

If you did not see this reasoning (and it is very tough to do so abstractly), once you reached the point of knowing that Q must perform at 8 or 10, why not try some hypotheticals to help eliminate answer choices? Very quickly you would discover that Q could not perform at 10, and that would lead you directly to the correct answer.

Now that we have established that Q performs at 10, from the last rule we can deduce that a folk group must play at 8, and hence answer choice (B) is correct.

Combining all of the information above leads to the following final setup to this tough game:

F: G H L ^{3}
R: P Q T ^{3}

North: P/G   ____   ____   X

P ⟶ 6/12

South:

X			/P
6	8	10	12
H̶		Q̶	G̶
Q̶			L̶
L̶			T̶
T̶			

$G_F > H_R$

[R / R]$_{10}$ or [F / F]$_{10}$

[L̶/T]$_{Stage}$

[G/H/L $_F$ Q$_R$]

P$_6$ ⟶ Q̶$_8$

Q$_8$ ⟶ P̶$_6$ ⟶ P$_{12}$

Given all of the rules above, you might expect that this game has some serious limitations, and indeed there are only four basic directions the game can take where the performers can be determined at each time (but the exact stage for all groups—at 8 and 10 in particular—cannot be determined). However, for most students these are very tough to identify in the time allotted, and thus we have chosen to display just the inferences above.

June 2006
Logic Games Section

SECTION IV
Time—35 minutes
22 Questions

Directions: Each group of questions in this section is based on a set of conditions. In answering some of the questions, it may be useful to draw a rough diagram. Choose the response that most accurately and completely answers each question and blacken the corresponding space on your answer sheet.

Questions 1-7

During an international film retrospective lasting six consecutive days—day 1 through day 6—exactly six different films will be shown, one each day. Twelve films will be available for presentation, two each in French, Greek, Hungarian, Italian, Norwegian, and Turkish. The presentation of the films must conform to the following conditions:

Neither day 2 nor day 4 is a day on which a film in Norwegian is shown.
A film in Italian is not shown unless a film in Norwegian is going to be shown the next day.
A film in Greek is not shown unless a film in Italian is going to be shown the next day.

1. Which one of the following is an acceptable order of films for the retrospective, listed by their language, from day 1 through day 6?

    (A)   French, Greek, Italian, Turkish, Norwegian, Hungarian
    (B)   French, Hungarian, Italian, Norwegian, French, Hungarian
    (C)   Hungarian, French, Norwegian, Greek, Norwegian, Italian
    (D)   Norwegian, Turkish, Hungarian, Italian, French, Turkish
    (E)   Turkish, French, Norwegian, Hungarian, French, Turkish

2. If two films in Italian are going to be shown, one on day 2 and one on day 5, then the film shown on day 1 could be in anyone of the following languages EXCEPT:

    (A)   French
    (B)   Greek
    (C)   Hungarian
    (D)   Norwegian
    (E)   Turkish

3. If two films in Italian are shown during the retrospective, which one of the following must be false?

    (A)   A film in French is shown on day 3.
    (B)   A film in Greek is shown on day 1.
    (C)   A film in Hungarian is shown on day 6.
    (D)   A film in Norwegian is shown on day 5.
    (E)   A film in Turkish is shown on day 4.

4. Which one of the following is a complete and accurate list of the days, any one of which is a day on which a film in Italian could be shown?

    (A)   day 1, day 3, day 5
    (B)   day 2, day 4, day 5
    (C)   day 2, day 5, day 6
    (D)   day 1, day 3
    (E)   day 2, day 4

5. If two films in French are going to be shown, one on day 3 and one on day 5, which one of the following is a pair of films that could be shown on day 1 and day 6, respectively?

    (A)   a film in French, a film in Turkish
    (B)   a film in Greek, a film in Hungarian
    (C)   a film in Italian, a film in Norwegian
    (D)   a film in Norwegian, a film in Turkish
    (E)   a film in Turkish, a film in Greek

6. If neither a film in French nor a film in Italian is shown during the retrospective, which one of the following must be true?

    (A)   A film in Norwegian is shown on day 1.
    (B)   A film in Norwegian is shown on day 5.
    (C)   A film in Turkish is shown on day 4.
    (D)   A film in Hungarian or else a film in Norwegian is shown on day 3.
    (E)   A film in Hungarian or else a film in Turkish is shown on day 2.

7. If a film in Greek is going to be shown at some time after a film in Norwegian, then a film in Norwegian must be shown on

    (A)   day 1
    (B)   day 3
    (C)   day 5
    (D)   day 1 or else day 3
    (E)   day 3 or else day 5

GO ON TO THE NEXT PAGE.

Questions 8-12

There are exactly five pieces of mail in a mailbox: a flyer, a letter, a magazine, a postcard, and a survey. Each piece of mail is addressed to exactly one of three housemates: Georgette, Jana, or Rini. Each housemate has at least one of the pieces of mail addressed to her. The following conditions must apply:

Neither the letter nor the magazine is addressed to Georgette.

If the letter is addressed to Rini, then the postcard is addressed to Jana.

The housemate to whom the flyer is addressed has at least one of the other pieces of mail addressed to her as well.

8. Which one of the following could be a complete and accurate matching of the pieces of mail to the housemates to whom they are addressed?

(A) Georgette: the flyer, the survey
    Jana: the letter
    Rini: the magazine
(B) Georgette: the flyer, the postcard
    Jana: the letter, the magazine
    Rini: the survey
(C) Georgette: the magazine, the survey
    Jana: the flyer, the letter
    Rini: the postcard
(D) Georgette: the survey
    Jana: the flyer, the magazine
    Rini: the letter, the postcard
(E) Georgette: the survey
    Jana: the letter, the magazine, the postcard
    Rini: the flyer

9. Which one of the following is a complete and accurate list of the pieces of mail, any one of which could be the only piece of mail addressed to Jana?

(A) the postcard
(B) the letter, the postcard
(C) the letter, the survey
(D) the magazine, the survey
(E) the letter, the magazine, the postcard

10. Which one of the following CANNOT be a complete and accurate list of the pieces of mail addressed to Jana?

(A) the flyer, the letter, the magazine
(B) the flyer, the letter, the postcard
(C) the flyer, the letter, the survey
(D) the flyer, the magazine, the postcard
(E) the flyer, the magazine, the survey

11. Which one of the following CANNOT be a complete and accurate list of the pieces of mail addressed to Rini?

(A) the magazine, the postcard
(B) the letter, the survey
(C) the letter, the magazine
(D) the flyer, the magazine
(E) the flyer, the letter

12. If the magazine and the survey are both addressed to the same housemate, then which one of the following could be true?

(A) The survey is addressed to Georgette.
(B) The postcard is addressed to Rini.
(C) The magazine is addressed to Jana.
(D) The letter is addressed to Rini.
(E) The flyer is addressed to Jana.

GO ON TO THE NEXT PAGE.

Questions 13-17

A summer program offers at least one of the following seven courses: geography, history, literature, mathematics, psychology, sociology, zoology. The following restrictions on the program must apply:

   If mathematics is offered, then either literature or sociology (but not both) is offered.

   If literature is offered, then geography is also offered but psychology is not.

   If sociology is offered, then psychology is also offered but zoology is not.

   If geography is offered, then both history and zoology are also offered.

13. Which one of the following could be a complete and accurate list of the courses offered by the summer program?

   (A)   history, psychology
   (B)   geography, history, literature
   (C)   history, mathematics, psychology
   (D)   literature, mathematics, psychology
   (E)   history, literature, mathematics, sociology

14. If the summer program offers literature, then which one of the following could be true?

   (A)   Sociology is offered.
   (B)   History is not offered.
   (C)   Mathematics is not offered.
   (D)   A total of two courses are offered.
   (E)   Zoology is not offered.

15. If history is not offered by the summer program, then which one of the following is another course that CANNOT be offered?

   (A)   literature
   (B)   mathematics
   (C)   psychology
   (D)   sociology
   (E)   zoology

16. If the summer program offers mathematics, then which one of the following must be true?

   (A)   Literature is offered.
   (B)   Psychology is offered.
   (C)   Sociology is offered.
   (D)   At least three courses are offered.
   (E)   At most four courses are offered.

17. Which one of the following must be false of the summer program?

   (A)   Both geography and psychology are offered.
   (B)   Both geography and mathematics are offered.
   (C)   Both psychology and mathematics are offered.
   (D)   Both history and mathematics are offered.
   (E)   Both geography and sociology are offered.

GO ON TO THE NEXT PAGE.

Questions 18-22

Exactly eight computer processor chips—F, G, H, J, K, L, M, and O—are ranked according to their speed from first (fastest) to eighth (slowest). The ranking must be consistent with the following:

    There are no ties.
    Either F or G is ranked first.
    M is not the slowest.
    H is faster than J, with exactly one chip intermediate in speed between them.
    K is faster than L, with exactly two chips intermediate in speed between them.
    O is slower than both J and L.

18. Which one of the following could be true?

    (A)   F is ranked first and M is ranked eighth.
    (B)   G is ranked fifth and O is ranked eighth.
    (C)   J is ranked third and L is ranked seventh.
    (D)   K is ranked second and H is ranked third.
    (E)   M is ranked seventh and L is ranked eighth.

19. H CANNOT be ranked

    (A)   second
    (B)   third
    (C)   fourth
    (D)   fifth
    (E)   sixth

20. If O is faster than F, then which one of the following chips could be ranked second?

    (A)   G
    (B)   H
    (C)   M
    (D)   J
    (E)   L

21. If M is faster than J, then the fastest ranking J could have is

    (A)   second
    (B)   third
    (C)   fourth
    (D)   fifth
    (E)   sixth

22. Which one of the following must be true?

    (A)   J is ranked no faster than fifth.
    (B)   K is ranked no faster than third.
    (C)   L is ranked no faster than fifth.
    (D)   M is ranked no faster than third.
    (E)   O is ranked no faster than eighth.

S T O P

IF YOU FINISH BEFORE TIME IS CALLED, YOU MAY CHECK YOUR WORK ON THIS SECTION ONLY.
DO NOT WORK ON ANY OTHER SECTION IN THE TEST.

JUNE 2006 LOGIC GAMES SECTION

1.	E	8.	B	15.	A	22.	C
2.	D	9.	B	16.	D		
3.	A	10.	E	17.	E		
4.	B	11.	B	18.	B		
5.	D	12.	E	19.	E		
6.	E	13.	A	20.	B		
7.	D	14.	C	21.	D		

This is an Unbalanced: Overloaded Basic Linear game.

FF GG HH II NN TT[12]
**   **   **

I ⟶ ⬚IN

G ⟶ ⬚GI

G ⟶ ⬚GIN

$$\underset{\substack{1 \\ \cancel{N}}}{\rule{2em}{0.4pt}} \quad \underset{\substack{2 \\ \cancel{N} \\ \cancel{G}}}{\rule{2em}{0.4pt}} \quad \underset{\substack{3 \\ \cancel{N}}}{\rule{2em}{0.4pt}} \quad \underset{\substack{4 \\ \cancel{N}}}{\rule{2em}{0.4pt}} \quad \underset{\substack{5 \\ \cancel{G}}}{\rule{2em}{0.4pt}} \quad \underset{\substack{6 \\ \cancel{N} \\ \cancel{G}}}{\rule{2em}{0.4pt}}$$

This game is Unbalanced: Overloaded because there are twelve films available to fill six slots. Only six of the films are selected, and the other six are not selected. Note that this scenario allows for films of some languages *not* to be selected as there is no rule specifying that a film in each language must be shown. Thus, for example, it is possible for both Turkish films not to be shown.

The first rule leads to N Not Laws on day 2 and day 4.

The second rule creates a conditional relationship (note the "unless"), and the conditional relationship leads to an I Not Law on day 6. Note that an N Not Law is *not* created on day 1 because N can move independently of I. I and N are not in a general block; they only appear as a block *when* I is present. Because of this interaction between I and N, combining the second rule with the first rule leads to I Not Laws on day 1 and day 3 (if N cannot be shown on day 2, then I cannot be shown on day 1, etc.).

The third rule contains similar language to the second rule, leading to another conditional relationship, this time between G and I. Because of this relationship, G Not Laws can be created on days 2, 5, and 6 (days 2 and 5 because I cannot be shown on days 3 and 6; day 6 because G must always be shown before I).

The last two rules can be combined into one super-rule where the presence of G creates a GIN block. G is thus a very powerful variable in this game and must be tracked at all times.

Question #1: Global, Could Be True, List. The correct answer choice is (E)

The first rule eliminates answer choice (B). The second rule eliminates answer choices (A), (C), and (D). Consequently, answer choice (E) is correct. Note that in answer choice (E) the N film can stand alone without the presence of I because the second rule involving I and N is only activated when I is present.

Question #2: Local, Could Be True, Except. The correct answer choice is (D)

If I is shown on day 2 and day 5, then the second rule indicates that N must be shown on day 3 and day 6:

$$\underline{\quad}\ \ \underline{\ \text{I}\ }\ \ \underline{\ \text{N}\ }\ \ \underline{\quad}\ \ \underline{\ \text{I}\ }\ \ \underline{\ \text{N}\ }$$
$$\ \ \ \ 1\ \ \ \ \ \ 2\ \ \ \ \ \ 3\ \ \ \ \ \ 4\ \ \ \ \ \ 5\ \ \ \ \ \ 6$$

Consequently, answer choice (D) is correct because both N films have already been shown, so they cannot also be shown on day 1.

Question #3: Local, Cannot Be True, FTT. The correct answer choice is (A)

If both Italian films are shown, due to the Not Laws there are a limited number of placement options available for the two: only day 2, day 4, and day 5 exist as available options. Thus, the two films are shown on either days 2 and 4, or days 2 and 5 (days 4 and 5 are not an option because there would be no room for N to follow the first I). Once you recognized this situation, the best course of action is to make two quick hypotheticals next to the problem. Of course, in each scenario, the second rule dictates that N must be shown on the days following I:

Hypothetical #2: $\underline{\quad}\ \ \underline{\ \text{I}\ }\ \ \underline{\ \text{N}\ }\ \ \underline{\quad}\ \ \underline{\ \text{I}\ }\ \ \underline{\ \text{N}\ }$

Hypothetical #1: $\underline{\quad}\ \ \underline{\ \text{I}\ }\ \ \underline{\ \text{N}\ }\ \ \underline{\ \text{I}\ }\ \ \underline{\ \text{N}\ }\ \ \underline{\quad}$
$$\ 1\ \ \ \ \ \ 2\ \ \ \ \ \ 3\ \ \ \ \ \ 4\ \ \ \ \ \ 5\ \ \ \ \ \ 6$$

As proven by the two scenarios, N must be shown on day 3, and thus answer choice (A) cannot be true and is therefore correct.

Question #4: Global, Could Be True, List. The correct answer choice is (B)

As discussed in the prior question, the only placement options available to I are day 2, day 4, and day 5. Accordingly, answer choice (B) is correct.

Question #5: Local, Could Be True. The correct answer choice is (D)

If the two French films are shown on day 3 and day 5, then there is not a third French film available to be shown, and answer choice (A) can be eliminated. The Not Laws created during the game setup eliminate answer choice (C) (I cannot be shown first) and answer choice (E) (G cannot be shown sixth). Answer choice (B) is incorrect because if G is shown first, then from the combination of the second and third rules I must be shown second, and N must be shown third, but that creates a conflict because F has already been assigned to day 3. Thus, answer choice (D) is correct.

Question #6: Local, Must Be True. The correct answer choice is (E)

If no Italian film is shown, then from the second rule we can deduce that no Greek film is shown either (this inference is the result of the contrapositive of the third rule). Thus, if no French, Italian, or Greek films are available, only Hungarian, Norwegian, and Turkish films can be shown. Because H and T are randoms, the focus of this question must be on N. From the initial Not Laws, we know that N cannot be shown on day 2 or day 4. Consequently, H or T must be shown on day 2 and day 4. This information proves answer choice (E) correct.

Question #7: Local, Must Be True. The correct answer choice is (D)

The condition in the question stem asserts that both an N and a G film will be shown, and that information in combination with the super-rule creates the following relationship:

$$N > \boxed{G\ I\ N}$$

Because of the size of the block behind N, N cannot be shown in any of the last three slots. From the Not Laws, we also know that N cannot be shown on day 2, and hence the only days remaining for N to be shown are day 1 and day 3. Therefore, answer choice (D) is correct.

This is a Grouping Game: Defined-Moving, Balanced, Numerical Distribution.

On the surface, this game appears fairly easy: five pieces of mail addressed to three different housemates. However, there is a great deal of uncertainty because number of pieces of mail each housemate receives is not fixed.

With only five pieces of mail for the three housemates, and with each housemate receiving at least one piece of mail, there are only two possible numerical distributions in this game:

> 3 - 1 - 1: one housemate receives three pieces of mail, and each of the other housemates receives one piece of mail.

> 2 - 2 - 1: two housemates receives two pieces of mail each, and the other housemate receives one piece of mail.

The last rule ties into these two distributions by establishing that the housemate receiving F *must* be in the group of 3 in the 3-1-1 distribution, or in one of the groups of 2 in the 2-2-1 distribution.

The other two rules are fairly generic. The first rule establishes two Not Laws on G, and leaves G with only three options for mail: F, P, and/or S. This rule also establishes that L and M will always be addressed to J or R. This has important consequences when paired with the second rule.

The second rule is conditional, and can be diagrammed as follows:

$$L_R \longrightarrow P_J$$

From this rule, we can deduce that when L is addressed to R, and consequently P is addressed to J, that F or S is addressed to G:

$$L_R \longrightarrow P_J \longrightarrow F/S_G$$

In this chain relationship, F, or F and S, must be addressed to G. At a minimum, S must always be addressed to G since addressing F to G would require S to be addressed to G as well, per the actions of the last rule.

The rules and relationships above can be compiled to form our main diagram:

F L M P S [5]
    *   *

$$L_R \longrightarrow P_J$$

$$F \longrightarrow min\ 2$$

3-1-1 (F must be in the group of 3)
or
2-2-1

$$\frac{F/P/S}{\cancel{G}} \quad \frac{}{J} \quad \frac{}{R}$$
$$\cancel{L}$$
$$\cancel{M}$$

Inference:

$$L_R \longrightarrow P_J \longrightarrow F/S_G$$

With the information in the setup, we are ready for the questions.

Question #8: Global, Could Be True, List. The correct answer choice is (B)

In this List question each of the incorrect answer choices can be eliminated by a simple application of the rules:

Answer choice (A) is incorrect because P is not addressed to any of the housemates. Consider that in a game with only three rules, one of the ways they will test you is to see if you understood the basic constraints on variable use and assignment (e.g. every piece of mail is addressed to a housemate and every housemate has at least one piece of mail addressed to her).

Answer choice (C) is incorrect because M is addressed to G, a violation of the first rule.

Answer choice (D) is incorrect because from the second rule when L is addressed to R, then P must be addressed to J.

Answer choice (E) is incorrect because from the last rule the housemate to whom the flyer is addressed must receive at least two pieces of mail.

Thus, answer choice (B) is proven correct by process of elimination.

Question #9: Global, Could Be True, List. The correct answer choice is (B)

This is the hardest question of the game, with fewer than 50% of students answering this question correctly. The key to the question is realizing that the question stem contains the word "only." The use of this word in the question stem indicates that the test makers are looking for a list where each piece of mail could be the *only* piece of mail addressed to J. Thus, the answers do not list all of the pieces of mail that could be addressed to J, but rather the pieces of mail that could be addressed to her in scenarios where she receives only one piece of mail. This is one reason F does not appear in any choice—the appearance of F would automatically eliminate the answer in easy fashion (probably too easy of a fashion for Law Services' taste).

A question like this is most easily solved when you have created as many game scenarios as possible, so the best strategy with this game is to skip it, and then return at the end after you have solved the other questions (and hopefully created applicable hypotheticals that can then be used to solve this question more quickly; question #12, for example, helps to show that L could be the sole piece of mail addressed to J).

Let's consider two other approaches to this question. The first involves looking at the relationships and abstractly solving the problem. With this approach, we would focus on the second rule, which ends with P being addressed to J. The actions of this rule prohibit the two randoms—M or S—from being the sole piece of mail addressed to R. If M or S is the sole piece of mail addressed to J, then

L must be assigned to R, enacting the second rule and forcing P to be assigned to J. Eliminating M and S from contention knocks out answer choices (C), (D), and (E). The difference between answer choices (A) and (B) is the presence of L in answer choice (B), and a mental calculation shows that L could be the sole letter addressed to R because F, P, and S could conveniently be addressed to G and M could be addressed to R.

The process described above is admittedly difficult, but sometimes considering the different solution avenues is helpful because many questions are solved not with just one path of attack but with a combination of approaches.

Another method of solving this question is to use hypotheticals to confirm and eliminate variables. For example, our inference involving the second rule sets the stage for a hypothetical where P is the only piece of mail addressed to J:

> When L is addressed to R, then P is addressed to J, allowing F and S to be addressed to G. M, a random, can then be addressed to R or G:

$$
\begin{array}{ccc}
\text{M/} & & \\
\text{S} & & \text{/M} \\
\underline{\text{F}} & \underline{\text{P}} & \underline{\text{L}} \\
\text{G} & \text{J} & \text{R}
\end{array}
$$

Establishing that P can be the sole piece of mail addressed to J eliminates answer choices (C) and (D), neither of which contain P.

As the three remaining answers only address L or M (or neither), we do not have to worry about S. This is odd because S is a random, and one would normally expect that a random would be a likely variable that could be the sole piece of mail addressed to J. This suggests that instead of examining M—the other random—first, we should instead examine L first. Indeed, L can be the only piece of mail addressed to J, as shown by the following hypothetical:

$$
\begin{array}{ccc}
\text{S} & & \\
\text{P} & & \\
\underline{\text{F}} & \underline{\text{L}} & \underline{\text{M}} \\
\text{G} & \text{J} & \text{R}
\end{array}
$$

This information eliminates answer choice (A), leaving only M under consideration.

As mentioned before, neither of the two randoms—M or S—can be the sole piece of mail addressed to R. If M or S is the sole piece of mail addressed to J, then L must be assigned to R, enacting the second rule and forcing P to be assigned to J.

Regardless of which method or combination of methods you use to solve the problem, the correct answer choice is (B).

Question #10: Global, Cannot Be True, List. The correct answer choice is (E)

This question, as distinguished from question #9, asks for you to consider the listed pieces of mail in each answer in combination, and to determine which combination cannot be addressed to J. As we know from the combination of the first and second rules, when L is *not* addressed to J, then L must be address to R. When L is addressed to R, then P must be address to J. Answer choice (E) contains neither L or P, which violates this relationship. Consequently, the combination in answer choice (A) cannot occur, and (E) is correct.

Question #11: Global, Cannot Be True, List. The correct answer choice is (B)

This is the fourth List question in this game. This question is identical to question #10, but this time the focus is on R, not J.

As shown in the discussion of the second rule, when L is addressed to R, the consequence is that F or S or both must be addressed to G. If both L and S are addressed to R, then F must be addressed to G, but there is no other piece of mail available to be addressed to G, creating a violation of the third rule (the other two variables are P and M; P must be addressed to J when L is addressed to R, and M can never be addressed to G according to the first rule). Therefore, answer choice (B) cannot occur and is correct.

Question #12: Local, Could Be True. The correct answer choice is (E)

If M and S are addressed to the same housemate, they cannot be addressed to G from the first rule, leaving only J and R as options. If M and S are addressed to J, then L would be addressed to R, ultimately creating a violation of the third rule because F would be the sole piece of mail addressed to G (P would be addressed to J, and S would already be addressed to R). Thus, M and S cannot be addressed to J, and M and S must be addressed to R.

With M and S addressed to R, we can infer that L must be addressed to J (if L were addressed to R, F would be the sole piece of mail addressed to a housemate, a violation of the last rule). G would have the option of P, or F and P or both, meaning that regardless of who F is addressed to, P must be addressed to G:

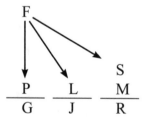

As F is the uncertain variable in this question, seek answer choices containing F. Answer choice (E) contains F, and reflects the fact that F could be addressed to J. Answer choice (E) is thus correct.

This is a Grouping Game: Undefined.

The game scenario establishes that there are seven prospective courses available for a summer program, with the stipulation that at least one is offered. As the group size is undetermined, this game is Undefined.

There are four rules in this game, and each is diagrammed below:

Rule #1

$$M \longrightarrow \begin{array}{c} L \\ \text{or (not both)} \\ S \end{array}$$

Rule #2

$$L \longrightarrow \begin{array}{c} G \\ + \\ \cancel{P} \end{array}$$

Rule #3

$$S \longrightarrow \begin{array}{c} P \\ + \\ \cancel{Z} \end{array}$$

Rule #4

$$G \longrightarrow \begin{array}{c} H \\ + \\ Z \end{array}$$

These four rules yield several inferences:

Rule #2 and Rule #3 Combined

The third rule requires that P to be offered but the second rule requires that P not be offered. Thus, the sufficient conditions in each rule cannot occur simultaneously, and we can infer that L and S are never offered together:

$$L \longleftarrow\!\!\!|\!\!\!\longrightarrow S$$

The presence of this inference actually makes the "but not both" phrase in the first rule superfluous; regardless of that phrase in the first rule, the combination of the second and third rules makes it impossible for L and S to be offered together.

Rule #3 and Rule #4 Combined

The fourth rule requires that Z to be offered but the third rule requires that Z not be offered. Thus, the sufficient conditions in each rule cannot occur simultaneously, and we can infer that G and S are never offered together:

$$G \longleftrightarrow\!\!\!|\!\!\!\longrightarrow S$$

Note that the presence of S in the two inferences means that when S is offered, neither G nor L is offered, and from the third rule Z cannot be offered either (although from that same rule P would be offered).

Rule #2 and Rule #4 Combined

The second rule contains a sufficient condition of G, and the fourth rule has G as the sufficient. Thus, these two rules can be linked:

```
                        H
          G ─────────→  +
                        Z

 L ─────────→  +


           P̸
```

Of course, we can also add in the contrapositive of the third rule (which could also be described as recycling the first inference) and add the fact that S cannot be offered:

```
                        H
          G ─────────→  +
                        Z

 L ─────────→  +


           P̸ ─────────→ S̸
```

Note also that the inference regarding S could have been made through Z as well.

Thus, when L is offered, the fate of every course is determined except for that of M. This inference is tested in question #14.

The last point of note is that there are no randoms in this game. Every one of the variables is addressed at least one of the rules, meaning that every variables can be checked against a rule.

The combination of the information above leads to the final setup for this game:

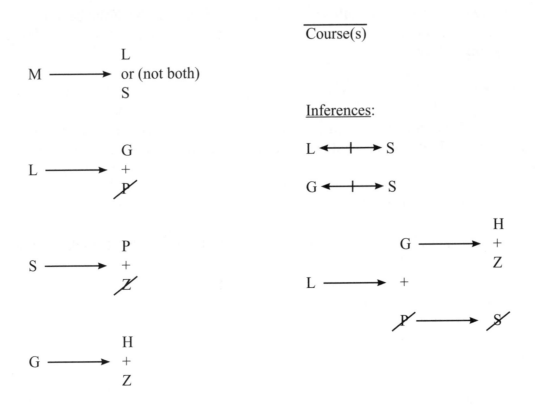

Question #13: Global, Could Be True, List. The correct answer choice is (A)

Answer choice (A) is the correct answer. Neither of the listed courses are sufficient conditions in any of the rules, and so they both can be offered without affecting other variables.

Answer choice (B) is incorrect because according to the last rule when G is offered then Z must also be offered.

Answer choice (C) is incorrect because according to the first rule when M is offered then L or S must also be offered.

Answer choice (D) is incorrect because according to the second rule when L is offered then G is offered and P is not offered.

Answer choice (E) is incorrect because according to the second rule when L is offered then G is offered. In addition, according to the inference made in the setup, L and S cannot both be offered.

Question #14: Local, Could Be True. The correct answer choice is (C)

From the discussion of inferences, when L is offered, then G, H, and Z must be offered, P and S cannot be offered, and M may or may not be offered. As this is a Could Be True question, immediately attack the uncertainty in this question: M. Only answer choice (C) addresses M, and as it could be true that M is not offered, answer choice (C) is correct.

Question #15: Local, Cannot Be True. The correct answer choice is (A)

The question stem specifies that H is not offered. As the fourth rule lists H as a necessary condition, taking the contrapositive of the fourth rule reveals that G cannot be offered. G is not one of the answer choices, however. But, G is a necessary condition on the second rule, and taking the contrapositive of that rule reveals that L cannot be offered:

$$\cancel{H} \longrightarrow \cancel{G} \longrightarrow \cancel{L}$$

Accordingly, answer choice (A) is correct.

Question #16: Local, Must Be True. The correct answer choice is (D)

If M is offered, then from the first rule L or S but not both must offered. This creates two distinct possibilities:

$$
\begin{array}{c}
\quad\quad\quad\quad\quad\quad\quad\quad\quad\quad H \\
\quad\quad\quad\quad\quad\quad G \longrightarrow + \\
\quad\quad\quad\quad\quad\quad\quad\quad\quad\quad Z \\
M \longrightarrow L \longrightarrow + \\
\quad\quad\quad\quad\quad\quad \cancel{P} \longrightarrow \cancel{S}
\end{array}
$$

or

$$
\begin{array}{c}
\quad\quad\quad\quad\quad\quad\quad\quad P \\
M \longrightarrow S \longrightarrow + \\
\quad\quad\quad\quad\quad\quad\quad\quad \cancel{Z}
\end{array}
$$

Answer choice (A) is incorrect because if S is offered with M then L cannot be offered.

Answer choice (B) is incorrect because in one scenario P is offered, but in the other P is not offered. Thus, P does not have to be offered when L is offered.

Answer choice (C) is incorrect because if L is offered with M then S cannot be offered.

Answer choice (D) is the correct answer. When M and L are offered, then a total of five courses are offered. When M and S are offered, then at least three courses are offered. In each instance, at least three courses are offered, and thus this is the correct answer.

Answer choice (E) is incorrect because when M and L are offered, then a total of five courses are offered. If this answer read, "at most four *additional* courses are offered," then it would be correct.

Question #17: Global, Cannot Be True, FTT. The correct answer choice is (E)

As discussed in the setup to the game, combining the third and fourth rules leads to the inference that G and S cannot be offered together. Thus, answer choice (E) cannot be true and is the correct answer.

This is a Basic Linear Game: Balanced.

F G H J K L M O ^{8}

The last three rules form a powerful sequential relationship that largely controls the placement of variables in the game. While you could show all of the Not Laws that result from the sequence on your diagram, to do so would not be a valuable use of your time; the sequence provides enough visual information so that you can rely upon it without drawing our every Not Law. The one inference we have drawn out on the diagram is that O must be ranked seventh or eighth (the two blocks push O into one of the last two spaces).

Question #18: Global, Could Be True. The correct answer choice is (B)

Answer choice (A) is incorrect because M cannot be ranked last.

Answer choice (C) is incorrect because if J is ranked third, then from the fourth rule H must be ranked first, a violation of the second rule.

Answer choice (D) is incorrect because when K is ranked second then L must be ranked fifth, and when H is ranked third, then J must be ranked fifth, and according to the first rule there are no ties.

Answer choice (E) is incorrect because there is no available ranking for O when M is seventh and L is eighth.

Accordingly, answer choice (B) is proven correct by elimination.

Question #19: Global, Cannot Be True. The correct answer choice is (E)

Given that H is a variable that causes fewer problems when it is ranked highly, and this is a Cannot Be True question, there is reason to suspect that the further "back" H is pushed, the more problems it will create. Indeed, when H is ranked sixth, then J must be ranked eighth, leaving no room for O. Hence, H cannot be ranked sixth and answer choice (E) is correct.

Question #20: Local, Could Be True. The correct answer choice is (B)

If O is faster than F, then O must be ranked seventh, and F must be ranked eighth. Further, from the second rule, we can infer that G is then ranked first:

$$\frac{G}{1} \quad \frac{}{2} \quad \frac{}{3} \quad \frac{}{4} \quad \frac{}{5} \quad \frac{}{6} \quad \frac{O}{7} \quad \frac{F}{8}$$

The blocks can then be placed in only two arrangements:

#1: KL in 2-5

$$\frac{G}{1} \quad \frac{K}{2} \quad \frac{M}{3} \quad \frac{H}{4} \quad \frac{L}{5} \quad \frac{J}{6} \quad \frac{O}{7} \quad \frac{F}{8}$$

#2: KL in 3-6

$$\frac{G}{1} \quad \frac{H}{2} \quad \frac{K}{3} \quad \frac{J}{4} \quad \frac{M}{5} \quad \frac{L}{6} \quad \frac{O}{7} \quad \frac{F}{8}$$

As only H or K can be second, answer choice (B) is correct.

Question #21: Local, Must Be True, Maximum. The correct answer choice is (D)

If M is faster than J, then at least three chips must be faster than J: H, M, and F or G. Thus, the earliest J could be is fourth, eliminating answer choices (A) and (B). However, in order to be certain that J can be fourth, try a hypothetical and confirm that J can be fourth:

$$\frac{F/G}{1} \quad \frac{H}{2} \quad \frac{M}{3} \quad \frac{J}{4} \quad \frac{K}{5} \quad \frac{}{6} \quad \frac{}{7} \quad \frac{L}{8}$$

Unfortunately, this hypothetical fails because the first four spaces are occupied, forcing K to be ranked fifth and thus L must be ranked eighth, leaving no room for O. Therefore, answer choice (C) is also incorrect.

J in fifth will work, as shown by the following hypothetical:

$$\frac{F/G}{1} \quad \frac{M}{2} \quad \frac{H}{3} \quad \frac{K}{4} \quad \frac{J}{5} \quad \frac{G/F}{6} \quad \frac{L}{7} \quad \frac{O}{8}$$

Answer choice (D) is therefore correct.

Question #22: Global, Must Be True. The correct answer choice is (C)

Answer choice (A): As shown by the third diagram in the explanation to question #20, J can be ranked faster than fifth.

Answer choice (B): As shown by the second diagram in the explanation to question #20, K can be ranked faster than third.

Answer choice (C): This is the correct answer. F or G must be first, and K must be ranked three slots faster than L, and so K can be ranked no faster than second, and thus the earliest L can be ranked is fifth.

Answer choice (D): M can be ranked second, as shown by the following hypothetical:

$$\frac{\text{F}}{1} \quad \frac{\text{M}}{2} \quad \frac{\text{K}}{3} \quad \frac{\text{G}}{4} \quad \frac{\text{H}}{5} \quad \frac{\text{L}}{6} \quad \frac{\text{J}}{7} \quad \frac{\text{O}}{8}$$

Answer choice (E): As shown by the third diagram in the explanation to question #20, O can be ranked faster than eighth.

September 2006
Logic Games Section

SECTION V
Time—35 minutes
22 Questions

Directions: Each group of questions in this section is based on a set of conditions. In answering some of the questions, it may be useful to draw a rough diagram. Choose the response that most accurately and completely answers each question and blacken the corresponding space on your answer sheet.

Questions 1-5

At each of six consecutive stops—1, 2, 3, 4, 5, and 6—that a traveler must make in that order as part of a trip, she can choose one from among exactly four airlines—L, M, N, and O—on which to continue. Her choices must conform to the following constraints:

Whichever airline she chooses at a stop, she chooses one of the other airlines at the next stop.
She chooses the same airline at stop 1 as she does at stop 6.
She chooses the same airline at stop 2 as she does at stop 4.
Whenever she chooses either L or M at a stop, she does not choose N at the next stop.
At stop 5, she chooses N or O.

1.   Which one of the following could be an accurate list of the airlines the traveler chooses at each stop, in order from 1 through 6?

(A)   L, M, M, L, O, L
(B)   M, L, O, M, O, M
(C)   M, N, O, N, O, M
(D)   M, O, N, O, N, M
(E)   O, M, L, M, O, N

2.   If the traveler chooses N at stop 5, which one of the following could be an accurate list of the airlines she chooses at stops 1, 2, and 3, respectively?

(A)   L, M, N
(B)   L, O, N
(C)   M, L, N
(D)   M, L, O
(E)   N, O, N

3.   If the only airlines the traveler chooses for the trip are M, N, and O, and she chooses O at stop 5, then the airlines she chooses at stops 1, 2, and 3, must be, respectively,

(A)   M, O, and N
(B)   M, N, and O
(C)   N, M, and O
(D)   N, O, and M
(E)   O, M, and N

4.   Which one of the following CANNOT be an accurate list of the airlines the traveler chooses at stops 1 and 2, respectively?

(A)   L, M
(B)   L, O
(C)   M, L
(D)   M, O
(E)   O, N

5.   If the traveler chooses O at stop 2, which one of the following could be an accurate list of the airlines she chooses at stops 5 and 6, respectively?

(A)   M, N
(B)   N, L
(C)   N, O
(D)   O, L
(E)   O, N

GO ON TO THE NEXT PAGE.

Questions 6-11

The members of a five-person committee will be selected from among three parents—F, G, and H—three students—K, L, and M—and four teachers—U, W, X, and Z. The selection of committee members will meet the following conditions:

> The committee must include exactly one student.
> F and H cannot both be selected.
> M and Z cannot both be selected.
> U and W cannot both be selected.
> F cannot be selected unless Z is also selected.
> W cannot be selected unless H is also selected.

6. Which one of the following is an acceptable selection of committee members?

(A) F, G, K, L, Z
(B) F, G, K, U, X
(C) G, K, W, X, Z
(D) H, K, U, W, X
(E) H, L, W, X, Z

7. If W and Z are selected, which one of the following is a pair of people who could also be selected?

(A) U and X
(B) K and L
(C) G and M
(D) G and K
(E) F and G

8. Which one of the following is a pair of people who CANNOT both be selected?

(A) F and G
(B) F and M
(C) G and K
(D) H and L
(E) M and U

9. If W is selected, then anyone of the following could also be selected EXCEPT:

(A) F
(B) G
(C) L
(D) M
(E) Z

10. If the committee is to include exactly one parent, which one of the following is a person who must also be selected?

(A) K
(B) L
(C) M
(D) U
(E) X

11. If M is selected, then the committee must also include both

(A) F and G
(B) G and H
(C) H and K
(D) K and U
(E) U and X

GO ON TO THE NEXT PAGE.

<u>Questions 12-17</u>

Within a five-year period from 1991 to 1995, each of three friends—Ramon, Sue, and Taylor—graduated. In that period, each bought his or her first car. The graduations and car purchases must be consistent with the following:

Ramon graduated in some year before the year in which Taylor graduated.

Taylor graduated in some year before the year in which he bought his first car.

Sue bought her first car in some year before the year in which she graduated.

Ramon and Sue graduated in the same year as each other.

At least one of the friends graduated in 1993.

12. Which one of the following could be an accurate matching of each friend and the year in which she or he graduated?

(A) Ramon: 1991; Sue: 1991; Taylor: 1993
(B) Ramon: 1992; Sue: 1992; Taylor: 1993
(C) Ramon: 1992; Sue: 1993; Taylor: 1994
(D) Ramon: 1993; Sue: 1993; Taylor: 1992
(E) Ramon: 1993; Sue: 1993; Taylor: 1995

13. Which one of the following could have taken place in 1995?

(A) Ramon graduated.
(B) Ramon bought his first car.
(C) Sue graduated.
(D) Sue bought her first car.
(E) Taylor graduated.

14. Which one of the following must be false?

(A) Two of the friends each bought his or her first car in 1991.
(B) Two of the friends each bought his or her first car in 1992.
(C) Two of the friends each bought his or her first car in 1993.
(D) Two of the friends each bought his or her first car in 1994.
(E) Two of the friends each bought his or her first car in 1995.

15. Which one of the following must be true?

(A) None of the three friends graduated in 1991.
(B) None of the three friends graduated in 1992.
(C) None of the three friends bought his or her first car in 1993.
(D) None of the three friends graduated in 1994.
(E) None of the three friends bought his or her first car in 1995.

16. If Taylor graduated in the same year that Ramon bought his first car, then each of the following could be true EXCEPT:

(A) Sue bought her first car in 1991.
(B) Ramon graduated in 1992.
(C) Taylor graduated in 1993.
(D) Taylor bought his first car in 1994.
(E) Ramon bought his first car in 1995.

17. If Sue graduated in 1993, then which one of the following must be true?

(A) Sue bought her first car in 1991.
(B) Ramon bought his first car in 1992.
(C) Ramon bought his first car in 1993.
(D) Taylor bought his first car in 1994.
(E) Taylor bought his first car in 1995.

GO ON TO THE NEXT PAGE.

<u>Questions 18-22</u>

A child eating alphabet soup notices that the only letters left in her bowl are one each of these six letters: T, U, W, X, Y, and Z. She plays a game with the remaining letters, eating them in the next three spoonfuls in accord with certain rules. Each of the six letters must be in exactly one of the next three spoonfuls, and each of the spoonfuls must have at least one and at most three of the letters. In addition, she obeys the following restrictions:

The U is in a later spoonful than the T.
The U is not in a later spoonful than the X.
The Y is in a later spoonful than the W.
The U is in the same spoonful as either the Y or the Z, but not both.

18. Which one of the following could be an accurate list of the spoonfuls and the letters in each of them?

   (A)   first: Y
           second: T, W
           third: U, X, Z
   (B)   first: T, W
           second: U, X, Y
           third: Z
   (C)   first: T
           second: U, Z
           third: W, X, Y
   (D)   first: T, U, Z
           second: W
           third: X, Y
   (E)   first: W
           second: T, X, Z
           third: U, Y

19. If the Y is the only letter in one of the spoonfuls, then which one of the following could be true?

   (A)   The Y is in the first spoonful.
   (B)   The Z is in the first spoonful.
   (C)   The T is in the second spoonful.
   (D)   The X is in the second spoonful.
   (E)   The W is in the third spoonful.

20. If the Z is in the first spoonful, then which one of the following must be true?

   (A)   The T is in the second spoonful.
   (B)   The U is in the third spoonful.
   (C)   The W is in the first spoonful.
   (D)   The W is in the second spoonful.
   (E)   The X is in the third spoonful.

21. Which one of the following is a complete list of letters, any one of which could be the only letter in the first spoonful?

   (A)   T
   (B)   T, W
   (C)   T, X
   (D)   T, W, Z
   (E)   T, X, W, Z

22. If the T is in the second spoonful, then which one of the following could be true?

   (A)   Exactly two letters are in the first spoonful.
   (B)   Exactly three letters are in the first spoonful.
   (C)   Exactly three letters are in the second spoonful.
   (D)   Exactly one letter is in the third spoonful.
   (E)   Exactly two letters are in the third spoonful.

S T O P

IF YOU FINISH BEFORE TIME IS CALLED, YOU MAY CHECK YOUR WORK ON THIS SECTION ONLY.
DO NOT WORK ON ANY OTHER SECTION IN THE TEST.

SEPTEMBER 2006 LOGIC GAMES SECTION

1.	D	8.	B	15.	A	22.	A
2.	B	9.	A	16.	E		
3.	C	10.	E	17.	E		
4.	E	11.	B	18.	B		
5.	B	12.	B	19.	D		
6.	E	13.	B	20.	E		
7.	D	14.	C	21.	D		

This is an Unbalanced: Underfunded Basic Linear game.

L M N O [4]

This game is Unbalanced: Underfunded because there are only four airlines to fill the six stops. Thus, some airlines must be used multiple times. Note also that the game does not specify that every airline is used. Thus, some viable solutions will not contain all four airlines. This makes the game much trickier. Remember, always read the rules carefully to see if every slot is filled, and if every variable must be used. In this game every slot is filled, but not every variable must be used. That creates a greater number of possible solutions.

* With the first rule, instead of drawing Not-blocks for each airline such as not LL, etc, we chose to create an A̸A to represent that the same "Airline" cannot appear consecutively.

* The second and third rules can be diagrammed internally, meaning directly on the main diagram. Simply draw a double arrow between stops 1 and 6, and another arrow between stops 2 and 4.

* The fourth rule is drawn as two separate Not-blocks, but the operational effect of neither L nor M appearing before N is that if N appears in stops 2-6, then O must precede it. N can appear in stop 1 because neither L nor M would precede it.

* The last rule creates a dual-option on stop 5, and the interlaced effects of all of the rules create a limited scenario in each part of the dual-option. Thus, the last rule creates two basic templates for the game. Let us examine each.

If N is chosen for stop 5, then from the first rule N cannot be chosen for stops 4 and 6. If N cannot be chosen for stop 6, then from the second rule N cannot be chosen for stop 1. Similarly, if N cannot be chosen for stop 4, then from the third rule N cannot be chosen for stop 2. From the fourth rule we can infer that L and M cannot be chosen for stop 4, and thus O must be chosen for stop 4. When O is chosen for stop 4, from the third rule we can infer that O must be chosen for stop 2. If O is chosen for stops 2 and 4, then from the first rule O cannot be chosen for stops 1 and 3. Only L or M is then available for stop 1 (and from the second rule, stop 6 as well):

N chosen for stop 5:

L/M	O		O	N	L/M
1	2	3	4	5	6
N̶	N̶	O̶	N̶		N̶
O̶			L̶		
			M̶		

If O is chosen for stop 5, then from the first rule O cannot be chosen for stop 4 or stop 6. If O cannot be chosen for stop 4, then from the third rule O cannot be chosen for stop 2. If O cannot be chosen for stop 6, then from the second rule O cannot be chosen for stop 1. Of course, from the fourth rule, if O cannot be chosen for stops 1 or 2, then N cannot be chosen for stops 2 or 3 (and then from the third rule N cannot be chosen for stop 4):

O chosen for stop 5:

				O	
1	2	3	4	5	6
O̶	O̶	N̶	O̶		O̶
	N̶		N̶		

Taking a moment to examine the restriction on each stop, only L or M is available to fill stops 2 and 4.

O chosen for stop 5:

	L/M		L/M	O	
1	2	3	4	5	6
O̶	O̶	N̶	O̶		O̶
	N̶		N̶		

Thus, the final rule—in combination with the other rules—triggers a powerful chain reaction where two very strong templates emerge for the game. This template approach—which will be discussed in much more detail in a later lesson—should not be new to you as this approach was discussed several times in the Linear Setup Practice Drill in this Homework. With these two templates in hand, we are now ready to efficiently attack the game.

Question #1: Global, Could Be True, List. The correct answer choice is (D)

Answer choice (A) is incorrect because M is chosen consecutively for stops 2 and 3, a violation of the first rule. Answer choice (B) is incorrect because stops 2 and 4 are different airlines, a violation of the third rule. Answer choice (C) is incorrect because M is immediately followed by N in stops 1 and 2, a violation of the fourth rule. Answer choice (E) is incorrect because stops 1 and 6 are different airlines, a violation of the second rule. Thus answer choice (D) is correct. Note that answer choice (D) only uses three of the airlines and does not use airline L.

Question #2: Local, Could Be True, List. The correct answer choice is (B)

If N is chosen for stop 5, from our template we know that N cannot be chosen for stop 1, and this information eliminates answer choice (E). The template also indicates that O must be chosen for stop 2, and this fact eliminates answer choices (A), (C), and (D). Thus, answer choice (B) is correct. Please note that there are other reasons to eliminate some of the answers, such as the fact that answer choices (A) and (C) violate the fourth rule.

Question #3: Local, Must Be True, List. The correct answer choice is (C)

If O is chosen for stop 5, then O cannot be chosen for stop 4, and from the third rule, O cannot be chosen for stop 2. This fact eliminates answer choices (A) and (D). Answer choices (B) and (E) can be eliminated because they violate the fourth rule. Thus, answer choice (C) is correct. Note that answer choices (A), (B), and (D) can also be eliminated because our O in 5 template shows that M must be second if L is unavailable.

Question #4: Global, Cannot Be True, List. The correct answer choice is (E)

An examination of our two templates reveals that O in stop 1 and N in stop 2 is not possible, and hence answer choice (E) is correct. Because of the actions of the second and third rules, when O and N are chosen for stops 1 and 2, then neither O nor N can be chosen for stop 5, a violation of the last rule.

Question #5: Local, Could Be True, List. The correct answer choice is (B)

If O is chosen for stop 2, then from the third rule O must be chosen for stop 4. Applying the first rule, O cannot be chosen for stop 5, and thus N must be chosen for stop 5. Because answer choices (A), (D), and (E) do not place N in stop 5, they can all be eliminated (answer choice (A) can also be eliminated because it violates the last rule).

In addition, if O is chosen for stop 2, then from the first rule O cannot be chosen for stop 1, and from the second rule O cannot be chosen for stop 6. This information eliminates answer choice (C), and thus answer choice (B) is correct.

Interestingly, every question in this game is a List question. This unusual occurrence is likely a result of the powerful interaction of the rules, and the fact that there are only two main directions the game can go. Most of the List questions in this game ask about partial lists, and this helps mask the true effects of the interaction of the rules.

This is a Grouping Game: Defined-Fixed, Unbalanced: Overloaded, Numerical Distribution.

Aside from the first rule that serves to better establish the distribution, all of the rules are conditional. In games that rely solely on conditional rules, you are generally not able to make definitive inferences about where variables must be placed, but rather you must understand the relationships between certain variables and how they may or may not be grouped with one another. That means that a traditional diagram where definitive inferences are represented on the base is not going to occur. Instead, we must set the base of five slots, diagram the rules and make conditional inferences, and then proceed to attack the questions based on that information.

Parents: F G H³
          *
Students: K L M³
          * *
Teachers: U W X Z⁴
              *
10 ⟶ 5

K/L/M ____ ____ ____ ____
Student

Rules:

F ⟷ H

M ⟷ Z

U ⟷ W

F ⟶ Z
Z̸ ⟶ F̸

W ⟶ H
H̸ ⟶ W̸

Inferences:

F ⟷ W   (from the 2nd and last rules)

F ⟶ M   (from the 3rd and 5th rules)

With exactly one student selected, there are only two possible parent-teacher distributions, namely fixed 2-2 and 1-3 distributions (3-1 is impossible because F and G cannot be selected together, and 0-4 is impossible because U and W cannot be selected together). Thus, there are only two possible distributions in the game:

P	S	T
2	1	2
(G, F/H)		
1	1	3
		(X, Z, U/W)

However, these distributions only play a role in the last two questions.

Question #6: Global, Could Be True, List. The correct answer choice is (E)

Answer choice (A) is incorrect because only one student is selected (K and L are both selected here).

Answer choice (B) is incorrect because if F is selected Z must also be selected.

Answer choice (C) is incorrect because if W is selected H must also be selected.

Answer choice (D) is incorrect because U and W cannot be selected together.

Answer choice (E) is the correct answer choice.

Question #7: Local, Could Be True. The correct answer choice is (D)

If W and Z are both selected, then H must also be selected, and F, M, and U all cannot be selected.

Answer choice (A) is incorrect because U cannot be selected.

Answer choice (B) is incorrect because K and L cannot both be selected (two students).

Answer choice (C) is incorrect because M cannot be selected.

Answer choice (D) is the correct answer choice.

Answer choice (E) is incorrect because F cannot be selected.

Question #8: Global, Cannot Be True. The correct answer choice is (B)

From the inferences we know that F and M cannot be selected together (F requires Z, and Z cannot be with M), so answer choice (B) is correct.

Question #9: Local, Could Be True-Except. The correct answer choice is (A)

From the inferences we know that W cannot be selected with F (W requires H, and H cannot be with F), so answer choice (A) is correct.

Question #10: Local, Must Be True. The correct answer choice is (E)

The final two questions address the distributions possible in this game. If only one parent is selected, and you know that only one student will be selected, then the other three spots must be filled by the four teachers (1-1-3). Looking at the teachers, you see from the rules that U and W cannot both be selected (and thus one of U or W is out), so the other two teachers—X and Z—must both be selected in order to fill the three spaces. Since X must be included, answer choice (E) is correct.

Question #11: Local, Must Be True. The correct answer choice is (B)

If M is selected then K and L (the other two students) are both out. Further, from the rules and inferences Z and F are also out (neither can be with M). And you also know that U and W cannot be together, so one of them is out. That gives you all five of the non-selected people: K, L, Z, F, and U/W. From that you can see that everyone else must be selected in order to fill the five spaces. So M, G, H, X, and U/W are selected, and answer choice (B) is the correct answer.

This is an Advanced Linear Game: Unbalanced: Underfunded.

The five-year period forms a natural base for this game, and the car purchases and graduations should be stacked on top of the base. The remaining variable set—the three friends—should be used to fill in the spaces in the car and graduation rows, as such:

Car: _____ _____ _____ _____ _____

Grad: _____ _____ _____ _____ _____

      1   2   3   4   5

The friends variable provides uncertainty in this game, namely because the number of variables is fewer than the available slots. At first, it appears that the three friends will fill three spaces in each row (the graduation row and the car row), leaving two empty space variables (E's) to fill the two remaining slots in each row. If this was the case, the Underfunded aspect of the game would be easily deflected. But, the second-to-last rule makes it clear that R and S will graduate in the same year, meaning that there are three E's in the graduation row (along with an RS block and variable S). In the car row there are 2 or 3 E's, depending on when R buys his car (R could conceivably buy a car in the same year as S or T). Let's look at each rule, with the exception of the last rule, which can be represented right on the diagram (subscripts are used to represent the car/graduation elements):

First rule:

$$R_G > T_G$$

Second rule:

$$T_G > T_C$$

Third rule:

$$S_C > S_G$$

Fourth rule:

$$\boxed{\begin{array}{c} R_G \\ S_G \end{array}}$$

These four rules can be combined into one super-sequence:

$$S_C > \boxed{\begin{array}{c} R_G \\ S_G \end{array}} > T_G > T_C$$

This sequence is immensely powerful in this game because it limits the placement of a number of variables. In fact, the sequence is so powerful that there are only two possibilities for the graduation row. However, other than mentioning this fact, we tend not to diagram out those options because the sequence is so strong that we do not need to expend the time diagramming out the options. Let us instead look at the complete diagram to the game, adding in Not Laws and the dual options created by the super-sequence:

R S T ^{3}

$$S_C > \boxed{\begin{array}{c} R_G \\ S_G \end{array}} > T_G > T_C$$

Car:

S/	S/		T/	/T
T̸	T̸	T̸	S̸	S̸
		S̸		

Grad:

E				E
1	2	3	4	5
R̸	T̸	E̸	R̸	R̸
S̸			S̸	S̸
T̸				T̸

From the sequence, the graduations of the three friends must be after Sue bought her car but before Taylor bought his car, and thus 1991 and 1995 in the graduation row must be empty (E). In addition, because three separate yearly events occur after S bought her car, Sue can only have bought her car in 1991 or 1992 (and this is represented by a dual-option). Similarly, because three separate yearly events occur before T bought his car, Taylor can only have bought his car in 1994 or 1995 (represented by another dual-option).

Note that the last rule, which states that "at least one of the friends graduated in 1993," is represented by an E Not Law under 1993 in the graduation row.

Question #12: Global, Could Be True, List. The correct answer choice is (B)

The question stem specifies that graduation years are under consideration. As we discussed above, 1991 and 1995 cannot be years in which any friend graduated, and thus answer choices (A) and (E) can be eliminated. Answer choice (C) can be eliminated because R and S graduated in the same year, and answer choice (D) can be eliminated because R and S graduated earlier than T (and in this answer T graduated in 1992 whereas the other two graduated in 1993). Hence, answer choice (B) is proven correct by process of elimination.

Question #13: Global, Could Be True. The correct answer choice is (B)

As shown on our diagram above, none of the friends graduated in 1995, a fact that eliminates answer choices (A), (C), and (E). S graduated no later than 1992, eliminating answer choice (D). Consequently, answer choice (B) is correct. Note that the Not Laws also eliminate all four incorrect answer choices.

Question #14: Global, Cannot Be True, FTT. The correct answer choice is (C)

This is the hardest question of the game. This question is difficult because it is presented in terms of falsity. Remember, always convert questions into "true" terms, and so "must be false" becomes "cannot be true."

Answer choice (C) cannot be true because in 1993 neither S nor T bought a car; only R could have bought a car in 1993, and thus only one friend could have bought a car in 1993. The other four answer choices could occur, and are thus incorrect.

Question #15: Global, Must Be True. The correct answer choice is (A)

As we discussed in the setup to the game, none of the friends graduated in 1991, and therefore answer choice (A) is correct. As is often the case, a major inference in the game is directly tested.

Question #16: Local, Could Be True, Except. The correct answer choice is (E)

The condition in the question stem creates the following chain:

$$S_C > \boxed{\begin{matrix} R_G \\ S_G \end{matrix}} > \boxed{\begin{matrix} T_G \\ R_C \end{matrix}} > T_C$$

This chain address all six events involving the friends. Answer choice (E) cannot occur because R bought his car earlier than T bought his car, and hence R cannot have bought his car in 1995. Answer choice (E) is thus correct in this except question.

Question #17: Local, Must Be True. The correct answer choice is (E)

If S graduated in 1993, then R also graduated in 1993, forcing T to graduate in 1994 and T to buy his first car in 1995:

Car:	S/	/S			T

Grad:	E	E	$\boxed{\begin{matrix} R \\ S \end{matrix}}$	T	E
	1	2	3	4	5

Accordingly, answer choice (E) is correct.

This is a Pure Sequencing game, but one that adds a layer of interest by creating three groupings of the letters. This game contains two templates.

There are six letters and three spoonfuls. Because each spoonful must contain between one and three letters, there are two unfixed numerical distributions present:

6 letters-to-3 spoons distributions:	3	2	1
	2	2	2

Let's examine each rule in order:

Rule #1:

This is a simple sequencing rule that can be represented as:

$$T > U$$

The immediate implication of this rule is that U cannot be in the first spoonful and T cannot be in the third spoonful.

Rule #2:

This rule is worded in a slightly trickier fashion than the prior rule. By stating that "U is *not in a later* spoonful than the X," the test makers allow for X and U to be in the same spoonful. Thus, the rule is properly represented as:

$$U \geq X$$

The first two rules can be linked to form the following sequence:

$$T > U \geq X$$

Because U cannot be in the first spoonful, we can infer that X also cannot be in the first spoonful.

Rule #3:

This is a simple sequencing rule that can be represented as:

$$W > Y$$

The immediate implication of this rule is that Y cannot be in the first spoonful and W cannot be in the third spoonful.

Rule #4:

This rule creates a vertical block as follows:

$$\boxed{\begin{array}{c} Y/Z \\ U \end{array}}$$

Adding this rule to the sequence involving U gives us the following setup:

T U W X Y Z [6]

$$T > \boxed{\begin{array}{c} Y/Z \\ U \end{array}} \geq X$$

W > Y

$\overline{\text{S1}}$	$\overline{\text{S2}}$	$\overline{\text{S3}}$
U̸		Z̸
X̸		W̸
Y̸		

However, the final rule has a powerful effect on the game. Because U can only be in the same spoonful as Y or Z, *but not both*, there are only two basic directions the game can take:

Option #1: U and Y in the same spoonful

$$\begin{array}{c} T \\ ---- \\ W \end{array} > \boxed{\begin{array}{c} Y \\ U \end{array}} \geq X$$

Z?

In this option, the UY block links to both the first and third rules, forcing both T and W to precede the UY block. X is either in the same spoonful as the UY block, or in the next spoonful. Z is a random.

Option #2: U and Z in the same spoonful

$$T > \boxed{\begin{array}{c} Z \\ U \end{array}} \geq X$$

W > Y

In this option there are two separate chains, but none of the letters is a random. In both sequences X is a letter that must be carefully watched due to the "greater or equal to," relationship with U.

Question #18: Global, Could Be True, List. The correct answer choice is (B)

This is a basic List question, so apply each of the rules to all of the contending answer choices, eliminating Loser answer choices as you go through.

The format of this question is a bit difficult to read. It would have been nice if Law Services provided vertical space between each answer choice, but they chose not to do that. To combat this problem, at your discretion you can simply separate each answer choice with a horizontal line. Thus, with four quick lines you can visually separate each answer choice and avoid confusion.

Answer choice (A) is incorrect because according to the third rule Y is in a later spoonful than W.

Answer choice (C) is incorrect because according to the third rule Y is in a later spoonful than W.

Answer choice (D) is incorrect because according to the first rule U is in a later spoonful than T.

Answer choice (E) is incorrect because according to the second rule U cannot be in a later spoonful than X.

Answer choice (B) is thus proven correct by process of elimination.

Question #19: Local, Could Be True. The correct answer choice is (D)

If Y is the only letter in one of the spoonfuls, then Option #2 applies, and our rule configuration is:

$$T > \boxed{\begin{array}{c} Z \\ U \end{array}} \geq X$$

$$W > Y$$

Three answer choices can thus be easily eliminated:

Answer choice (A) is incorrect because Y cannot be in the first spoonful as Y must be in a later spoonful than W.

Answer choice (B) is incorrect because Z cannot be in the first spoonful as T must be in an earlier spoonful.

Answer choice (E) is incorrect because W cannot be in the third spoonful as W must be in an earlier spoonful than Y.

At this point only answer choices (C) and (D) remain in consideration. Let's examine both:

Answer choice (C) is incorrect because if T is in the second spoonful, then X, U, and Z must be in the third spoonful. Because W must be in an earlier spoonful than Y, W must go in the first spoonful, but then there is no spoonful where Y can be placed where Y is the only letter in that spoonful. Thus, T cannot be placed in the second spoonful and remain in accordance with the question stem conditions, and so (C) is incorrect.

Answer choice (D) is the correct answer. If X is in the second spoonful, then U and Z must also be in the second spoonful and T must be in the first spoonful. W must then be in the first spoonful (if W is in the second spoonful there are four letters in the second spoonful), and Y can be the only letter in the third spoonful, in accordance with the condition in the question stem.

Question #20: Local, Must Be True. The correct answer choice is (E)

The question stem stipulates that Z is in the first spoonful. Under Option #2, Z cannot be in the first spoonful, and thus this question operates under Option #1, with the following setup:

$$
\begin{array}{c}
T \\
\text{-- -- } > \\
W
\end{array}
\boxed{\begin{array}{c} Y \\ U \end{array}} \geq X
\qquad
\underset{S1}{\underline{Z}} \quad \underset{S2}{\underline{}} \quad \underset{S3}{\underline{}}
$$

Because each spoonful must contain at least one letter, at the very least letter X must be in the third spoonful, and thus answer choice (E) is correct. As an aside, letters U and Y could also be in the third spoonful but they do not have to be in the third spoonful.

Question #21: Global, Could Be True, List. The correct answer choice is (D)

The question asks for a list of the letters that could be the only letter in the first spoonful. From our initial discussion of the rules we determined that U, X, and Y could never be in the first spoonful. Thus, answer choices (D) and (E), which both contain X, can be eliminated. Letter T is common to all three remaining answer choices ((A), (B), and (D)), and thus the real difference between the three answer choices comes down to W and Z. Under Option #1, Z is a random, and could be the only letter in the first spoonful:

$$
\begin{array}{ccc}
 & & Y \\
 & W & U \\
\underline{Z} & \underline{T} & \underline{X} \\
S1 & S2 & S3
\end{array}
$$

As answer choices (A) and (B) do not contain Z, they are both incorrect. Thus, answer choice (D) is proven correct by process of elimination.

Question #22: Local, Could Be True. The correct answer choice is (A)

If T is in the second spoonful, either Option could apply. However, certain inferences follow from the given rules. Because U is in a later spoonful than T, U must be in the third spoonful along with Y or Z (but not both). And because of the second rule, X must also be in the third spoonful. Thus, the third spoonful must contain three letters. This information is sufficient to eliminate answer choices (D) and (E).

The assignment of three letters to the third spoonful also places the game in the 3-2-1 unfixed distribution. Since the third spoonful already has three letters, the other two spoonfuls must have one or two letters (one spoonful has one letter and the other spoonful has two letters). This information eliminates answer choices (B) and (C). Thus, answer choice (A) is correct, and is proven possible by the following hypothetical:

```
                      X
          W           Y
          Z     T     U
         ___   ___   ___
         S1    S2    S3
```

APPENDIX

Test-by-Test Game Use Tracker

This appendix contains a reverse lookup that cross references each game according to the source LSAT. The tests are listed in order of the PrepTest number (if any). The date of administration is also listed to make the process easier. If a test is not listed, then no questions from that exam were used in this book.

Games listed under each test begin by listing the *Logic Games Bible Workbook* chapter the game appears in, the game date, and then the question numbers.

For information on obtaining the publications that contain the entire LSATs listed below, please visit our Free LSAT Help area at www.powerscore.com/lsat/help/pub_ident.cfm

PrepTest 39—December 2002 LSAT

Chapter 4, Page 154, Section #1: December 2002 Questions 1-5
Chapter 4, Page 155, Section #1: December 2002 Questions 6-11
Chapter 4, Page 156, Section #1: December 2002 Questions 12-18
Chapter 4, Page 157, Section #1: December 2002 Questions 19-23

PrepTest 40—June 2003 LSAT

Chapter 3, Page 83, Game #10: June 2003 Questions 18-23

PrepTest 43—June 2004 LSAT

Chapter 3, Page 76, Game #3: June 2004 Questions 1-5
Chapter 3, Page 78, Game #5: June 2004 Questions 13-17
Chapter 3, Page 81, Game #8: June 2004 Questions 18-22

PrepTest 44—October 2004 LSAT

Chapter 3, Page 79, Game #6: October 2004 Questions 7-12
Chapter 3, Page 80, Game #7: October 2004 Questions 18-22

PrepTest 45—December 2004 LSAT

Chapter 3, Page 77, Game #4: December 2004 Questions 1-6
Chapter 3, Page 82, Game #9: December 2004 Questions 7-12

PrepTest 47—October 2005 LSAT

Chapter 4, Page 174, Section #2: October 2005 Questions 1-5
Chapter 4, Page 175, Section #2: October 2005 Questions 6-11
Chapter 4, Page 176, Section #2: October 2005 Questions 12-17
Chapter 4, Page 177, Section #2: October 2005 Questions 18-22

PrepTest 48—December 2005 LSAT

Chapter 4, Page 192, Section #3: December 2005 Questions 1-6
Chapter 4, Page 193, Section #3: December 2005 Questions 7-12
Chapter 4, Page 194, Section #3: December 2005 Questions 13-17
Chapter 4, Page 195, Section #3: December 2005 Questions 18-22

PrepTest 49—June 2006 LSAT

Chapter 4, Page 212, Section #4: June 2006 Questions 1-7
Chapter 4, Page 213, Section #4: June 2006 Questions 8-12
Chapter 4, Page 214, Section #4: June 2006 Questions 13-17
Chapter 4, Page 215, Section #4: June 2006 Questions 18-22

PrepTest 50—September 2006 LSAT

Chapter 4, Page 232, Section #5: September 2006 Questions 1-5
Chapter 4, Page 233, Section #5: September 2006 Questions 6-11
Chapter 4, Page 234, Section #5: September 2006 Questions 12-17
Chapter 4, Page 235, Section #5: September 2006 Questions 18-22

PrepTest 51—December 2006 LSAT

Chapter 3, Page 74, Game #1: December 2006 Questions 6-10
Chapter 3, Page 75, Game #2: December 2006 Questions 16-22

MORE INFORMATION

Additional PowerScore Resources ▮▮▮▮▮▮▮▮▮▮

Because new LSATs appear every several months, and access to accurate and up-to-date information is critical, we have devoted a section of our website to *Logic Games Bible Workbook* students. This online resource area offers updates on recent LSAT Game sections, discussions of additional Logic Game concepts, and general information. The *LSAT Logic Games Bible Workbook* online area can be accessed at:

www.powerscore.com/lsatbibles

If you would like to comment on the *Logic Games Bible Workbook*, or make suggestions for additional sections, please send us a message at lsatbibles@powerscore.com. We thank you for purchasing this book, and we look forward to hearing from you!

CONTACTING POWERSCORE

POWERSCORE INTERNATIONAL HEADQUARTERS:

PowerScore Test Preparation
57 Hasell Street
Charleston, SC 29401

Toll-free information number: (800) 545-1750
Website: www.powerscore.com
Email: lsat@powerscore.com

POWERSCORE LSAT PUBLICATIONS INFORMATION:

For information on the *LSAT Logic Games Bible*, *LSAT Logical Reasoning Bible*, *LSAT Reading Comprehension Bible*, *LSAT Deconstructed Series* or *LSAT Logic Games Ultimate Setups Guide*.

Website: www.powerscore.com/pubs.htm

POWERSCORE FULL-LENGTH LSAT COURSE INFORMATION:

Complete preparation for the LSAT.
Classes available nationwide.

Web: www.powerscore.com/lsat
Request Information: www.powerscore.com/contact.htm

POWERSCORE VIRTUAL LSAT COURSE INFORMATION:

45 hours of online, interactive, real-time preparation for the LSAT.
Classes available worldwide.

Web: www.powerscore.com/lsat/virtual
Request Information: www.powerscore.com/contact.htm

POWERSCORE WEEKEND LSAT COURSE INFORMATION:

Fast and effective LSAT preparation: 16 hour courses, 99th percentile instructors, and real LSAT questions.

Web: www.powerscore.com/lsat/weekend
Request Information: www.powerscore.com/contact.htm

POWERSCORE LSAT TUTORING INFORMATION:

One-on-one meetings with a PowerScore LSAT expert.

Web: www.powerscore.com/lsat/content_tutoring.cfm
Request Information: www.powerscore.com/contact.htm

POWERSCORE LAW SCHOOL ADMISSIONS COUNSELING INFORMATION:

Personalized application and admission assistance.

Web: www.powerscore.com/lsat/content_admissions.cfm
Request Information: www.powerscore.com/contact.htm